ERIN MILLER

Final Flight Final Fight

My grandmother, the WASP, and Arlington National Cemetery

First published by 4336 Press, LLC 2019

Copyright © 2019 by Erin Miller

The events described within are written to the best of the author's recollection.

First edition

ISBN: 978-1-7335606-0-3

Editing by Kelly Davis
Cover art by Jasmine Eskandari
Cover art by Shane Yeager & Celene Di Stasio @ DC Visionaries (Cover Photography)

This book was professionally typeset on Reedsy.
Find out more at reedsy.com

For Gammy

Foreword

Give honor...to whom honor is due— Romans 13:7

I was having a rough day and no one could understand what I was going through. I felt alone, isolated, and tired of putting up with the hostility, harassment and denigration by some insecure male fighter pilots who couldn't handle that women could fly planes and shoot the gun just as well or better than they could. I sort of knew what I was signing up for when Congress finally repealed the law and then the Pentagon changed the policy prohibiting women from becoming fighter pilots just because we had ovaries. I was in the 9th class of women allowed to attend the Air Force Academy and one of only two women in my pilot training class, so I was getting used to competing and succeeding in the very male-dominated military world. I was eager for the opportunity to serve our country as a fighter pilot, prove women could do it, and pave the way for other women and girls behind me. I felt I was tough enough for the challenge, but I am also human and had days where I was discouraged, alone, and contemplating getting out of the military altogether.

On one of those days, I decided to attend a lunch at the officers' club for an organization called The Daedalians, which was a "fraternity" of military pilots, past and present. I was usually the only woman at these meetings, but it was a special group of patriots and pilots with amazing stories of flying in World War II, Korea, and Vietnam. I loved to hear their stories and feel connected to a long tradition of fighting for our country in the air. That particular day, in walked three women much older than I dressed in military uniforms with wings. I was confused. I thought the military only opened up pilot training to women around 1980, four years before I entered basic training, while restricting us to non-combat aircraft, whatever that means. (We used to joke that it meant we could get shot at but we couldn't shoot back.)

These confident, affable and feisty women sat down at my table and introduced themselves as Women Airforce Service Pilots (WASP) who flew planes for America during World War II. Here in my presence were these amazing female pioneers who ferried planes around the country, trained men to become pilots, and towed targets for the gunners on the ground to use for target practice. Dawn Seymour, Ruth Helm, and Eleanor Gunderson were the coolest and most inspiring ladies I had ever met and became life-long friends of mine from that day forward.

The three WASP were so excited to meet *me* and hear my flying stories in the mighty A-10 Warthog. They peppered me with questions with a twinkle in their eyes and the excitement of children. I asked them about their flying experiences and was moved by the tales they told of being young, independent women in the 1940s who loved to fly and answered the nation's call to serve to free up male pilots for combat roles. A total of 1102 women served as WASP: 28 Originals, who qualified — with 500 or more hours — in 1942 to ferry aircraft for the Ferrying Division, Air Transport Command; and 1074 who completed training, first in Houston (April and May, 1943), and after that in Sweetwater, Texas. Thirty-eight WASP perished while serving their country in WWII. The WASP were supposed to be militarized, but Congress didn't approve it reportedly due to cultural hang-ups about women serving as military pilots (I was very familiar with that dynamic!)

By the end of the lunch meeting, the discouragement I was feeling that day was long gone and I was inspired by these wingwomen and patriots to continue to serve and fly for our country. Over the following years, our friendships deepened and I counted on our times together for comradery, advice, and inspiration. In our visits together, I heard more stories about their training and flying including the challenges they also encountered with men who didn't think women should be pilots. Finally, I met some women who could relate to what I was going through a generation later! My WASP friends taught me to keep a positive attitude and not focus on how others were treating me or their biases against us. They were so proud of me and the other women who followed in their jet stream to become combat pilots and they made sure I knew it. They were living vicariously through me in some ways, as I was blessed to continue to fulfill the dreams that they still had in their hearts to serve their country and fly. I learned so much from Dawn, Ruth, and Eleanor and was honored to invite them as front row guests in the hangar when I took over command of an A-10 Fighter Squadron, the first woman in US history to command a combat flying unit.

The WASP were skilled pilots, mastering many aircraft like the P-51, T-6, and B-29. When the war was over, they were abruptly disbanded, kicked out, and told to go home to give the flying assignments back to the men. Some WASP went on to fly as civilians, while others started a family and settled back into more culturally accepted roles for women at the time. I met many other WASP over the years, and one thing that struck me was they weren't bitter about their unequal treatment and sudden disbandment. The WASP who I knew were all grateful for the amazing opportunities they had and looked back with fondness on that extraordinary defining season of their lives.

The WASP contribution to our country in WWII was not appropriately recognized for over thirty years, unfortunately. It was a big and long overdue fight, but in 1977 they were finally given retroactive veterans' status including medals, access to VA healthcare and other earned benefits, and the right to be buried at veterans cemeteries across the country with full military honors just like their male counterparts. Mission complete. Honor finally given to these feisty, barrier-breaking patriots.

Or so we thought.

Fast forward to December 2015. After 26 years serving our country in uniform, I had just completed my first year deployed to a new battlefield called the U.S. House of Representatives. Christmas of 2015 was behind us, and while taking the tree and lights down, I was also preparing to head back to DC and planning to tackle the priorities for my district in 2016. I never could have predicted what would become our first urgent and top priority. I was in my kitchen in Tucson doing dishes when a group text came in from one of my staff with a link to a story about a WASP who passed away and was denied having her ashes placed in the hallowed ground for our nation's heroes—Arlington National Cemetery.

I initially could not believe what I was reading—it had to be "fake news!" There must be some mistake. I directed my team to investigate the situation and get back to me right away. That's when I first learned about Elaine Danforth Harmon, one of these extraordinary female pilots, whose ashes were sitting on the shelf in her family's closet since her dying wish to be laid to rest at Arlington had been denied. My team reported back to me quickly to confirm that, unfortunately, the story was accurate, and Elaine's family appropriately wasn't going to take "no" for an answer. Elaine's feistiness was passed down to her daughter and granddaughters who went to the media and social media on a campaign to right this wrong. Erin Miller, granddaughter of Elaine and author of "Final Flight, Final Fight" summed it up well: "Arlington said 'no' to the wrong family!"

In my decades in uniform as a fighter pilot, retiring as a Colonel, I have more experience than I want to with buffoonerous (not a real word but we use it all the time in fighter squadrons) bureaucratic decisions by the military that are wrong, stupid, and make the military look really bad. I quickly realized this situation fell squarely in this category. Here we were at the end of 2015, the same year the Pentagon (finally) decided to open up all positions in the military to qualified women. There was no way they were also closing the gates to Arlington on the very women who paved the way for us! They wouldn't be that stupid or cruel. Turns out they would.

"Final Flight, Final Fight" tells the story of Elaine Danforth Harmon's service as a barrier-breaking WASP and the fight to fulfill her dying wishes to be laid to rest at Arlington as she deserved. Erin took detailed notes during the journey which allows the reader to truly experience how ordinary citizens like her and her family can bring about change through advocacy, perseverance, and mobilization of others for a cause greater than themselves. This book will inspire you with the story and legacy of Elaine and the WASP while also hopefully building your faith that Washington, D.C. isn't always as dysfunctional as it appears nearly all of the time. In the fight for Elaine and the WASP, which I was honored to lead in Congress, Democrats and Republicans came together to right a wrong. Erin takes you with her on that mission through the halls of Congress, on social media, and in multiple media interviews to raise awareness, build support and effect change. Erin also discovered more about her own grandmother, known to her as "Gammy," and the magnitude of her service than she had ever fully understood while Gammy was living. For so many reasons, I was infuriated to find out about the latest discrimination against Elaine, the WASP, and military women. This was personal. Like Erin and her family, I wasn't going to rest until the 21 gun salute was fired, taps was played, and an American flag was folded and handed to Elaine's daughter "on behalf of a grateful nation" by an honor guard at Arlington.

"Final Flight, Final Fight" is an easy-to-read, compelling story of Elaine and the WASP service and the fight to give them the honor they deserve. This book will continue to educate people about the WASP and help perpetuate their legacy for the next generations. When visitors from all over the world come to the hallowed ground of Arlington, they will continue to learn about the WASP thanks to Elaine's family refusing to let the gates of Arlington be shut on their pioneering feisty patriotic loved one.

Rest in peace, Elaine, for the final fight was finally won. Thanks, Erin, for documenting Elaine's service, the legacy of the WASP, and this final fight to give them the honors that we owe them as a grateful nation. It was a privilege to be your wingwoman in this noble battle.

-Senator Martha McSally

Acknowledgement

I described this book to someone as one long acknowledgment. I am grateful to everyone in it who had a hand in accomplishing the mission and to those who worked against us - it only made us more determined. Thank you to Mom and my sisters Tiffany and Whitney, Dad, and our extended family. Thank you to Gammy for setting the example.

Thank you to Martha McSally for her passionate commitment to ensuring equal recognition for the women of the WASP and her personal attention during the process described in this book.

Special thanks to the following people for assisting with the development of the book: editor Kelly Davis; designer Jasmine Eskandari for the cover design; Shane Yeager and Celene Di Stasio at DC Visionaries for the cover photography; all of the women of the WASP, especially Bernice "Bee" Falk Haydu, who was kind enough to read and comment on the book; my developmental readers and supporters: Gabee Lepore, Gina Andracchio, Joshua Greenfield, Tara Lane Bowman, Sarah Byrn Rickman, Crispin Burke, Trisa Thompson, Jennifer Backman, Tara Copp, Alan Farkas; Sarah Parry Myers for her support and provision of her interview with my grandmother, so I could hear her voice while I wrote; Carey Lohrenz and Steve Snyder for their encouragement and advice on publishing; Dr. Peggy Chabrian, Kelly Murphy & the Women in Aviation International staff for marketing support and their dedication to honoring the legacy of the WASP by ensuring women keep flying!

To all the families, friends, and supporters of the Women Airforce Service Pilots: my grandmother said all the women of the WASP were her friends, whether she had met them or not, and I consider all of you my extended family. Please keep telling people about the WASP – let's continue to grow our extended family!

Glossary

AP: Associated Press news service.

CPTP: Civilian Pilot Training Program. Flight training offered by the Civilian Aeronautics Administration that taught civilians to fly during the World War II era.

FAA: Federal Aviation Administration. United States government agency that regulates civil aviation.

FOIA: Freedom of Information Act. The law under which people may request copies of United States government documents.

SPARS: United States Coast Guard Women's Reserve. Established by Congress and signed into law in 1942. The name is derived from combining the first letters of the Latin motto of the Coast Guard, *semper paratus*, with the English translation, "always ready."

VA: United States Department of Veterans Affairs. Previously known as the Veterans Administration. United States federal agency that regulates programs pertaining to those who have served in the armed forces.

WAAC: Women's Auxiliary Army Corps. Created by law in 1942 as a female auxiliary unit to the United States Army.

WAC: Women's Army Corps. Created by law in 1943 to convert the

WAAC to active duty status. The program continued until 1978 when it was integrated into the male Army components.

WAFS: Women's Auxiliary Ferrying Squadron. Group of female ferrying pilots led by Nancy Love to fly warplanes from factories to air bases.

WASP: Women Airforce Service Pilots. Group of women formed in 1943 to fly military planes for the United States. Composed of members of the WAFS and WFTD as well as new trainees.

WASP AIR Act: Women Airforce Service Pilots Arlington Inurnment Restoration Act. Short title of House bill H.R. 4336.

WAVES: Women Accepted for Volunteer Emergency Service. United States Navy organization created for females during World War II that continued until 1978 when the women's units were integrated into the male Navy components.

WFTD: Women's Flying Training Detachment. Precursor training program for female pilots before the WASP. Led by Jackie Cochran.

I would like to be buried in Arlington Cemetery. Proof of my veteran status is necessary. It requires a copy of my DD-214. I have put copies of that form in various places.

If for some reason (and there should be no reason) I can't be in the Columbarium at Arlington, then there is still one burial site available at Rock Creek Cemetery where Daddy is buried.

Carpe Diem,
Elaine

1

Final Flight

May 2014

"I hope that I die tomorrow," Gammy said to me as she sat on the edge of her new bed and gazed at the hardwood floor.

I ran through the responses that would be appropriate but Gammy didn't need to hear something appropriate. She would have dismissed an inauthentic reply anyway.

"I understand," I replied.

In May of 2014, her doctors at the Veterans Affairs (VA) hospital diagnosed a rash, originally thought to be another episode of recurring shingles, as skin cancer. Since Gammy had already been doing chemotherapy treatments for several years to fight off breast cancer, the doctors were not sure she could handle surgery. They did some tests and determined she had a strong heart considering she would be turning 95 at the end of the year. However, there was still a possibility that the anesthesia would be too hard for her and she would die in surgery. Rather than look at this as a risk, Gammy saw her circumstances as a prime opportunity for unintentional euthanasia.

Her doctor scheduled surgery to remove the skin in the affected area. I was at Gammy's house the day before so we could get her things together for her stay in the hospital. I had gone to the VA hospital in Washington, D.C., that morning to pick up the medications for her post-surgery recovery. A few days earlier, my family had decided that it would be better if Gammy moved out of the second floor bedroom into a ground floor room. She was no longer able to walk up and down the stairs. She had to crawl. Gammy took it as a challenge. If crawling was what she had to do to get back and forth to her bedroom, she did it. Now we were forcing her to take the easy way out and she resented it.

I spent time with Gammy during the day to help her move her things downstairs and clean up. Someone from VA had delivered a proper hospital bed for her new room, so Gammy was surrendering her old bed too. As if leaving her room wasn't difficult enough, she would have a constant reminder that she was now so infirm that she needed a bed with rails to keep her from falling out of it.

Gammy and I sat upstairs on the edge of her double bed with the faded wooden headboard while she rummaged through little boxes from atop her dresser. I could see she was taking this opportunity with me not only to clean, but also to continue to organize for her eventual death. For years, Gammy had been discarding things because she was always concerned about "not being a burden." Her goal was to leave as little as possible for her family to deal with after she was gone. Gammy picked up a small dusty blue box of costume jewelry.

"Do you want any of this jewelry?" she asked.

I looked at the old pieces Gammy was flipping through and I politely declined.

"Women don't dress up enough anymore. We used to always wear all sorts of jewelry," she lamented.

She twirled a worn down metallic brooch in her hands and I could tell that her mind was wandering. I imagined that Gammy was thinking about the glamorous 1950s captured in a few photos in which she and my grandfather wore tailored suits at dinner and managed to look suave even as Mom and her siblings hung playfully over the dining chairs. I glanced down at my gray sweatpants and running shoes and had to agree that times had changed. I watched as she continued to rummage through small cardboard boxes and then I spotted a small pair of gunmetal gray wings stretching from a diamond-shaped shield.

"What about those?" I asked.

"Oh, you can have those. You should have those." Gammy handed the pair of wings to me and sighed. I knew they weren't her original ones, since those were in the museum, but I thought it was a good keepsake anyway. The wings reminded me of all the times I had seen her go out in uniform to share the story of her service in the war – lectures I had never attended.

"How are you doing?" I asked.

"Just tired." She replaced the dusty lid on the box and set it back on the dresser.

I supervised Gammy as she made her final backwards crawl down the stairs to her new room. On the desk next to her new bed, I arranged personal items like her glasses, medicine, and tissues. Her new bedroom was still her active office whose floor-to-ceiling shelves filled with books and memorabilia about World War II, airplanes, the early days of baseball, and the Women Airforce Service Pilots, or "WASP," provided comfort in the transition. Her honorable service certificate and service medals were displayed in a frame placed among the books on the shelves. Gammy's passion for sharing the history of the WASP surrounded her in her final days. It seemed to me that she owned every book written about the WASP, many of which were signed by the authors, including a few of her fellow pilots. Fans and researchers still sent letters requesting information about her service in the WASP. There were 8 x 10 photo prints awaiting her autograph, which Gammy supplied until her hand no longer cooperated.

Gammy sat down to rest on her new bed, let out a sigh, and said, "Well, I'm pooped."

"Can I get you anything?" I asked.

Lost in thought, she looked around her new room for a minute before responding. "I am just so old. I am too old. People weren't meant to live this long. I have had a fine life. I don't know why I am still here. I am bored. I can't eat. It's just – I just don't know. I hope that I don't live through this surgery tomorrow. I hope that I get anesthesia and don't wake up," Gammy replied.

While I was sad to hear her express this morbid desire, I knew she also had a point. The fact that Gammy was complaining was significant. I had never known my grandmother to be a complainer. She had lived through the Great Depression and World War II and still had a positive attitude. Even in the face of adversity, she always took things at face value and assumed that she would come through it all fine. But her quality of life had deteriorated and now she was being taken out of the only bedroom she had known for decades. At least she was still in her white brick house on the hill in the woods in her beloved state of Maryland, which, according to Gammy, was the only place worth living. New Zealand was a close second. I was not certain why New Zealand received high praise from my finicky Gammy, but I recalled upon her return from a vacation to the land of the kiwi that she had many compliments for the green rolling hills dotted with sheep. Or perhaps she had a permanent adrenaline rush associated with that country from the bungee jump she had done while visiting. "They let me jump for free because I am over 75," she informed me with a smile, always happy to take advantage of a bargain.

The surgery went well. After testing, the doctors determined they had removed enough of the skin cancer to declare the operation a success. I visited Gammy while she was recovering at the Veterans Affairs hospital. She rested, tucked under several thin white blankets, in the adjustable hospital bed. I had always viewed Gammy as upbeat, even managing at times to joke about dying as her body succumbed to old age, but today she was dejected.

"Do you want that?" Gammy asked. "I won't eat it. They are always trying to get me to eat." She pointed to the lunch tray hovering over her hospital bed. "They" (the nurses) were "always" trying to get her to eat because she had lost so much weight in the previous year. Gammy and I were about the same height and she had always outweighed me. In fact she used to tell me that I needed to put on weight. But now she was the thinner one and I had to remind her to eat. Gammy didn't enjoy eating anymore because she had lost her sense of taste.

"No thank you, Gammy. How are you feeling?" I tucked the corner of one of the blankets back under her shoulder.

"Mad," she answered.

I laughed and asked why.

"Because I am still here," Gammy replied.

2

Final Fight

W hen a pilot passes away, the aviation community says she took her "final flight." In April 2015, about a year after saying she was angry for her continued physical existence, Gammy took her final flight after succumbing to all the cancer that had invaded her body. A decade of chemotherapy for breast cancer – metastasized everywhere, including the brain – along with a hip replacement, radiation treatments, and surgery for skin cancer, eventually extinguished the toughest of humans, a rugged World War II pilot who seemed indestructible.

Gammy had arranged to donate her body to the Maryland State Anatomy Board, which administered a program for scientific research on human bodies; this was one example of her investment in the education of future generations. A representative from the state took Gammy's body away from the hospice in the early morning hours after she passed away. Even in death she wanted to be of service. The Anatomy Board also cremated at no charge, another way Gammy tried to ease the burden on our family. She thought researchers might learn something from her cancer-ridden body. We did not know how long we would have to wait until the Anatomy Board returned her to us. Information about the body's purpose or how long it would be studied was not disclosed to the family. All they told us was it could be up to eighteen months, and so we were prepared to wait a year and a half to hold a funeral for Gammy.

I sometimes joked that my family displayed the stereotypical WASP attitude of the other sort, "White Anglo-Saxon Protestant," which meant we collectively avoided dealing with emotions by burying them with productivity. The morning that Gammy passed away was filled with a flurry of activity surrounding the practical aspects of dealing with the death of a family member. No time for sadness! Too much to do!

As the appointed executrix of the estate, Mom immediately began addressing matters. The first thing I saw when I woke up later in the morning after Gammy had died was Mom at the dining room table poring over documents pulled from Gammy's fireproof file box. She leaned her head of silver hair on her hand and examined some papers through her glasses, which had to perch perfectly on her nose since one side arm was missing. Another part of the plan to not be a burden on the family was to have a well-organized estate. Gammy's estate planning skills would have earned accolades from my law school professor who taught the trusts and estate law class. There were hanging folders containing important personal documents: *Family trust*, *Investments*, and one simply titled *Death*, which also held a copy of my grandfather's will on crinkly parchment dated 1944.

Even though I was a relatively new attorney, Mom asked me to go through the box to organize and analyze its contents, along with a separate stack of documents, and explain their legal functions to her. I sat at the table for a while stacking and marking these documents with adhesive flags for different purposes. I read through the will and discovered Gammy had left her grandchildren a gift.

"Gammy is giving each of the grandkids a thousand dollars. You should send receipts for them to sign when you mail the checks out,"

I advised Mom for bookkeeping purposes.

"Okay, that's a good idea." Mom grabbed a pen to jot down a reminder for herself among her copious notes regarding Gammy's estate.

Finally Mom pulled out a letter-sized envelope with the words "funeral arrangements" scrawled across the front in Gammy's hand-writing and asked me to read its contents. Inside was Gammy's version of letterhead (a photocopied Women Airforce Service Pilots logo) with handwritten detailed instructions on her desired funeral and burial arrangements.

I would like to be buried in Arlington Cemetery. Proof of my veteran status is necessary. It requires a copy of my DD-214. I have put copies of that form in various places.

If for some reason (and there should be no reason) I can't be in the Columbarium at Arlington, then there is still one burial site available at Rock Creek Cemetery where Daddy is buried.

We had known that she wanted to be laid to rest at Arlington, so this was not news to us. Gammy had attended several funerals at Arlington National Cemetery for her fellow WASP and she had told Mom after one of the funerals that her choice would also be Arlington. There were indeed many copies of her DD-214, the document showing her separation from active duty service, although Gammy did not receive it until decades after her final military flight. Gammy had been meticulous about keeping multiple copies of documents in an organized system. I recalled how she gave me photocopies of photographs over the years; it seemed to me that spending time with the photocopy machine had become another of her hobbies.

Mom and I spent the rest of the day at Gammy's house with Mom's three siblings, known to me as Aunt Chris, Uncle Rob, and Uncle Bill. Gammy and my grandfather, Robert Harmon, had moved into the classic American white brick house on a hill in the woods a few years after the war. My grandfather passed away in 1965, before I was born. To my sisters, cousins, and me this house was always "Gammy's house." I was fortunate to spend a lot of time there growing up because it was only one and a half miles away from my childhood home. When Gammy's four children had their own children, the white house on the hill became the hub of our extended family. Each year there, Gammy dressed up as Uncle Sam on the Fourth of July to celebrate her favorite holiday: the birthday of the United States of America. Inevitably, a cousin would almost catch on fire playing around with fireworks or almost break a bone jumping off the stone wall in the vast leafy backyard leading to the tennis court. Gammy's house was where we gathered on Christmas day to open presents and eat breakfast while passing the phone around to speak with family members who couldn't make it in person, and where, on New Year's Eve, Gammy showed herself to be the most laid-back grandmother in America as she permitted her numerous grandkids to run amok in the house until well after midnight banging pots and pans and turning the living room into a pillow fort castle. She stayed elsewhere in the house completing crossword puzzles, occasionally showing herself only to fuel us with junk food and marvel at our endless energy. As the family matriarch, Gammy was the glue of our family, not only keeping us together, but also instilling in us the American values that had shaped her own life and underpinned her expectations of being placed at Arlington National Cemetery after her passing.

With the family gathered at Gammy's house to help organize her belongings, I explained the pertinent documents and Mom handed the funeral arrangements letter to one of her three siblings so they could read it in turn. Aunt Chris started to read it first, but passed it off when she began to cry and had to leave the room. The family agreed that a memorial service should coincide with the Arlington National

9

Cemetery funeral ceremony, aware that it could be many months away. My grandfather's brother, Ernest Harmon, a doctor who had served in the United States Air Force as a flight surgeon, had been buried at Arlington a few years earlier, so we had family members familiar with the current process at that cemetery.

I started to imagine Gammy's Arlington National Cemetery funeral: simple, but elegant and respectful. As her grandkids gathered around with some extended family members, an Air Force honor guard would perform funeral rites and hand Mom, the eldest child, a folded United States flag. And afterwards maybe we would have a small gathering with sandwiches at the Women In Military Service For America Memorial next door to the cemetery in Arlington, another request from her funeral arrangements letter. I knew Gammy wanted her grave site to act as a marker for the WASP so that visitors might be inclined to research the group's service to keep its history alive. I imagined my involvement with her funeral would entail nothing more than wearing appropriate attire and showing up on time.

We all got to work cleaning out the house. Gammy had been gone fewer than twelve hours and we were already discarding her things. It was surreal and cathartic. Each person took a room and I ended up in Gammy's office-turned-bedroom.

I sat on the old stool at her bedside desk still littered with used tissues and medicine bottles. I opened the desk drawers, the contents of which immediately reminded me that Gammy was a child of the Great Depression era. She had kept numerous balls of rubber bands and hundreds of unused paperclips in her desk, saving everything that "might" be useful to someone someday: several pairs of scissors of varying ages, old reading glasses, bent letter openers, and incomplete sets of playing cards. None of these items was a surprise to find in the desk of a woman who had washed resealable plastic sandwich bags so she could reuse them or had baked with the same piece of tinfoil until the numerous holes resulting from such frugality rendered it ineffective.

I laughed when I found a stack of unused greeting cards. When we received birthday or holiday cards from Gammy, she had always used a paper clip to attach a small note of her sentiments rather than write on the card – so we could use it again.

My youngest sister Whitney showed up in the middle of the cleaning session, having driven down from her house in New Jersey.

"Hey, how's it going?" Whitney asked as she entered Gammy's office bedroom with her hair in a ponytail and a trash bag in hand, ready to assist.

"Look what I found." I held up the pile of blank greeting cards and smiled.

Whitney laughed. "Hey, those blank cards came in handy sometimes!"

I continued to dig through Gammy's desk. I found some old receipt books from the 1960s and 1970s for weekly receipt of rent in amounts like $25 from former occupants of Gammy's extra bedrooms. I couldn't decide if that was expensive for that era or if it was a bargain. According to Mom, Gammy "enjoyed the parade of renters and wanted to help them by keeping rent at a minimum." Never one to overreact, I recalled when Gammy had casually reported "he's dead" after she went to check up on one renter in his room when his employer had telephoned to inquire about his whereabouts. Not long after, another renter moved in.

I found a thoughtful notebook labelled "Information for the next owners of my home" in which Gammy detailed the quirks of her house and how to deal with them. I came across a receipt dated 1943 for an hour of flying at a cost of $7.50 at College Park Airport. Hidden away among old office supplies, there was a small jewelry bag containing entangled necklaces. I set about unthreading the knots in the chains and discovered Gammy's Congressional Gold Medal necklace. I fished it out and put it aside in the "important stuff" pile. Gammy had told me on several occasions that she was ready to die, and now that she was gone, organizing all her things was a natural transition to life

11

without her. I hadn't had time to fully process my feelings about her death, but I knew she would want us to take proper care of her historic items.

I discovered a slender velvet bag among the assortment of random items in her desk. I opened the bag and pulled out a black pen with President Barack Obama's signature on the side. I felt something crunchy inside the bag and pulled out a little note scrawled in Gammy's distinctive cursive handwriting: *This is the pen President Obama used to sign the Congressional Gold Medal bill for the WASP.*

"Oh, Gammy," I said to myself, "only you would keep something from the President of the United States stuffed in a desk drawer behind crumbling forty year-old rubber bands."

I brought the pen and the items from the "important stuff" pile out to the dining room and placed it with her other WASP memorabilia that we had collectively gathered throughout the day. Gammy had already given a lot of her personal WASP articles and documents to the College Park Aviation Museum located at the airport where she had learned to fly. There were numerous aviation museums and other repositories of World War II artifacts that would have appreciated Gammy's WASP items but she had instructed us to give her things to the College Park Aviation Museum, to the archives at Texas Woman's University, or to the WASP museum in Sweetwater, Texas.

"Erin, do you want Gammy's dictionary?" Mom asked me as I turned to leave the dining room.

I looked over at the huge dictionary on its wooden perch next to Gammy's floral patterned armchair.

"I – I don't know what I would do with it," I responded. "I can look words up on the internet now."

"I know." Mom's face conveyed a look of disappointment yet understanding.

There were several of us in the house that day filling bags and sorting items to throw away or donate to charity. Even after an entire day, we had only made a dent in the assortment of things at

Gammy's home. For someone who had been discarding things for years to avoid burdening her children, there was still no shortage of stuff to sort through. I stood in the living room and thought of how much more there was to do: the worn furniture still needed to go, along with the stained area rugs. This room was where Gammy had proudly placed her overstuffed Christmas tree each year. It was always difficult to make out the actual pine underneath the layers of ornaments, lights, tinsel, and garlands. On Christmas Day a mountain range of presents blocked access to the tree as well. For the most part Gammy wrapped gifts in decades-old department store boxes, which she reused annually, in such a way that ribbon alone held the paper – no tape allowed – and collected any wrapping paper that didn't get too mangled. "Unwrap things carefully so I can use the paper again," she instructed us each Christmas morning. All those decorations, boxes, and wrapping accessories must have been stored somewhere in the house, which meant their future whereabouts also had to be determined.

The following day I went back to work – partially to escape the fractured family environment at Gammy's house, but also because I felt that skipping more than one day of work was unnecessary. Gammy's death wasn't a surprise; she was 95 years old and had been sick for a long time. I was fine. Once at the office, however, my mind wandered away from the tasks at hand. I thought I was catching the flu because my body was sore. We had a baby shower for a coworker. As someone led the room in silly shower games, I realized how not fine I was. Maybe it was a delayed reaction to Gammy's death. Little more than 24 hours since Gammy had left us, I was at the celebration of a new life. It was fitting; it was the cycle of existence. In any case, I abruptly left the shower, mumbled something to my boss (who was surprised that I had even presented myself at work that day), and drove home in tears as Charlie Puth crooned "When I See You Again," from the car's stereo.

Mom's cousin Sally called that evening to give her condolences and to tell me about submitting a "noteworthy obituary" in *The Washington Post*. After Sally's father (my grandfather's brother Ernest Harmon) died, she learned that the time limit for requesting one was 30 days. That evening I looked up the noteworthy obituary section online and submitted the required information.

The next day I also called *The Baltimore Sun* to see if they would be interested in doing an expanded obituary for Gammy, since she had grown up in Baltimore. I connected with a reporter named Fred Rasmussen, who was excited to learn about the Baltimore native who had been a World War II pilot. Convinced that the newspaper would publish the story, Fred encouraged me to write about Gammy and suggested that I look at previously published obituaries for guidance.

I was under the impression that Fred wanted me to write an obituary for Gammy, so that's what I did. After reading some of the obituaries online and following a similar format, I wrote a brief version of Gammy's story from her childhood in Baltimore to her service in World War II. The reader would learn of her adventurous, straightforward attitude and how she inspired us to be like her. While I was writing, I realized how much about her life and her service with the WASP I didn't know beyond a superficial level. Whether motivated by their humble personalities, sadness about being forced out of military aviation, a feeling that what they did wasn't interesting to anyone else, or some other reason, many women of the WASP didn't discuss their service with their families. But after doing the basic research necessary to write her obituary, I realized a great historic person was waiting to be discovered behind the woman I had always called Gammy.

A few days later, the obituary Fred had written based on my submission was published in *The Baltimore Sun* and featured a huge print of the classic photo of Gammy in her bomber jacket. Mom bought several copies of the newspaper to distribute to family members. I was happy that *The Baltimore Sun* recognized the relevance and importance of what Gammy had done in World War II, even though it was a short period of service during her 95 year existence.

As a result of the publication of Gammy's obituary in May 2015, we received a letter of condolence from Senator Barbara Mikulski. Senator Mikulski had represented Maryland in the United States Senate since 1987 and before that she had been in the House of Representatives for ten years. The senator had even congratulated Gammy in person at the Congressional Gold Medal ceremony for the WASP at the US Capitol in 2010. The letter praised Gammy's service as a member of the WASP and her trailblazing spirit. It also conveyed that the senator was honored that Gammy "was able to receive the veteran's status that she worked so hard for despite many obstacles."

The Washington Post had been communicating off and on with us, continuously promising that they would call us for more information. Finally I received a call from a reporter who wrote some of their obituaries. During our conversation I explained Gammy's history in the Women Airforce Service Pilots, what she and the WASP did during the war, and that they were the first women to fly military aircraft for the United States.

"What did your grandmother do after the war ended?" the reporter asked me.

"She came home to Maryland, raised four children with my grand-father, then on her own after he died in 1965," I replied.

"But what did she do for work?"

"She did a few different jobs but eventually was a real estate appraiser for about 25 years," I explained.

"So being a real estate appraiser was her main occupation?" he inquired.

"Yes, I guess so. But I think you're missing the significance of her wartime service, that is why her death would be noteworthy," I pointed out.

"Well, did she even fly planes?" he asked with an air of incredulity.

I had to hold myself back from answering immediately because I was offended by this man's question and I wanted to be polite when discussing my recently deceased grandmother. His total ignorance that Gammy and the other women of the WASP program had flown during the war was ridiculous. I was aware that many people had never heard of the WASP, but I had explained Gammy's World War II service in my submission to the newspaper. Gammy was one of the first women to fly planes for the military. She and the rest of the WASP were not officially designated as part of the military when they served, so they had to fight with Congress in the 1970s to be granted retroactive military status. When they were awarded the Congressional Gold Medal in 2010, the story was on the front page of the newspaper this writer represented! Gammy was present in the Oval Office when President Obama signed the bill authorizing the medal. Yet, this man seemed to have no idea who the women of the WASP were, despite my explanation over the phone and the information provided in the online submission form. Even with access to a magical tool called the internet, this reporter was clueless.

Mom called me later in the day, upset because the reporter had subjected her to the same ignorant conversation. I was then doubly offended – by his disrespect toward Gammy and then by his conde-scending conversation with Mom.

"*The Post* has really gone downhill," Mom remarked – an under-statement considering how angry she was. Mom was so flummoxed by her earlier conversation that she emailed the newspaper's obituary department that night and informed them that their reporter was missing the point of the story.

I very much appreciate The Washington Post publishing a news obituary on my mother, Elaine Danforth Harmon. However, after speaking with the reporter this morning, I am concerned about the focus of the story. My mother was a Women Airforce Service Pilot in WWII. There are only a little over 100 of the original 1,074 or so left. These women were pioneers, the first women to fly military aircraft in the US. They were role models. They broke gender barriers. They were trailblazers. As a member of the WASP, she was a recipient of the Congressional Gold Medal.

My mother was very much a part of the effort in getting the WASP official recognition as veterans. For many years she spoke at area schools and various events about her experiences. I also know she would like to acknowledge the many years of excellent health care she received at the Washington VA Medical Center from their truly top-notch doctors, nurses, and hospital staff.

With Memorial Day weekend coming up it would seem ideal to focus on this aspect of her life more than how many years she worked as a real estate appraiser. There is lots of information about her on the internet.

* * *

The next day we received a call from General Wilma Vaught, a retired Army Brigadier General and the first woman to reach that rank from the comptroller field. General Vaught was not only a good friend of Gammy's but also the driving force behind the successful completion of the Women In Military Service For America (WIMSA) Memorial in 1997. Gammy was a charter member of the memorial, honoring women of the armed forces in a museum setting just outside the gates of Arlington National Cemetery.

General Vaught alerted us to Gammy's obituary printed that day in *The Washington Post*. We hadn't even realized it was published since the reporter had also failed to mention when the obituary might be printed. General Vaught was "completely horrified" at the pathetic obituary and said she would be giving *The Washington Post* a piece of her mind as soon as possible. General Vaught was probably what many people would imagine one of the first female Army generals to be: although short in stature, she was forceful in words and actions with a gruff voice to match, not someone from whom a "talking to" would be a fun experience.

Mom called out to me from the dining room with the phone in her hand, "Erin, General Vaught says *The Post* obituary is already published!"

I immediately opened my laptop on the coffee table in the living room to look for the obituary on the internet while Mom continued to chat with General Vaught. Scrolling among the lines of black and white text on the newspaper's website, between obituaries about a switchboard operator and a physician were a few lines about "Elaine D. Harmon, appraiser, pilot."

I heard Mom hang up with General Vaught, so I carried my laptop into the dining room to show Mom what I had found. Mom glared at the computer screen, shook her head, and remarked, "This reporter represents the exact type of misogynist man who prevented Gammy and other women from being officially recognized as part of the military in World War II."

"*The Post*," was now officially "an irrelevant news source" in Mom's opinion. She banged out another email to the newspaper that night condemning the terrible write-up:

...you not only missed the story, you ignored the story. It is incomprehensible that on the approach to Memorial Day, The Washington Post was incapable of properly and respectfully crediting a veteran Women Airforce Service Pilot who broke gender barriers, was among the first group of women to fly military aircraft, and received a Congressional Gold medal...[the reporter] said to me,"She ONLY flew planes for a little over a year, she was an appraiser for 25 years."

18

The switchboard operator and physician may have made some remarkable contributions to society during their lives, but we had no idea since the reporter apparently only based his obituaries on the jobs the subjects of those obituaries did. After explaining our experiences with this reporter to my sister Tiffany, she said, "Gammy got a Congressional Gold Medal, it's not like they pass those things out like candy!" The obituary also prompted Tiffany to send the newspaper a lengthy email of her own:

...I can tell you definitely that our grandmother would have hated what you wrote about her and if she knew the writer she would have had no problem telling him that he completely dropped the ball and is a poor reporter.

General Vaught had also alerted us to another issue. "It says here in *The Baltimore Sun* obituary, which was very respectful by the way, that Elaine wanted to be at Arlington."

"Yes, she left instructions to request Arlington as her final resting place," Mom informed the General over the phone.

"I've heard a rumor, nothing confirmed officially that I can find, but through the grapevine they say WASP are no longer allowed at Arlington National Cemetery."

"How can that be?" Mom asked. "I've been to WASP funerals there with my mother."

"This is what I've heard. I wanted to tell you so that in case they say no, you won't be surprised," General Vaught explained.

We were shocked to hear this. Mom was in disbelief because she had attended multiple funeral services with Gammy over the years for other women of the WASP at Arlington National Cemetery. Most had been buried with their husbands, but Mom knew of two women whose cremains had been placed in Arlington's beautiful Columbarium on their own, just as Gammy had requested. Only a few weeks had elapsed since Gammy had died, and before the state had even returned her cremains to us, we already had a potential problem with her last request to be laid to rest at Arlington National Cemetery.

3

Final Flight

May 2004

G ammy, dressed in her Women Airforce Service Pilots uniform, of a color called Santiago blue, complete with beret atop her head of short gray hair, made her way through the crowd along the National Mall in Washington, D.C., alongside my boyfriend and me.

"Here, you all need these," Gammy said as she handed us two lanyards with "VIP Guest" badges hanging from them. We hung them around our necks as we approached the security guards regulating entry at a cordoned off area. We displayed our badges to gain entry to the seating area in front of the stage erected on the grass strip between the Washington Monument and the Lincoln Memorial.

"This is cool," my boyfriend announced. "Aren't you impressed?"

"Yeah, it's exciting," I replied.

"You're probably used to it," he offered.

"I don't usually do things like this with her, so this is new to me too," I said.

We found three available seats and then under the sun, which was surprisingly forgiving for a May day in Washington, we waited for the ceremony to begin. As a member of the Women Airforce Service Pilots located in the vicinity of Washington, D.C., Gammy had played a small role in supporting the development of the project we were there to dedicate. The crowd numbered in the thousands, including hundreds of World War II veterans, many in uniform. I was proud to be sitting with one.

A voice from the speakers flanking the stage announced the beginning of the ceremony. "Ladies and Gentlemen, welcome to the dedication ceremony of the World War II Memorial. Welcome the Honorable Marcy Kaptur." Representative Kaptur had initiated legislation in Congress to authorize the building of the World War II Memorial. She explained in her speech that the inspiration came from the Durbin family in her home state of Ohio who wanted "a place where America's grandchildren could come to know the reasons why America fought." Unfortunately Mr. Roger Durbin, a World War II veteran, had passed away before the memorial he worked so hard to establish was completed. His granddaughter spoke at the memorial dedication ceremony on his behalf.

Tom Brokaw, the journalist who reported and wrote extensively about the "Greatest Generation," spoke of how the responsibility to honor and remember those who served in World War II had now fallen on the succeeding generations. "We are honored and obligated to honor you with our lives by fulfilling our duty, the duty to carry on your noble mission."

President George W. Bush asked all the men and women in the audience who had fought or lived through World War II to stand up. His own father, former President George H.W. Bush, a Navy veteran, stood up. Gammy stood up. I applauded as our country formally recognized the monument to honor all those who had served during World War II in some capacity. At the time, I took for granted that everyone, including all departments of the United States government, saw Gammy as a veteran. I knew it had been a difficult road to achieve that belated designation of "veteran" for Gammy and the other women of the Women Airforce Service Pilots, but in my mind all that controversy had been resolved long ago. On that beautiful sunny day, I was just one of the millions of Americans watching our country dedicate another memorial on the National Mall.

4

Final Fight

May 2015

A round Memorial Day, the official holiday at the end of May in honor of those who died in service to the country, but also the unofficial beginning of summer in the United States, Mom went to retrieve Gammy's ashes from the state crematorium. She returned with a small black plastic box – Gammy's informal urn – that was heavier than it looked. I opened it only once to confirm the contents. Inside was a thick, transparent plastic bag containing Gammy's cremated remains. We already had Gammy's honorable discharge certificate and service record (often referred by its government form number, "DD-214"); and now we had the certificate of cremation and the cremains, the final items required to complete the application process for inurnment at Arlington National Cemetery.

"Do you think I should investigate what General Vaught told us about Arlington denying the WASP before I apply?" Mom asked me, holding the phone in her hand as she flipped through the Arlington National Cemetery paperwork on the table.

"Mom, we can't argue with them for saying no unless they have actually said no. You have to apply and see what happens," I replied.

"Okay, I guess we'll see what happens then." Mom dialed the phone number to Arlington National Cemetery's administrative office. I heard her read off information from Gammy's documents. "The WASP. Right, the Women Airforce Service Pilots. Yes, we have the cremation certificate. Yes, okay. Thank you." Mom ended the call.

"That didn't sound bad, what did they say?" I asked.

"The woman on the phone didn't seem concerned about what kind of service Gammy did. She said we have to wait to be assigned a date and that's it. Maybe General Vaught heard wrong," Mom replied. She looked at the black box sitting on the table. "Where are we going to keep Gammy? I don't want Rosco to get into the ashes," she added, out of concern that one of the dogs would snoop around the urn.

Rosco, one of my two Shiba Inus, was good 98 percent of the time, but when he did eat something, it was always something bad for him: two whole corn cobs, a bottle of anti-diarrhea pills, xylitol sweetened gum – things requiring trips to the emergency veterinary clinic. Not being experts on how to properly display or retain a plastic box of ashes while also keeping it out of reach of the dogs, Mom decided the safest place to keep it would be high up in the closet and I agreed. Ironically, Gammy had kept my Great Great Aunt Helen's ashes in her own closet for over 20 years while searching for the paperwork to apply for Helen to be at Arlington National Cemetery. Helen Harmon was eligible to be inurned in Arlington National Cemetery because she had served in the United States Naval Reserve during World War I. She was one of the women casually referred to as "Yeomanettes," who opened the door for women to later serve in the United States Naval Reserve as WAVES (Women Accepted for Volunteer Emergency Service) during World War II. The problem was Gammy couldn't find Helen's paperwork and then the government's copies were destroyed in a fire at a storage facility at the National Personnel Records Center in St. Louis, Missouri in 1973. Gammy had persisted until she sorted out the situation and Helen was finally inurned on May 1, 1988, about

26 years after she had died.

While Gammy's ashes waited in the closet, calls and cards of condolences continued to trickle in as people saw the news about her passing. In June, Mom and I went to The American Legion Post 156 in Ellicott City, a nearby town in Maryland, for a special ceremony. One of its members, Michael Lauriente, had invited us to accept an honorary posthumous certificate of membership for Gammy. The American Legion's national organization had opposed veteran's status for the WASP in the 1970s during the Congressional hearings, although some of the individual lodges were supporters of the WASP. Now Gammy would be on the permanent Post rolls of The American Legion as an honorary perpetual member.

* * *

Summer 2015

"I got a call from Arlington today," Mom announced from her seat at the dining room table one day in late July when I arrived home from work. "They said no."

"What? That's crazy. What was their explanation?" I asked.

"The guy who called me said that since the WASP were active duty designees, they aren't eligible at Arlington," Mom replied.

"What does that mean?" I retorted. "That since the government decided the WASP were veterans 35 years late, they aren't as good as other veterans? How is that Gammy's fault? This is ridiculous. You have to contact Senator Mikulski. Based on her letter, she is under the impression that Gammy was a veteran."

"I told him they must be wrong because Gammy went to several funerals there for the WASP, including for Toby Felker, who wasn't inurned with her husband. I even went with her to a few of the funerals!" Mom recounted the call to me in disbelief. "The guy on the phone explained the Army had a misinterpretation of policy and the cemetery should not have been placing WASP at Arlington National Cemetery on their own merit, but only as spouses if they were eligible. He said we can apply for an exception to policy. But I don't think we should have to ask for an exception. She should be there on her own merit from her service as a WASP. Can you help me look at the laws and figure out what they're relying on for this decision?"

"Of course!" I replied.

That day in late July was the beginning of our first dive down the rabbit hole of internet research into this term "active duty designee" to find background information to accompany our request to the senator to investigate the rejection of Gammy's cremains by Arlington National Cemetery.

After hours of research among Gammy's documents and books, and what was available on the internet, I informed Mom of my conclusions. "Mom, 'active duty designee' does not seem to be a legal term. I think the Army made it up. The only place I find it used is on this archived Arlington National Cemetery web page that says the WASP and other active duty designees *are* eligible to be at the Columbarium in Arlington, which the Army is now saying is a mistake. I don't understand why they are trying to say they aren't accepted anymore. When did this change?"

"I'm filling out a Freedom of Information Act request to the Army to ask for the written decision letter of this policy," Mom exclaimed with pride from her bed as she squinted at the laptop computer monitor perched on her legs.

After Mom drafted her letter of outrage, which Whitney and I edited, she assembled the requested information and sent if off to Senator Mikulski's office in early August. Then the waiting began. We had no illusions that there would be a speedy reply.

The reason we chose to contact the senator may need some further explanation for people not familiar with laws and jurisdictions in the

United States. The Constitution of the United States of America lays out the jurisdiction of the federal, or national, government. Things that are not delineated in the Constitution are under the jurisdiction of the states, which also have their own laws. On a basic level, the armed services and issues related to them, such as military cemeteries, are under the purview of the federal government. Therefore the laws related to the military cemeteries are created by the United States Congress. Congress is composed of two bodies: the Senate and the House of Representatives. There are two senators from each state. The state delegation to the House of Representatives, often referred to only as "the House," is composed of a varying number of members based on the population of the state they represent. Maryland had eight representatives at the time.

Since we wanted a federal law changed, or at least investigated, we needed to contact someone in Congress. Senator Mikulski had been there almost 40 years; therefore, she was the most senior federal elected official to Congress from our home state of Maryland.

The federal government also has many agencies that administer the laws created by Congress and create their own internal regulations pursuant to those laws. The Social Security Administration regulates payments for workers who retire or are disabled, the Department of the Interior administers federal land and parks, and the Department of Veterans Affairs administers benefits like healthcare to those who have served in the armed forces. The military has an agency for each branch (Department of the Army, Navy, etc.) We were fighting the interpretation of a federal law by the Department of the Army, a federal agency, and needed someone in the best position to advocate for us in the federal government, and we figured it should be the most senior federal official from our state.

While we waited for a response from the senator's office, we also waited for the birth of my youngest sister Whitney's first child. I drove a few hours to Whitney's house in New Jersey one weekend to wait with her.

"Are you having labor pains yet?" I asked Whitney. I was immersed in the hot tub, but she only had her feet dangling in the water since she was about 40 weeks pregnant.

"No," she replied with a pouty face. "If I don't deliver in a week, they're going to induce me. I've been walking and walking and walking and doing a lot of those things that supposedly encourage labor to start. They're all lies!" Whitney sighed. "Did Mom send the letter to Mikulski?"

"Yes," I replied. "And she did a FOIA request for the decision memo. I have learned that Mom gets really excited about making Freedom of Information Act requests." We both laughed.

At the medical office the next day, the doctor exclaimed Whitney was less than one centimeter dilated – the birth of her baby was still in a holding pattern. Responding to the look of frustration on Whitney's face, the doctor remarked, "It's better than zero!" Whitney was not amused, but the doctor smiled and I laughed.

I had to go back to work and secretly hoped the baby would stay put until the next weekend. I drove up again the following Friday. After spending more time in the hot tub chatting with Whitney who kept telling the baby it was time to come out, around midnight, she finally declared with great relief, "I think I am having labor pains!" And my niece Isabella was born the next evening at 7:45 p.m. Life was routine for the next month and a half, interspersed with visits to Whitney's house to see the new baby, while we waited for a response from the senator's office.

On October 3, 2015, a couple weeks after the official end of summer, I pulled the mail from the mailbox and flipped through the envelopes and catalogs as I walked back to the house. Upon noticing one specific envelope with a return address of Arlington National Cemetery, my heart began to race. I walked straight through the house, discarded the other pieces of mail on the dining table, and started to open the Arlington letter. I had no expectations of either good or bad news, but I was anxious to read the reply inside. Would it say Gammy could be at

Arlington National Cemetery, that the representative who had called earlier that summer was mistaken? Unfortunately, the news inside was disappointing and reiterated what the cemetery representative had told Mom on the phone back in July. In the letter, the Executive Director of Arlington National Cemetery referenced our request to Senator Mikulski and explained that "active duty designees" like the Women Airforce Service Pilots are not eligible for inurnment. In the letter, he explained that Arlington National Cemetery had been incorrectly inurning WASP since at least 2002 when the prior contradictory guidance had been issued, erroneously confirming the group's eligibility. In short, the women of the WASP who were already resting at Arlington National Cemetery without an eligible spouse were there by mistake.

However, the letter gave specific references to the law on which the Army's decision was based. It had taken over five months to get a written explanation, but finally we had something concrete to dispute.

My anxiety turned to anger. I hadn't been too upset since Mom's phone conversation a couple months earlier because the situation had been ambiguous. But with the written denial staring me in the face, I became determined to ensure that my vision of a funeral for Gammy at Arlington National Cemetery became a reality. And I knew that our entire family would want this too.

After firing off a few expletive-laden messages to friends and family, I reviewed the research I had done since the phone denial a few months earlier. I dug deeper into federal law, legislative history, and news articles to figure out if the Army's decision made any legal sense. I spent time in Mom's basement digging through boxes of old documents and books from Gammy's house. Fortunately, Gammy had kept a lot of her paperwork and memorabilia which eased the research.

Gammy had left behind a library of what seemed like every book that had even mentioned the WASP, many of them signed by the authors: an autographed copy of Tom Brokaw's *Greatest Generation*, a gift from

Secretary of Defense William Cohen in 1999; an autographed copy of WASP Bee Haydu's book *Letters Home*, "To Elaine, My good WASP friend. Always blue skies and CAVU;" and a copy of the September 20, 1977 Congressional transcript of the House Veterans' Affairs Committee hearing on granting veterans' status to the WASP, signed by Congresswoman Margaret Heckler, "To Elaine Harmon, With warmest wishes & grateful thanks for your courageous & gallant service, Margaret M. Heckler."

Flipping through one of her scrapbooks, I noticed a photo of Representative Marcy Kaptur with Senator Bob Dole alongside Gammy. It was taken at a luncheon in 1997 for supporters of the World War II Memorial – a luncheon that Roger Durbin, the inspiration for the memorial, had also attended. Looking through old photos, I started to get a peek into this world that Gammy had been a part of, at which point I realized that I had much to learn about who Gammy, or rather Elaine Danforth Harmon, was.

Holding Tom Brokaw's book in hand, I thought back to that day on the National Mall when Gammy was a "VIP" guest at the World War II Memorial dedication. I had no idea at the time that eleven years later Tom Brokaw's words of instruction to take responsibility for honoring the members of the World War II generation would resonate so personally. Like Mr. Durbin's granddaughter, I needed to speak for my own grandmother who was no longer here to speak for herself. Thus began my personal mission to honor Gammy and her colleagues by fighting for their equal recognition at Arlington National Cemetery – learning along the way why Gammy had fought to preserve the history of the Women Airforce Service Pilots of World War II.

* * *

According to the Arlington letter, the Army's decision was based on the wording of Public Law 95-202 from 1977, the law that was the subject of the Congressional hearing transcript I had found. This law had granted the WASP and other similarly situated groups the right to petition the Department of Defense for retroactive recognition as veterans. The language of the law was specific to benefits under "laws administered by the Veterans Administration." But Arlington National Cemetery was run by the Department of the Army, which narrowly interpreted those words to exclude her service with the Army during World War II as not recognized in its department. However, just because the law was written that way didn't mean it was right and it did not mean that my family had to accept it without question.

The simple explanation was that the Army claimed that the women of the WASP were only veterans at the Department of Veterans Affairs, not the rest of the federal government. The unbelievable truth was that although I had taken Gammy for cancer treatment for years at a Veterans Affairs hospital, where she was considered a veteran, she was not considered a veteran at Arlington National Cemetery, run by the Department of the Army. Her service was good enough to qualify her for decades of health care, including expensive chemotherapy and radiation treatments, but not a spot for her ashes in a cemetery. As my dad the Vietnam War veteran put it, "They spent a lot of money keeping her alive long enough to decide she wasn't good enough to be buried."

The Department of Veterans Affairs administers 136 national cemeteries. Gammy would have been accepted at any of those, but she had requested to be laid to rest at Arlington National Cemetery. Even though her funeral arrangements letter had designated an alternative burial spot with my grandfather, I thought Gammy was correct to write "there should be no reason" she should not be allowed at Arlington National Cemetery. The statement also showed an eerie foresight on Gammy's part. She and the other women of the WASP had been fighting for 70 years to have the same recognition as their male counterparts, so she had a reason to be skeptical about the certainty of her funeral and burial request. The women of the WASP had appeared in their military uniforms at the request of the United States Air Force and other groups at official events for many years as examples of living history, the first women to fly planes for the military. I knew decades had passed between their wartime service and the moment the WASP were formally designated as veterans, but I had always thought of Gammy as a veteran, unaware that her status was viewed by the government as being on a lower tier than others who had served the country. I was incredulous staring at this letter full of bureaucratic nonsense.

Mom was down at the beach house on the day the letter arrived, so I had to call her on the phone to tell her about it.

"Mom, we got a letter from Arlington," I said into the phone with the letter in my hand. I stood in the dining room looking through the windows at the trees whose leaves were glistening in the evening sunlight, showing off the beginnings of the yellow and orange shades of fall.

"What does it say?" Mom asked on the other end of the line.

"It says the same thing they told you on the phone. She isn't allowed at Arlington," I replied.

The line was quiet for a moment as Mom absorbed the information I had relayed.

"Any word from the senator's office?" she asked.

"Not yet," I told her.

"I guess we have to wait and see if the senator comes up with anything," Mom said.

"We need the senator or someone else in Congress to do something about this. I've been looking through all the laws and regulations again today after I got this letter," I explained.

"And...?" Mom asked.

"If I were a lawyer for the Army and they told me to decide if this regulation permitting WASP and the others to be inurned at Arlington was in accordance with the law, I would have come to the same conclusion, in a legal sense. Not that I agree with it, obviously."

"So what are you saying?" Mom asked.

After a moment of silence to acknowledge the monumental task ahead, I admitted, "We need Congress to pass a law so we can bury Gammy."

5

Final Flight

The WWII trailblazer who happened to be my grandmother

To understand why we didn't accept Arlington National Cemetery's rejection of Gammy's ashes and instead bury her in my grandfather's plot at another cemetery – the alternative spot she had designated in case there were problems – requires explanation about Gammy's life and why her time in the WASP was so meaningful to her that she wanted it honored at one of the most well-known cemeteries in the world.

I would fight for my grandmother because I loved her but I realized nobody outside our family was going to care about helping me bury "Gammy," the neighborhood's most famous Halloween witch and grandmother whose burned, yet undercooked, lasagna I had to eat growing up. They were going to care about Elaine Danforth Harmon, the hero, trailblazer, and patriot who volunteered to serve her beloved United States during World War II as one of the first female pilots to fly military airplanes.

I didn't know Gammy as a trailblazing woman of history. As children, most people have a cadre of family members and their adult acquaintances swirling around them. We view these people in our

35

circle in relative terms: my mom, my grandmother, my aunt. But it is not until we approach adulthood and we start taking on our own burdens and dealing with the problems of the world that we realize our family members are also their own individuals. We discover other dimensions of their lives, what it was like before they had kids of their own, or the problems they tackled while we were young and unaware of it all. The larger the degree of generational separation, the less we are likely to discover about the people behind the affectionate nicknames. We often have less time to spend with them. There is a disconnect between the person who we think we know and the greater picture of who they truly are. Such was the case with Gammy.

Growing up, I had a close relationship with Gammy, which initially developed simply because we lived near each other. I could have even walked to her house, but I don't remember ever doing so, as that would have required crossing a busy thoroughfare that ran from Maryland into the city of Washington. My other grandparents were much older and they lived over 350 miles away in western New York, so I had not seen them often. Gammy's husband, my grandfather Robert Harmon, passed away before I was born. Gammy was not only my closest grandparent, but she became my only grandparent when I was about 12 years old.

When I was born in 1976, she and the other WASP were in the midst of lobbying for their veteran status on Capitol Hill. Since Gammy's house was conveniently located on the outskirts of Washington, some of the WASP from out of town would stay with her when they had meetings about the pending legislation. Bee Haydu and Marty Wyall were two of the many WASP who spent time at Gammy's home. It was during these lobbying years that many of them got to know each other for the first time, as they had often worked closely with only their classmates during the war.

By the time I was old enough to realize what she and the other WASP had done in the war, their lobbying efforts had been completed for a number of years. As a child, I had no idea what they had to do to earn the right just to be called veterans. I used to see Gammy put on her WASP uniform and travel to different schools, museums, air shows, or other community events, to give talks about what she had done during the war. Somehow, she never made a formal WASP visit to my school.

As a young girl, I thought everyone's grandmother had flown planes in the war. I thought it was a grandma's job. I received many confused looks from other children when I asked whether their grandmothers talked about flying planes during the war. I told people that Gammy had flown planes in World War II as if it was a given that they knew about the WASP, only 13 of whom hailed from our state. Some kids didn't believe me. Some adults didn't believe me either. Maybe the other kids would have believed me if she had visited our school or if the story of the WASP had been printed in our history textbooks; at the time, I never questioned why I had not learned about them in school. If I had not been related to a member of the WASP, I would likely have never known about them. Gammy understood this, and it bothered her; particularly after a decade spent convincing Congress of the value and validity of their service, she wanted to ensure the next generation knew about the role of the WASP during World War II. Thereafter, Gammy took every opportunity available to educate people by sharing her personal experience of flying military planes in 1944.

Gammy used to receive fan mail, as I called it. Adults and children wrote to thank her for visiting or to ask questions about her service. A lot of kids did research papers about the WASP and wanted Gammy's input on their projects. I never did any school projects or papers about her or the WASP because, although Gammy spent so much time sharing her story as a way to educate the public, in our family setting, she didn't make a big deal out of what she had done. She preferred to talk to me about how my tennis game was coming along or what books I was reading rather than shine a light on her own achievements. I saw her as "Gammy, my grandmother," not "Gammy, historic World War

II pilot," so it never occurred to me that she was a worthy subject for a school project. Gammy had photographs of herself that she signed upon request and mailed out to people on a regular basis. I thought this was all completely normal. Some grandmothers did needlepoint; Gammy gave talks about flying planes for the United States Army during World War II. Only as I grew older did I realize that not much about Gammy was normal.

After the war, Gammy's next adventure was raising her children and eventually helping out with her grandchildren. She had attended clown school in the 1970s and loved to joke around with her grandkids. True to her Great Depression upbringing, she admonished us if we did anything she perceived as wasteful like leaving lights on when we left a room or taking more food than we ended up eating. *"Don't let your eyes be bigger than your stomach!"* She generally didn't cook, which she told me was a result of her own children being too picky. When she did cook, I usually wished she hadn't because it was often an unenjoyable (and sometimes unidentifiable) meal.

Gammy was a sturdy, athletic woman with styled short gray hair who was still slightly taller than I was when I became an adult. She always made an effort to look presentable, which she accomplished with great frugality. Birthday and holiday presents were usually something practical – a grammar book, a dictionary, mittens – or something close to her heart, like the year we all received red T-shirts featuring the state flag of her beloved Maryland.

Gammy once paid an aerobatic pilot at a local air show to take me up in his plane and do spins, loops, and other feats. When the pilot saw that it was me, a scrawny seven year old, and not Gammy who he had been hired to take up, he questioned her about it on the side.

"She'll be fine. She's tough!" Gammy told him while giving me a smile.

When the pilot asked if I was scared as he was strapping me into the back seat of the old biplane, I confidently barked, "No way!"

During the flight he tried his best to scare me, occasionally yelling back, "Here comes another trick!" before rolling or diving the plane. I had fun but tried not to lose my cookies, lest I embarrass Gammy. When we landed, I was afraid I would vomit all over the pilot's shoes. Luckily all the greasy, sugary funnel cake I had consumed pre-flight stayed put.

I think Gammy genuinely believed I would become a professional tennis player for all the tennis we played together; she even sent me to sleepaway tennis camp (where I was *not* one of the shining stars – but I was decent). We had to play at local tennis courts together because she didn't keep up the maintenance on the tennis court in her own backyard; weeds grew through cracks in the pavement. She was a resourceful person, which came in handy when my best friend Amy accidentally whacked me in the face with her racket at tennis one morning. Gammy had a roll of toilet paper in the car to sop up the blood spewing from my nose.

"You'll be fine, don't worry," Gammy consoled me as the crumpled, bloody wads of paper piled up on the tennis court while a distraught Amy looked on, probably wondering why we weren't already headed to a hospital. When Gammy dropped me off at home (still not having visited the hospital), she didn't have much to say to the nine-year old me except to suggest I put a bag of frozen peas on my possibly broken nose.

Staying home from school often meant a day at Gammy's house, which was generally what one would think of as a grandmother's house – filled with family mementos and lots of books. There was a United States flag flying daily off the front porch. By the front door she had a glass case displaying porcelainized baby shoes of her children, which I always found strange, but I guessed that was the trend in the 1940s and 1950s when Mom and her siblings were born. There was a huge painting of my great grandfather Ernest E. Harmon that hung over the sofa in the living room that had always struck me as grand and austere, like being in a museum. In the hallway was a grandfather clock that never seemed to function properly, either ringing at odd times or not at all. I often spotted Gammy's WASP uniform hanging in the hall closet near the clock. The hardwood floors had once been covered with cream-colored wall-to-wall shag carpeting, but she tore it up when I was in elementary school after I had started refusing to go to her house because the years of accumulated dust in the carpet strands irritated my sinuses.

However, staying home from school with Gammy did not mean avoiding educational activities. She owned a television, but I rarely watched it. Everything we did together was a learning opportunity: word games like Boggle or Scrabble, or reading books together. We also enjoyed working on her favorite pastime: crossword puzzles, especially those published in *The New York Times*.

"Do you know what ort means?" Gammy asked one day while we did a crossword together at the dining room table.

"No," I replied. "What is it?"

"I guess you ought to look it up," Gammy replied.

In a scene that was repeated on many occasions with each of her grandchildren, I walked over to the wooden dictionary stand in the living room upon which sat the oldest and largest book I had ever seen in person – Gammy's dictionary. I flipped through the thin pages and took note of how many words had been circled or underlined, a sign Gammy had already looked them up.

As I came upon the "O" section, I said to Gammy, "You already circled ort. You already looked it up. Why didn't you just tell me what it means?"

"You are more likely to remember it if you look it up yourself rather than if someone tells you," she explained.

Gammy was well known in our neighborhood for her dedication to Halloween. Rather than distribute commercially manufactured candy, she dressed up as a witch in an elaborate costume and passed out homemade caramel apples, which I often spent days making with her. She heated a big pot of caramel and then I stabbed the apples with pointed wooden sticks before dipping them in the melted

40

goo and setting them down in organized rows to dry on wax paper. Parents drove in from outside the neighborhood specifically to her house just to see their children get spooked by Gammy on her dark porch as she answered the door. She would quibble a bit with the kids before handing out the candy apples. After some alleged nationwide incidents of tainted candy, many parents stopped letting their children have homemade treats. Gammy then decided it was wasteful to make the apples and there was no fun in it anymore. With an air of contempt, Gammy explained to me that fear of contaminated candy, or of anything in life, was ridiculous.

Gammy was thoughtful and generous but also rigid and direct. When I once hid under my bed in a pointless hissy fit, she dragged me out by my feet, threw me over her shoulder and plopped me down among my cousins in her big blue radio-free station wagon to drive to a performance by the magician David Copperfield. But at least I was never left on the side of a highway in Maine like one of my cousins. Gammy returned for him eventually.

Whether it was school events like plays, project presentations, or graduation ceremonies, Gammy was there. And not just for me, but for her dozen grandchildren, so it was quite a time commitment. I chose to go to college at the University of California, San Diego, completely on the other side of the country from Maryland. But Gammy was at my graduation ceremony there too.

Even in her last years as I spent time going to and from the hospital with Gammy, I only felt that I was getting to know her in her current personage, although we occasionally spoke about things from long ago. After she was gone, I realized that in order to pursue this last request for her, it would become vitally important to come to know this other side, this person she was before she was "Gammy." I needed to see her as the rest of the world saw her: as a pioneer, as someone who inadvertently defied gender norms simply because she wanted to serve her country and fly airplanes.

When a grandparent dies, that personal history goes too. Generally

41

there are family stories and photos to keep the memory of that person alive. But Gammy was not an average grandparent and in addition the US Army refused to accept her ashes for inurnment at Arlington National Cemetery. I needed more than family stories and photos to convince the public that official recognition of Gammy's military service at the cemetery was worth their time, energy, and support. People needed to see that Gammy was more than my grandmother; she and her fellow pilots were an important part of the fabric of American history. What the women of the WASP did for our country made them, and Gammy, worthy of sharing the hallowed land at the nation's most well-known military cemetery for eternity. In order to convince anyone not related to me of this, I needed to see her not as I remembered her – the tennis lover, horrendous cook, and devoted Halloween celebrant – but as the rest of the world saw her, as a trailblazer in history.

My childhood memories of Gammy included the awareness that she had been a member of the WASP during World War II, which formed a core part of her identity, but she was also simply my grandmother. From her I learned how to improve my backhand, the value of a good education, and respect for what the United States represented in the world. I thought that helping to care for her as she bravely battled cancer would be my small attempt to repay everything she had done for me. But it was what happened after she died that would allow me to pay the highest respect to what her life represented. Fighting to secure a resting place for Gammy at Arlington National Cemetery also demonstrated what a great teacher she was – even though she was gone, she taught me to understand and appreciate the history of the Women Airforce Service Pilots and how to carry on her legacy of sharing the history of the WASP.

I cared because she was my grandmother.

Everyone else would care because she was a part of history.

I had already been researching some of the laws and history of the WASP since Arlington had first called to deny the request back in July.

Now that we had a letter in hand, it was obvious that I needed to have as much background information as possible to support an appeal of this decision. I approached this as someone who was not only a granddaughter, but also an historian, biographer, and detective. My focus was to learn about the WASP program, the legislative record pertaining to the WASP, and most of all, the woman who was to become "Gammy."

Fortunately, thanks to the influence of the Great Depression, Gammy had saved everything. I pieced together some memories of my conversations with her, information from the boxes of documents she left behind, her diary from WASP training, and stories from news articles about her and the WASP to construct my own biography of my grandmother – not the "Gammy" I knew, but the "Elaine Danforth Harmon" I didn't know.

* * *

Elaine Danforth Harmon

Elaine Danforth was born at home on 34th Street in Baltimore, Maryland on December 26, 1919. I imagined her upbringing was unusual for that era, or any era. Her father, Dave Danforth, was a professional baseball player from Texas. He met Elaine's mother, Margaret Oliphant, while he was playing for the Baltimore Orioles baseball franchise in Maryland. Margaret's father was a Baltimore city police detective and her mother rented out rooms in their house to baseball players, and Dave was one of them. Dave was a teammate of Babe Ruth on the Orioles roster in 1914, the same year he married 19-year-old Margaret. He was a teammate of Shoeless Joe Jackson on the World Series Championship White Sox team in 1917. During his playing time in Maryland, he also enrolled in the University of Maryland School

43

of Dentistry and eventually made dentistry his career. This career choice was not born out of a great passion for dental health, but from his childhood in Texas where he realized that during a time when professional baseball players also often held normal jobs to pay the bills, the only person in town who could take off work to play baseball was the town dentist.

Elaine recalled traveling around to different cities as a small child due to her father's baseball career. She used to complain to me how the world was a much "worse-off" place than when she was young.

"You know when I was a little girl, we didn't have all these problems this world has now. In New Orleans, when my dad was playing games, he used to give my sister and me a nickel and tell us to go into town on the streetcar to get ice cream," she once told me.

"How old were you?" I asked.

"I don't know, maybe four. We went into town and wandered around. Nobody bothered us and we went back later in the day. The world is much more difficult these days," she lamented.

"Well, maybe there were the same amount of problems but people didn't have television, so they didn't know as much about what was happening," I replied.

She looked at me with consternation, waved her hand, and said, "Oh fiddle faddle. You know what else? I used to take the train alone from Baltimore to Washington. My mom pinned a note to my chest with the address of my relatives down there and sent me on my way."

"What happened if you got lost?" I asked.

"That's what the note was for. Mother said to show someone the note and they would help me figure out where to go," she explained.

Elaine grew up with an independent streak and no hesitation about travel or facing the unknown. To fulfill her sense of adventure she eventually visited all the continents over the course of her lifetime. She was also generous and service-minded toward her community. During the Great Depression, people occasionally showed up at her family's home in Baltimore asking for food or money. Rather than turn them away, Elaine's mother always invited these strangers in to eat with them or made them a sandwich to take away. Elaine said the family philosophy was that those people needed help, her family was able to provide it, and they were honored to do so.

Elaine's mother Margaret was adamant about women maintaining their "proper" place in society. Margaret required that the family dress in proper attire for each meal. Girls should have skirts on and not be in play clothes. Sometimes Elaine changed outfits three times a day just to eat. Margaret not only demanded proper etiquette of her children but also excellent grammar, presumably so her three daughters would be worthy of becoming wives of upstanding men. She would have been proud to know that her daughter Elaine once gave each of her grandchildren a grammar book for Christmas. I have fuzzy memories of visiting my great grandmother Margaret. Although she was in her eighties at the time, I remember her intimidating stare and the fancy dresses she wore while holding her little white Maltese dog on her lap. I was certain she thought of me as a total "ragamuffin" since I typically wore a T-shirt and shorts, or pants with patches during the winter, usually had scraped knees and other injuries, and I ran around the house without end. I definitely never wore proper attire at her dinner table. Margaret died when I was six years old and I was fascinated to learn that she had never once worn a pair of pants. According to Margaret, pants were for men.

Elaine attended the University of Maryland at College Park for four years, graduating in 1940 with a degree in bacteriology. She kept herself busy at college as vice president of her sorority Kappa Delta, as a competitor on the rifle team, and as a member of the swim team. She was also a cheerleader. I did not find out she was a cheerleader until after I had graduated from college when I found an old black and white photo of her in a cheerleading outfit doing a 'C' jump. She was embarrassed about having been a cheerleader, but could not articulate the reason to me.

Dating my grandfather Robert Harmon during college kept Elaine busy as well. Robert had also grown up in an unusual family; his father was a pilot. Perhaps this helped them relate to one another. I envisioned Elaine and Robert having conversations which involved competition over whose father was cooler, the baseball player or the pilot. I wondered sometimes if her father-in-law's career in aviation had some influence on Elaine's interest in learning to fly, but unfortunately I never thought to ask her before she passed away. Robert's father died before Elaine met Robert, so maybe the mutual interest in flying was only a coincidence.

Robert's father was Ernest Emery Harmon, a pilot for the United States Army Air Corps during the First World War. I knew him as the military man in the fancy painting on the wall above the sofa in Elaine's house. When I was a kid, I assumed he must have been important because I figured artists didn't paint fancy portraits of inconsequential people. Ernest completed military pilot training in 1918. He became a test pilot and flight instructor for the United States, flying every plane available and becoming an expert on parachute mechanics along the way.

Ernest was the first pilot to fly the L.W.F. "Owl" bomber. In 1919 he became the first pilot to complete the "round the rim" flight, a three month journey through each state around the edge of the continental United States. He broke several speed records during his career and won many aviation competitions. In 1919 Ernest's wife Harriette became the first woman to fly in a plane from Washington, D.C., to New York City when she was his passenger as he piloted that route. Despite some nausea during the flight, she declared she was done with trains, cars, and any other mode of transportation besides airplanes.[1]

Ernest continued to play football after college at various bases during his Army Air Corps career. He used to recruit civilian players into the military if they would improve his own military football teams. Ernest became a mentor to one young man named Pete, a football

---

[1] "Woman Flyer's Trip from Capital 'Simply Perfect.'" *The Evening World.* May 31, 1919.

recruit from the University of Maryland, who thrived in the military environment. Pete eventually became General Pete Quesada who developed the concept of close air support, using it successfully during the D-Day invasion when he led the Ninth Air Tactical Command's support of invading ground troops.

On August 27, 1933, Ernest Harmon was flying from Washington to Long Island, New York, an itinerary he had flown numerous times. After encountering heavy fog, he ended up over Connecticut, where his plane crashed into some trees, throwing him from the plane and killing him. He was buried on August 30, 1933 in Arlington National Cemetery, only three days after he died. His wife Harriette was eventually buried alongside him. A daughter, Helen, who did not survive infancy, was also buried in their plot. In 1949, an act of Congress declared an air field in Stephenville, Newfoundland, Canada as Ernest Harmon Air Field.

During Elaine's senior year of college, she saw an advertisement in the University of Maryland newspaper, *The Diamondback*, for a Civilian Pilot Training Program (CPTP.) This program had been started by the federal government to increase the number of licensed pilots in the United States for what it perceived as necessary preparation for an impending entry by the United States into World War II. The program was affiliated with numerous colleges in the country, including Tuskegee University. Because of the desperate need for pilots, people previously excluded from flying planes were now offered an unprecedented opportunity to get a pilot's license. Despite being vice president of the Kappa Delta sorority chapter, competing on the swim team, the rifle team, and cheerleading, Elaine said the pilot program was the first thing that piqued her interest at college.

Elaine was under the age of 21, still unmarried, and female, so the CPTP program required permission from a parent for her to join. She sent the permission form to her father who also gave her the required 40 dollar fee. Elaine knew that her mother Margaret would never approve of such unladylike behavior as flying airplanes. Elaine said

47

she never even knew if her father told her mother; flying lessons became an unspoken secret between Elaine and her dad.

"We had to keep flying lessons secret from Mom," Elaine explained. "I did a lot of things growing up that she disapproved of."[2]

In contrast to the men who wanted to join the program – who simply paid the fee to sign up – Elaine had to compete for a spot that was only offered to one woman for every ten men who joined. Fortunately, there was a spot available for her. On her motivation for signing up, Elaine wrote in her unofficial mini-autobiography that she thought the CPTP would be "the most interesting activity I might ever have the opportunity to take advantage of."

There was an airport near the University of Maryland at College Park where Elaine learned to fly through this CPTP program. The College Park airport was the oldest continuously operating airport in the world, active since 1909 when Wilbur Wright began training pilots there. It was also the first place where Elaine flew a plane. The CPTP program consisted of a medical evaluation, 72 hours of ground school, and 35 hours of flight training. She loved this program and felt fortunate to have been accepted.

Likely because it was prohibitively expensive, Elaine didn't continue to fly immediately after she completed the CPTP program. She married Robert on July 26, 1941 and because the bombing of Pearl Harbor happened not too long after that on December 7, 1941, the two of them began to move around the country, working to support the war effort. Robert was classified as 4-F because of a heart condition, so he could not serve in the armed forces. However, as was the case with most Americans during that era, he wanted to contribute his talents where possible, so he found a job with Jack and Heintz, a company that manufactured airplane parts. Eventually he got transferred to a factory in the Philippines. There he assisted the war effort by managing the repair of aircraft in the Pacific theater of operations,

---

[2] Also referenced in interview between Elaine and Sarah Parry Myers, September 1, 2012, at Elaine's home in Maryland.

rather than having them transported back to the United States. This reduced the turnaround time required to get damaged planes back to the Pacific front. Elaine also worked in various capacities to support the war, such as using her bacteriology major from college to work at a military serum development lab in Ohio.

In 1943, Elaine saw a *Life* magazine cover story about the Women Airforce Service Pilots, nicknamed the "WASP," a program created in 1942 as a combination of two female pilot programs to free up male pilots to go overseas for combat during the war. After training, the women pilots would perform the same domestic flying duties as the men had been doing, allowing the Army to send more pilots overseas. Elaine wanted to join the WASP, but didn't know if her CPTP qualifications would be competitive enough to get her in. She assumed the other women applying would have years of experience and she wouldn't be a desirable candidate. As it turned out, there were many women in the WASP who had learned to fly in the CPTP program. By the time Elaine was ready to apply for the WASP, the number of flying hours required would have been fulfilled by her CPTP classes. Since it had been a few years since she finished the CPTP, Elaine wanted a few more hours at the controls of a plane to refresh her skills before applying to the WASP program. My mind flashed back to the day she had died when I discovered an old receipt in her desk showing payment for flying time at the College Park airport.

Her husband Robert encouraged Elaine to apply for the WASP program, so she put in her application with those of more than 25,000 other candidates. Only about 1800 applicants were accepted and 1074 graduated. Elaine was one of them.

Including those women from the Women Auxiliary Ferrying Squadron (WAFS) who were added in, the WASP program ultimately had 1102 total pilots.

While Elaine was in Florida, she received a telegram from the United States Army Air Forces ordering her to report to Avenger Field in Sweetwater, Texas on April 18, 1944. The telegram informed Elaine she had to travel at her own expense and would be paid $150 a month during training.

On the assigned day, Elaine made her way to Sweetwater's Bluebonnet Hotel, the designated meeting point. This was where she got her first glimpse of the other women who would eventually become some of her lifelong best friends. Elaine was a confident person, but upon seeing these other women at the hotel for the first time, she became self-conscious. She wrote in her diary, "I immediately felt inferior and decided that I wouldn't like any of these women." I was surprised to read this, because I had never seen her exhibit any signs of insecurity.

Elaine's attitude changed as soon as the women got to know each other. The pilot trainees stayed in barracks at Avenger Field, where all but the first few WASP classes were trained. Elaine shared her living space with five other women. She theorized that it probably was not insulated well because the temperature inside swung from freezing to sweltering depending on the weather. At times, the women dragged their metal cots outside to stay cooler at night under the open Texas sky. They slept under the stars and only had to worry about rattlesnakes invading their beds. Hot or cold, the area surrounding Avenger Field was almost always windy, amplifying whatever weather came through and blowing dust everywhere, including across the landing strip.

All the women stressed about "washing out" (pilot slang for "failing") and being sent home. In the mornings, they awoke to reveille and at night they turned in to taps, following tradition on military bases. The women followed military structure in their training and marched "everywhere" according to Elaine. They did PT (physical training) daily, about which Elaine wrote in her diary on May 2, 1944 that she enjoyed except that it was "disgusting if kept up too long." Elaine also described how a fellow trainee who was empty handed after mail call asked if anyone had an extra letter she could read.

This experience of being in close quarters and undergoing a demanding training regimen under military order brought these women together as close friends. Elaine felt that anyone who had been a WASP was her friend, even the ones she had never met. They had a common experience which bonded them for life and they always had something to talk about.

As a group, the women of the WASP learned to pilot every model of plane in the military's fleet. During training, they learned on planes like the BT-13, PT-17, PT-19, and AT-6. Some of these planes coincidentally had parts, in particular the instruments, made by Jack & Heintz. So, while Robert worked at the company that made parts for the planes, Elaine flew them. And on May 5, 1941, she soloed (flew alone) as a WASP trainee for the first time. From Elaine's diary I learned that she almost ran down her instructor during her first solo flight:

May 5, 1944

"I soloed today – I have never been happier in all my life. I had so much electricity, due to excitement, my watch even stopped running. I autographed my ship. Boy! It was the best ship I've ever flown. Just as I took off, they changed the tee setting & I came in and landed crosswind. Although I realized the wind wasn't straight I still didn't think to check the tee so I went around again, same pattern & just as I was on my last leg, I saw the T change and went around again. This time there was so much dust, I didn't want to land. I was blown into the other side of field, (almost ran instr. down) so I made my pattern on that side. This time I made a perfect landing."

During their time in training, a few of Elaine's roommates washed out. It was bittersweet to see her new friends leave – sad they had to go, but happy she remained another day. In her diary, she referred to many of the other trainees not by name, but by the state they came from, like "New York" (who had an attractive husband based on photos) or "Florida" (who recited her cockpit check procedures every night before her prayers).

"We had two classmates die in training accidents. The Army wouldn't pay to send the bodies home and you know, a lot of these families couldn't afford the shipping cost, but really they should not have had to pay at all. So we passed a hat around to collect money for them. It was a shameful situation," Elaine explained to me. Many Americans were not aware that the WASP were serving at all, much less that any died while doing so.

The two women in Elaine's class who died were Gleanna Roberts of Iowa, and Marjorie Laverne Davis of California. Since these women were designated as civilians, their caskets did not travel home draped with an American flag, as was customary for transporting deceased soldiers. Another custom, hanging a gold star in the grieving family's window, was not permitted for the families of these deceased pilots.

Elaine told me she didn't have many problems on a personal level with the male pilots. I didn't know if she glossed over these things to avoid intimate conversation because she was my grandmother or if she really didn't have many issues with discrimination. She said the main problem was the institutional gender discrimination by the government and society in general.

"Did the men have any issues with a woman teaching them?" I once asked her.

"No, at first they were hesitant, some of them, but once they realized I knew what I was doing, I did not have any problems," she explained. "We were all pilots. I know some of the other gals had more problems than I did. But we just wanted to fly."

Elaine felt the most discrimination from her own mother Margaret, who thought women shouldn't be flying planes because it was unlady-like. Elaine had avoided telling Margaret about the application to the WASP program, but when the time came to report for training, she couldn't hide it. Once Margaret found out, she did not speak to Elaine the entire time Elaine was serving in the WASP, about 10 months. Elaine wrote letters home and assumed Margaret read them. At least she knew her father Dave did.

"My mom thought we just wanted to hang around with the men. She thought I was becoming a loose woman," Elaine said with a smile during a CNN news interview in 2008. She was explaining the common misperception, also held by her own mother, of the WASP as a group of promiscuous young women chasing after male pilots.

Elaine graduated with class 44-W-9 in October 1944. The WASP had already learned that their program would be disbanded at the end of the year, despite the excellent performance of the pilots. This was heartbreaking news to the women in the program, but like Elaine, they appreciated each day they had the opportunity to fly, even more so knowing that it would soon come to an end. One of the more poignant memories Elaine had of her WASP days was Jackie Cochran crying as she informed the women who had just spent nine months learning to fly all models of military planes, and who had seen two classmates die, that the program would shortly be over.

After graduation, Elaine was transferred to Las Vegas Army Air Field in Nevada. There were already several women from previous WASP classes at the field later called Nellis Air Force Base, but Elaine didn't have occasion to work alongside them. Luckily, Elaine was fortunate to be transferred with her best friend from training, Maggie Gee, one of two Chinese American women in the WASP program.

Maggie was from Berkeley, California, and grew up in a tight-knit Chinese community. Before arriving in Texas to train with the WASP, she had been wearing a badge on her clothing which stated, "I'm Chinese," so she wouldn't be mistaken for a person of Japanese descent and taken away to an internment camp.[3] Maggie said one

---

[3] In 1942 the United States forcibly removed over 100,000 people of Japanese descent, including US citizens, from the West Coast of the United States and placed them in internment camps.

of the greatest benefits of joining the WASP program was getting to know people from across the country who, despite their different backgrounds, all considered serving their country as the highest priority.

Las Vegas was a small desert town at that time and only had a couple of casinos. Elaine and Maggie sometimes went to the casinos to hang out and eat dinner or dance. For the most part, they spent their time working. Maggie was assigned as a tow target pilot, dragging fabric targets behind her plane so gunners could practice shooting planes down.

As B-17s arrived at the Air Base, Elaine acted as co-pilot on at least one occasion. However, her main responsibility was to oversee male pilots on instrument training while flying a BT-13. She supervised the plane in flight while the male pilots had to be "under the hood," flying solely by looking at their instrument panels while the cockpit windows were draped in dark canvas.

"My job was to make sure they didn't fly the planes into Mt. Charleston," she joked with me on several occasions.

On December 20, 1944, Elaine and the rest of the WASP were officially released from duty and sent home. She never told me about her last flight as a WASP, but I imagined it was a typical flight to train another male pilot – one who would be staying on with the Army to fly while she had to go home. As the war evolved, the male pilots realized that these newly trained women could force them into ground combat positions and might displace them in the aviation industry once the war ended. These men lobbied Congress to deny women a formal place in the Army Air Forces. The militarization bill in the House of Representatives was defeated by 19 votes so the Army's promise to formalize the military status of the women serving in the WASP program was never fulfilled.

Like all of the women in the WASP, Elaine was heartbroken when the program was disbanded. During her time in the WASP, she had been able to pursue a potential career in aviation, which was snatched away when gender politics roared back to life as the war wound down.

Elaine took the train back to Baltimore in December of 1944 and was soon bored out of her mind. After spending most of the year in small desert towns in the sun and dust, she was back to Maryland's damp and chilly winter weather. Robert was still working in the Pacific to ensure America's damaged war planes were repaired and expeditiously returned to action. Elaine struggled with the transition from the busy and meaningful mission of flying military planes to having nothing to do.

To stay productive and get a change of scenery, Elaine took a trip to California to see a friend. Margaret did not approve of this decision either. In Margaret's opinion, Elaine had already done plenty to sully her reputation by flying military planes – not that Margaret had made an effort to understand what Elaine had done to contribute to the war effort. Margaret never asked.

"When I got home, none of my family ever asked what I had been doing while I was gone. I guess they weren't interested," Elaine explained.

Dave drove Elaine to Baltimore's Union Station so she could catch the train to Los Angeles to stay with a friend. Ultimately, Elaine ended up getting a job as an air traffic controller in Oakland, California. Down to her last dime, Elaine lucked into boarding with a family who agreed to hold off on collecting the rent. Elaine often walked to the airport because she had no money for the bus. She slept in a bedroom with the host family's teenage daughter and her friend. The family provided Elaine with breakfast and dinner and packed a bag lunch for her. After three weeks, Elaine was able to pay the family back when she received her first paycheck. She got another surprise that same week: Robert had wired 400 dollars from Asia.

"I felt rich that week!" Elaine recalled. She worked at the airport until Robert came back from the Philippines. Then the two of them returned to Maryland and started a family.

In 1947, another potential pathway to an aviation career opened when the newly formed United States Air Force offered Elaine a position in the reserve component. She went to meetings, but recalled that "nothing really happened there." She had an identification badge and could even go to the Officers' Club. Shortly after the Air Force had extended the offer, Elaine received a letter explaining that they had mistakenly reached out to her. Since Elaine was the mother of minor children, she was ineligible to be in the Air Force Reserve.

Elaine had followed the Army's orders and had gone home quietly. She made no fuss about the broken promise to make her an Army pilot. She didn't complain about the unequal treatment between not only male and female pilots, but between female pilots and females doing other jobs for the Army. She moved on with her life so that men could climb in the cockpits that she and the other WASP had occupied. "We did something great when the country needed us," she said often. The unrealized desire of the Women Airforce Service Pilots for proper recognition as members of the military never granted by the Army during the war would stew under the surface for over thirty years.

6

Final Fight

Fall 2015

few days after the first official rejection letter arrived from Arlington National Cemetery in October, a copy of the same letter with a cover letter from Senator Mikulski's office followed. The senator's letter was only four sentences, the final two of which were, "I am sorry that the response is not encouraging. I had hoped to resolve this matter to your satisfaction." I was frustrated with this answer, but I knew the senator herself had likely not even seen the information we had sent or had only received a passing summary of what it contained. I didn't want this standard treatment of our problem. I wanted someone to fight to fix this law in Congress, but it appeared asking wasn't enough to get Congress interested in fixing this problem. I decided we had to take a different approach.

I steered the strategy away from contacting more people in Congress (even though the ideal solution was a new law) and decided to focus on what I called, "shaming the Army into changing its decision by creating a public campaign in support of the WASP." This was no longer about Gammy; it was about equal recognition for all the women of the WASP. Although I only had a vague understanding of what they had done to gain veterans status in the 1970s, I figured if they succeeded back then, hopefully the public would support one more round of fighting for equal recognition of these trailblazing women.

I listened to Mom talk about writing letters to various government officials and imagined them getting tossed in the trash by the recipients or never arriving at all. At this point, six months had passed since Gammy's death and I even contemplated standing in front of Arlington National Cemetery with the box of Gammy's ashes and a sign featuring some catchy slogan about Arlington denying entry to World War II veterans.

On Veterans Day, an annual holiday celebrated on November 11 (Armistice Day in other nations), I sat on the sofa with my laptop doing research about the WASP. I caught Mom from the corner of my eye standing in the living room with a pensive look on her face.

"What are you thinking?" I asked, not looking up from my computer screen.

"I was thinking about going to Arlington to protest about Gammy," she replied.

"That's funny," I replied.

"Why?" Mom asked.

"I was thinking the same thing. We could stand there with a sign about how not all veterans are welcome or something like that," I suggested.

"So are we going to do it?" Mom asked.

"I decided it's not a good idea. I think we will get some attention, but it may be negative attention. And I think it will delegitimize our argument. It might make us look like we don't know what we are talking about, like we are just complaining. Also it's a graveyard. It might be seen as disrespectful," I replied.

"Yes, those are good points," Mom agreed. "I'm going to go work on another letter to the senator." She walked upstairs determined to write something more strategic and effective.

It would have been an unusual family bonding experience to spend the day with Mom protesting on Gammy's behalf at the gates of Arlington National Cemetery. However, I knew it wasn't a long term solution. I wanted to present a legitimate argument and explain what we needed. Mom and I had been scouring the internet and reading through Gammy's documents. I looked at the law and decided it would be ideal to either have the original law amended or to have a completely new law written to address this injustice. Given the initial response from our senator, I focused on publicizing the decision in the hope that the Army would change its policy to avoid bad press. We needed media attention to make the Army listen to us.

Deciding to use a vehicle that could attract more (and hopefully quick) visibility, I started relying on social media. I placed Gammy's WASP pilot wings that she had given me in front of her box of ashes and took a photo. That day, I posted it on Facebook and Instagram and explained that Gammy had flown planes in World War II but was denied a resting place at Arlington National Cemetery. Within a few hours, there was an overwhelming response from people who commented on how this rejection from Arlington National Cemetery was an injustice and we had to do something. Even though most of these people were not strangers, there were enough of them expressing outrage to give me confidence that a lot of people who didn't know us would be mad about this too, compelling them to act in support of reversing the Army's decision. I started thinking of other useful platforms, within the realm of social media and beyond, to share and disseminate this story effectively.

Mom sent her follow-up letter to Senator Mikulski in mid-November explaining that the letter we had received from the cemetery had not resolved the situation. She also made more Freedom of Information Act requests for a list of all WASP buried at Arlington National Cemetery and for memoranda related to the denial decision.

Understandably my entire family was angry, frustrated, and disap-pointed at what we viewed as a disrespectful decision by the Army. Therefore, if I was going to take the Army on, it was not going to be a solo mission. I needed to have both a support team and a strategy. I not only needed my family to be involved but also needed a network of experts, media, lawmakers, and grassroots supporters to ensure that the Army understood that public opinion was not supportive of its decision.

I had to do a lot more research because my general awareness that Gammy had flown planes for the WASP in World War II was not going to be an adequate argument to convince people that she deserved a spot in Arlington National Cemetery. At this point my answers to basic interview questions would have been terrible. *What kind of planes did she fly? What were her duties? Why should the WASP be eligible at Arlington National Cemetery? (Um...old ones? Flying? Because this is a load of B.S.?)*

This problem extended beyond the denial of a simple funeral request. The veterans benefits for which the WASP had already fought decades ago were only recognized by one agency in the federal government and that made no sense to me. The WASP were all at least 90 years old now and they couldn't exactly march on Capitol Hill like they had done in the 1970s. So I dusted off my history degree that Gammy approved of, along with the law degree she despised, and the cell phone she barely tolerated, and I started researching Elaine Danforth Harmon and the WASP. I had to figure out how to win a war of regulations against a bureaucratic behemoth named the United States Army.

Gammy took her last breath under a blue blanket emblazoned with gold WASP wings, anticipating that her dedication to preserving WASP history would continue with a permanent place for her ashes at Arlington National Cemetery. If the Army thought our family would acquiesce to their renewed attempt at discrimination, it had an unexpected battle looming on the horizon.

* * *

Around Thanksgiving, Mom thought it would be a good idea for me to meet someone who had been working on WASP issues for many years: Albert Lewis, son of WASP Dorothy "Dot" Lewis. We had much in common because he had already been researching WASP issues related to the status of the WASP since his own mother had passed away a couple years earlier. His WASP network included Professor Katherine "Kate" Landdeck at Texas Woman's University, which served as the official archives for the WASP. Not only had Kate been researching the WASP for decades, but Gammy was the first WASP Kate had interviewed for her graduate school work. She held a special place in her heart for Elaine Danforth Harmon. The network also included some WASP authors like Amy Nathan, Sarah Byrn Rickman, and Amy Goodpaster Strebe, along with WASP family like Julie Englund, daughter of WASP Irene Englund, the focus of another problem at Arlington National Cemetery in 2002 that I was planning to look into. I was glad to see Julie in our new email chains because I had found information on her earlier on in my research and thought we should find her.

As Mom and I sat with Albert at his dining table discussing what the two of them had in mind to spread the word around the WASP community, I sensed that it didn't match the scale of what I was envisioning.

"We have a mailing list for the newsletter, so we can write something for that," Albert suggested.

"I want to write another letter to the Acting Secretary of the Army. Maybe the people on the mailing list will write letters too," Mom replied from across the table.

As I watched this exchange go on, I pulled out my tablet to look at the website Albert had made at Fifinella.com a few years earlier to promote the WASP float for the Rose Parade. I wasn't against Mom or anyone writing letters, but I wanted to ensure we used all the tools available to us. Listening to their conversation about letter writing and looking at a static website reminded me of Gammy's stories of getting support in the 1970s. It was old-fashioned.

"So I think we need a multi-pronged social media and publicity attack," I blurted out from the end of the table. They both turned and looked at me. After a moment of reflection, Albert replied.

"Well, you're the young one around here, you work on that," he said.

"Okay," I replied. I thought the best way to go was to make several different approaches and see what struck a chord with people. Mom and Albert continued their chat about newsletters and mailing lists. I looked back at the tablet and started an internet search for websites and news stories that seemed relevant to a publicity campaign. I didn't know anything about public relations, but I was going to learn.

I was glad to know that Albert and this network of WASP family and supporters existed. I had a better understanding of who was already supporting us even though we hadn't yet begun a public campaign. I also became aware of the vast expertise on the history of the WASP available from the group. All I could think about was how frustrating it was that this undertaking was even necessary and how heartbreaking it would be if it was unsuccessful. Gammy was not here to fight another battle for her place in Arlington National Cemetery, but we had to try on her behalf. Even though I had yet to learn all the minutiae of the previous fight with Congress, I had done enough research to know that we had enormous obstacles to overcome in working to reverse a decision of the United States Army.

After our meeting, Mom drove us home on the Beltway, the famous circular freeway delineating the Washington, D.C., political bubble. I stared out the window from the passenger seat and admired the variety of autumn colors in the thick woods. My mind raced with ways to get the public to support us. *A petition? Website? Social Media? Television? All of the above?*

When I got home, the first thing I did was call my friend Shane Yeager who worked on digital video productions and websites for his own media company, DC Visionaries.

"Shane, I need a website," I said.

"When? For what?" he asked from the other end of the line.

"Right now. For my grandmother to get into Arlington National Cemetery. I can build basic websites, but I need a good one," I replied.

"Oh, wow, that's big. OK, I can find someone for you but I am going to Japan soon for work, so I can't help right now. When I come back in January, I can help," he explained.

"I want to do a social media campaign. I have no idea how to do that. Maybe when you get back, you can tell me more," I said.

"Of course, I will help any way I can," Shane offered.

After I hung up, I knew I didn't want to spend time building a website or waiting for someone else to build a website; I needed something right away, and more interactive than a website. I figured I could work with different social media sites. I thought of doing a petition on the website Change.org. One potential problem I considered was that I worked for the federal government. Although I worked at an agency unrelated to the issue at hand, I didn't want to jeopardize any part of the campaign due to my job. I gathered all my thoughts on the campaign and decided I would discuss it with my family that weekend at Whitney's house.

Later in the week, Whitney hosted Thanksgiving at her house in New Jersey, so we had plenty of time to plan the campaign over the four and a half day visit. The night I arrived, I got on the phone with my sister Tiffany in California. I told her about the meeting and that I wanted to do something on social media. It was immediately obvious that we were already on the same page.

"I was thinking we could start a petition on Change.org," she suggested.

"I was thinking the same thing!" I exclaimed. "But I work for the government, so I don't know if I should have my name on it. I don't know if they will care, but it seems like it could be one of those things that becomes a problem down the line."

"It's fine, I will create it under my name. I'll draft something and send it to you so you can edit it. Who are we supposed to address it to?" Tiffany wondered.

"I was thinking about that. There is nobody in charge right now since the previous Army Secretary already left and the Senate has not confirmed his replacement. I guess we have to address it to the guy that the Army is calling their current Acting Secretary of the Army," I suggested.

"Should we add the cemetery director too?" Tiffany inquired.

"Yes. Since nobody seems to be authorized to make an independent decision, I guess we should address it both of these people," I suggested to Tiffany. "Hopefully by the time the Senate confirmation hearing comes in January, we will know who can decide this and it will be on the new Army Secretary's radar."

The lawyer in me didn't want to address it to President Obama since we needed either the Army to figure out how to fix their own policy or Congress to amend the law, neither of which required the president, at least until a bill needed to be signed. And I didn't want any executive orders since Congress wasn't fond of President Obama's existing executive orders. I was also concerned that the president, as commander in chief, could take the Army's side of the situation.

"How many signatures do you think we will need to get it changed?" Tiffany asked me.

"I have no idea," I replied. "I was wondering the same thing. Some of the petitions I have signed have hundreds of thousands of signatures."

"I am pulling up the Change.org website right now to see what is out there," Tiffany said.

I put the phone on speaker mode and sat it next to me on the couch as I started searching the internet on my laptop to see if there were any news stories about petitions – hopefully about a petition related to the Army.

"I think I found something useful," I said as I perused the story on my laptop screen about a concert on an Army base in North Carolina.

"Oooh, this one is an Army story with a petition," I heard Tiffany say from the cell phone's speaker.

"Are you reading the one about the concert?" I asked.

"Yes!" she replied. "So, it says there was a concert planned at an Army base in North Carolina which had not been supported with public funding, although a similar concert that year had received public funding. After about six thousand signatures, the Army funded the concert."

"We have so many relatives. We can totally get six thousand signatures!" we both declared simultaneously to each other on the phone.

So Tiffany and I thought 6,000 signatures was a good number to shoot for. I realized there was a potential constitutional violation in the petition related to the concert issue which may have quickly forced the Army's hand, but we made 6,000 our goal anyway. Tiffany drew up a draft petition and we discussed some edits to it over the weekend. We had to be factual, but we also knew we had to tug at the heartstrings a bit and mention how our family was waiting to have a funeral for our heroic, trailblazing World War II pilot grandmother!

Tiffany officially launched our online petition called "Grant Military Honors to Women WWII Pilots" on the Change.org website on December 2, 2015. I was excited to share our petition. Tiffany, Whitney, and I wrote personal emails to almost everyone we knew asking them to sign the petition. I posted the petition information on the campaign's Facebook page. We all shared it on our personal Facebook pages, where, in turn, friends and family started sharing it and asking people to sign.

Shortly thereafter, I learned that Mom was annoyed with us for not running the petition wording by her.

"You don't explain how the previous Army memo said the WASP were allowed and then the new memo says they're not allowed. They're flip-flopping," Mom complained.

"Mom, people don't want to read too much. They need to know

FINAL FLIGHT FINAL FIGHT

the basic story: *My grandmother died. She wanted to be in Arlington Cemetery. They said no and we want them to say yes. The End.* If people want more information they can search for it online or contact us on the Facebook page. And we have the Fifinella.com website with all that information." My terse explanation did not help with her annoyance at all.

"Well, I disagree," Mom informed me.

"Okay, Mom," I replied. Campaigns need leaders, and I had unintentionally become the leader of this project. I had to remain objective and know how to best utilize my family members. Even Mom would not always agree with our tactics, but I needed to remain focused on the task.

The social media campaign quickly became an obsession for me. I spent the next few days sending emails and posting information on Facebook with the link to the petition. I even walked around to our neighbors and asked them to sign it. My cousin Sydney set up a table at her college with a scannable code linked to the petition and had students who walked past sign it. My extended family across the country shared the petition with everyone they knew. If all their friends and social media acquaintances signed on, I figured we would have the 6,000 signatures Tiffany and I had discussed before we even knew our next move.

Mom reached out to the WASP network she already knew from traveling with Gammy to events. She spoke at length with Julie Englund, to get her perspective from previous dealings with Arlington National Cemetery when her mother Irene was denied a military funeral there in 2002. Mom reached out again to Albert, and to Kate, the history professor at Texas Woman's University, who had already spent many years sharing the story of the WASP through various outlets. Mom contacted authors like Amy Nathan, Amy Goodpaster Strebe, and Sarah Byrn Rickman, who had each written books about women pilots during World War II, and who would not only lend their support to our campaign but would bring necessary legitimacy and expertise to our story.

I dubbed Mom "The Queen of Freedom of Information Act Requests." Her new favorite hobby was making FOIA requests for anything related to our problem. She wanted the internal Army legal memos detailing the decision to deny the "active duty designees" like WASP from Arlington National Cemetery. Mom also said she was composing a letter to the Army's proposed nominee for the position of Secretary of the Army. It took Mom a while to gather her thoughts, but she finally sent the letter to him via certified mail in early December of 2015.

I needed to learn how to effectively use more social media applications. Technically I had a Twitter account, but had only sent three test tweets since opening the account a couple years earlier. I started a new routine with my days. Each morning when I woke up, I spent at least an hour lying in bed doing things on social media. I searched for stories related to WWII, WASP, aviation, history, feminism, veterans, and anything else remotely related to our situation. I reached out to strangers online who had interests in these areas to inform them about the situation with Gammy and Arlington National Cemetery. I didn't know if what I was doing was effective, but I figured if I spent enough time experimenting with Twitter and other social media platforms, I would learn.

I obsessively refreshed the web browser on my phone to see how many signatures we were getting. Tiffany, Whitney, and our cousins did the same thing; we all texted each other to update ourselves on the numbers. The first few days my cousin Trisa and I had a continuous email conversation highlighting when a new benchmark had been met.

"500!"

"750!"

"1000!"

I read all the comments on the petition. They inspired me. When I saw signatures from people that I didn't know, I felt like we were succeeding because it meant that strangers were supporting our cause.

There were the occasional negative posts on our petition website or social media pages, usually disapproving of the WASP being buried in Arlington because they weren't combat veterans, didn't die in action, or weren't recognized as military at the time of service. I pointed out on multiple occasions that we were not trying to bury Gammy in the traditional sense, but to place her ashes in the cemetery, and the requirements for that were less strict. The good thing was we had so many people in favor of our position that I rarely interacted with the negative commentators because our supporters did it on our behalf! (And with colorful language at times.)

As the number of signatures increased, Mom's annoyance about the wording of the petition dissipated. She knew the accumulation of names was a good sign, but now she was starting to grasp the potential effects of the petition. One morning she asked me, "What is the point of doing this petition?"

"The point is to draw attention to the problem and show that people support a change in policy. Then hopefully we will get more attention and I can use it to get media coverage, and then get the attention of people who can change the rules or the law. But right now we need people to sign it, share it, and talk about it, so this campaign builds momentum," I explained.

"You mean like *trending*?" Mom asked. She smiled, awaiting my confirmation of her correct usage of social media slang.

"Yes Mom, like trending," I smiled in return at her acceptance of the big picture strategy.

We did not have to wait long to see the first glimpse of the ultimate goal coming into focus. The next morning, in my flannel pajama pants dotted with penguins (one of Gammy's favorite animals), I stood in the kitchen cooking eggs and potatoes on the stove when Mom came in, placed her tablet on the granite breakfast counter, and announced, "I think our petition is trending."

"What makes you think that?" I asked as I cracked a couple eggs into the frying pan.

She held up her tablet and said "When I go to the Change.org website, our petition is one of the ones on the front page."

I walked away from the eggs cooking on the stove to check the website.

"Oh my gosh! You are right! This is awesome!" I shrieked. With a spatula in one hand, I gave Mom a hug, then quickly ran back to the stove to flip the eggs.

"Gammy is trending!" Mom announced. "I'm going to go email some people!"

I had no clue how Change.org decided which petitions go on the front page of their website, but I was excited to see that enough people had been signing ours that it was now grouped with a small number of other petitions that already had hundreds of thousands of signatures. That helped us get a lot more signatures because anyone who logged onto the Change.org website saw our petition right away. Somewhere between my morning ritual of obsessively cruising social media and cooking eggs over medium, Gammy had gone viral.

7

Final Fight

Who is a veteran?

S
eeing Gammy in uniform was a regular occurrence, whether she was heading off to speak at a school, being featured in a photo in the newspaper, or going to visit the White House. Even though I didn't attend most of these events, I was often at her house when she left or returned, or else she would show me photos later on. I was accustomed to seeing her in uniform. To me it was no different than Dad's Marine Corps uniform or the Army uniform my great grandfather wore in the fancy painting over the sofa in Gammy's house. Growing up, I put Gammy, Dad, Great Grandpa, and the rest of the family and friends who served in the armed forces in the same category: veteran.

But it wasn't until the summer of 2015 that I realized the federal government still didn't put Gammy in that same category. I knew from Gammy that she and the other women of the WASP thought they would be commissioned into the Army during the war, but it didn't happen. Although there were lobbying efforts from both sides during the war, Gammy said she wasn't aware of the details, she did her job and left the politics to the politicians. In the 1970s there was a "big fight," as Gammy explained it to me in simple terms, but they were eventually declared to be veterans. That was the basic story I knew from childhood. But if the government truly considered them veterans, then this problem with Arlington National Cemetery wouldn't have come up. What I learned is that Gammy and the rest of the WASP were what I started calling "partial veterans." If you're thinking, "that makes no sense, a veteran is a veteran," then you're in the same mindset I was in my entire life until Arlington National Cemetery informed us Gammy wasn't the kind of veteran they bury.

In order to accurately advocate for a change in the law, I had to understand how the administration at Arlington National Cemetery and the related Army officials had arrived at this decision in the first place. That meant learning the history between the WASP and Congress, beyond Gammy's description of the "big fight." I spent time reading through the United States Code (federal laws), Congressional records, WASP books, and historic documents to piece together the missing details. I had to teach myself the history that Gammy had spent decades teaching to other people.

* * *

When Gammy joined the WASP, she was under the impression that eventually she would be commissioned into the Army. Gammy's friend Lorraine Zillner Rodgers (class 44-W-2) had even sent a telegram before reporting to Texas asking if she would become part of the Army. The response was: "It is probable WASPs will be militarized. If you are not prepared to follow through in this event, do not report at Sweetwater on 6 Sept."[4]

After Jackie Cochran and Nancy Love suggested recruiting women

---

[4] Telegram. Western Union to Lorraine Zillner from Jackie Cochran/General Arnold Sept 1, 1943. http://wingsacrossamerica.us/records_all/press_archive/sns2.pdf

to the Army in order to support the war effort and free up male pilots to fly combat missions, they were confronted with red tape and naysaying. Jackie and Nancy had seen the writing on the wall; waiting for Congress to decide if women could be pilots meant women would likely never fly a military plane because the war would end first. As an alternative, a proposal was made to add women under a civilian status to speed up the process, and then to convert the women over to official military status once they proved themselves to be excellent military pilots. Jackie and Nancy were both accomplished pilots and were confident about other women's potential as military pilots. The war was moving ahead and they couldn't wait for bureaucracy because the military needed more combat pilots as soon as possible. The women could take over the domestic flying duties so that the men could be transferred overseas.

The WASP program was a result of two previous programs involving female pilots. There was the Women's Auxiliary Ferrying Squadron (WAFS), which took experienced female pilots and assigned them to ferry aircraft around the country. There was also the Women's Flying Training Detachment (WFTD), to train female pilots. In August 1943 these programs merged and the Army assigned it a new name: the Women Airforce Service Pilots, or WASP. Gammy and the other women of the WASP always told me that the proper way to refer to them was "WASP," not "WASPs." She said, "the word pilots is already plural within the acronym, so there is no need to add another 's.'" I have since learned that it was not in fact incorrect to use "WASPs" in certain contexts, and to say "a WASP" was actually incorrect as it should have been "one of the WASP." However, Gammy repeated this often enough to me while I was growing up that when the extra "s" slipped out at the end, I felt Gammy looking down on me with contempt. So I referred to them as "WASP," with full awareness that it may have been grammatically incorrect.

The WASP did all the domestic flying duties that the men had been doing so that the men could go fly missions overseas. WASP missions included tow target training (flying a plane with a banner behind it which male trainees shot at to practice anti-aircraft fire), ferrying planes from factories to departure points, instructing male pilots, testing new or repaired airplanes, and flying planes for hours to break in the engines. They did the same military training as the men. If they didn't meet the standards, they washed out. They learned to fly every type of airplane in the fleet. They flew over 60 million miles in support of the war effort. 38 WASP died during this service.

As the women of the WASP proved that they were able to perform the same duties as the male pilots, the tide turned toward actively militarizing them. Representative Costello (CA-15) introduced bill H.R. 3358 in September 1943 to grant the WASP the military status they should have had from the start. The bill made its way through Congress, was resubmitted as H.R. 4219, and passed out of committee in March 1944. As far as Gammy knew, the WASP didn't form any lobbying groups or ask any organizations to lobby on their behalf. She told me that the "authorities" instructed them not to get involved with this legislation, "they wanted us to be good little girls, so we kept quiet."

A variety of people stepped up to actively oppose the legislation. Most notable was a group of civilian men who had either been training male pilots or were themselves training to be pilots. These men had avoided military service by helping to increase the pool of male pilots. When the Army began turning its focus to a land invasion, it again needed ground troops, and wanted these men to stop dealing with planes and instead to serve as ground soldiers. One clear way to avoid this was to force the women out of the cockpit positions they were fighting for, creating a renewed need for more male pilots. Despite the bill to militarize the WASP being "approved by the Armed Services (then called Military Affairs) committee and endorsed by the Secretary of War, the Army Chief of Staff, and the commander of the Army Air

Corps," it failed to pass by 19 votes.[5] Congress also decided to shelve the WASP program permanently at the end of 1944.

Women were serving in the armed forces during World War II in many capacities. The Army had about 100,000 women in the Army Auxiliary Corps by the end of the war. The Coast Guard and Marine Corps had formal female members. The Navy's WAVES (Women Accepted for Volunteer Emergency Service) had both enlisted and officer females in the Navy Reserve – with the idea to free up male sailors for duty at sea – the same idea behind the WASP. Although Congress and President Roosevelt approved other female programs for formal militarization, it was the female pilots of the WASP who were pushing the envelope of gender roles to an unacceptable limit. But Gammy and her fellow WASP flew with pride because they loved it, they loved their country, and they believed to their cores that their service was making a difference. The inaction of misinformed bureaucrats did not change the attitudes of the women of the WASP.

The WASP received a letter from General Henry "Hap" Arnold dated October 1, 1944, informing them that the program would be disbanded on December 20, 1944. When I started going through Gammy's things to gather useful documents and photos to support our fight against the Army, I found her original copy of this letter. She had kept it for over 70 years.

The gist of the letter was that the WASP had done their part and now men, who were more important, wanted their jobs back and the WASP were expected to accept it.

"...the war situation has changed and the time has come when your volunteered services are no longer needed. The situation is

---

[5] Sawyer, Kathy. "WASPs Lobby for Benefits." *The Victoria Advocate.* March 10, 1977. https://news.google.com/news-papers?nid=861&dat=19770310&id=OABaAAAAIBAJ&sjid=Ek-sNAAAAIBAJ&pg=7149,1658008&hl=en

that if you continue in service, you will be replacing instead of releasing our young men. I know that the WASP wouldn't want that."[6]

I had never seen this letter before. I knew that the WASP program had ended abruptly and generally knew that it was because male pilots had successfully campaigned to take the pilot positions, but I did not realize the extent of the sexist way in which they were terminated. I was not surprised at the condescending language of the letter; it was consistent with everything else I had learned about the program. Gammy had said she was sad when the program ended, as were all women in the WASP. But she also had the same attitude of most of the World War II generation: they had done their duty, and life went on. Gammy never had any in-depth conversations with me about her feelings on the gender issue underlying their unceremonious release from duty. I imagined that receiving that letter back in 1944 filled her with a spectrum of emotions from anger and frustration to sadness. "The WASP wouldn't want that" epitomized the condescension toward these women pilots by assuming that any interest the WASP had in aviation existed for the sole purpose of being placeholders for men. This letter was yet another motivator for me to ensure that Gammy received a proper resting place at Arlington National Cemetery.

Gammy and the rest of the WASP spent the next thirty years spread out across the United States and for the most part lost touch with one another as they moved on with their lives – changing last names when they got married and not establishing a widespread formal network to stay connected. Gammy didn't fly as a pilot again. I understood that flying was expensive, but I also learned that after the war the family had only one car, which Robert took to work each day, leaving Gammy home with the children. At that time, the seven miles from

---

[6] Letter from General Henry Arnold, Commanding General U.S. Army Air Forces. October 1, 1944. Personal collection of Elaine D. Harmon.

the city limits of Washington to their home in Maryland lacked much in the way of transportation services or other amenities. In addition to the cost of flying and arranging for child care, getting to the airport would have been difficult.

In 1965, the heart condition that had kept Robert from military service took his life. Mom was 19 years old and her youngest sibling was 12. Gammy kept the family together and a roof over their heads with a variety of jobs. Eventually she settled on real estate appraising as a career. Ironically, although the male pilots with whom Gammy had worked during the war had for the most part accepted her as an equal, the appraisal profession was different. She was in familiar territory as one of the only women in a male-dominated field. While she fought for equal treatment in her new profession, she and the rest of the WASP also fought for equal recognition as veterans on Capitol Hill.

In the 1970s, Congress introduced legislation to require the all-male service academies to admit women. The Navy, Army, and Air Force also started accepting women into flight training throughout the 1970s. While news about this filled the papers and the television reports, the Air Force Academy started boasting about how it would soon graduate the first women pilots for the armed forces. Naturally, Gammy and the other WASP took exception to these pronouncements, given that they had flown military aircraft 30 years prior to this. After decades of raising children and working other jobs, here was blatant evidence that the WASP, who had once graced the cover of *Life* magazine, had been discarded from American history. The women of the WASP decided to unite and demand the veteran's status they should have been granted during World War II. They were done being "good little girls."

Each time I heard Gammy talk about how she spent time looking for the other WASP in the 1970s while they organized their lobbying campaign, I was in awe. She once told me it took them about a year to contact and organize a good portion of the 1100 women who had served as WASP and were still alive. Mom remembered Gammy sitting at her typewriter at night banging out letters and addressing envelopes. Gammy had to remind me that after the war, the women all went home and really didn't keep in touch, except maybe with their closest friends. The documents related to WASP service had also been classified and Gammy told me she and the other women were instructed by the Army not to discuss what they had been doing in Texas.

I found some old color photos of Gammy with a few of her WASP friends, including Maggie Gee. On the back of one photo Gammy had written, "WASP Reunion, April 1969. Sweetwater, Texas." I knew they had started getting together again several years after the war ended. If this was the first reunion, I had no idea, but it must have at least been one of the earliest. One photo featured a group of 16 ladies including Gammy, who sat behind a handmade sign that read "Welcome Fifi's." Fifinella, or "Fifi" for short, was designed by Walt Disney as a stylized female gremlin who sported wings, a flying cap, and goggles, and the WASP adopted her as a mascot. Gammy and a few others in the photo were turned around and appeared to be laughing at one of their fellow pilots. These photographs didn't look much different from ones I had of my college friends and me getting together. Here was a group of ladies in shorts and sun dresses, smiling and laughing under the Texas sun as they reminisced about their time flying military planes – something the rest of the country had either never known about or had already forgotten.

By the time the women of the WASP needed to start lobbying for retroactive veterans benefits in the 1970s, some of them had already been getting together for reunions like I saw in Gammy's photos. They had created a newsletter and a mailing list for WASP news, and then used those tools to send out all the latest information on the campaign to get veterans' benefits. Several of the WASP started paper petitions and sat outside at events like county fairs to collect signatures to support their efforts on Capitol Hill. One smart WASP had a petition outside of several movie theaters showing the popular new movie

Star Wars. I laughed when I found a photo online of a few of the WASP holding a long roll of white butcher paper on the steps of a government building, showing off their petition signatures. Without realizing it, my sisters and I had started an electronic version of the campaign the WASP launched in the 1970s.

In 1972, Representative Patsy Mink of Hawaii introduced the first bill (H.R. 15035) in Congress attempting to recognize retroactively the military status of the WASP. Unfortunately there was still a lot of discrimination swirling about in the veteran community. The national office of The American Legion, the Veterans of Foreign Wars, and several other prominent groups opposed granting veteran status to the WASP, even as some of the local chapters sent statements to Congress in support of recognizing their service as military. The first House bill did not even make it to the Veterans' Affairs Committee for debate because of its controversial nature.

Senator Barry Goldwater of Arizona, who had flown with some of the women during the war, supported this move for veteran status. He introduced legislation in 1975 in the Senate under bill S.1345 to grant the WASP veteran status for the purposes of all laws administered by the Veterans Administration.[7] Representative Mink introduced another House version under H.R. 6595. Again, both of these bills failed because of the controversy about the WASP.

In 1977, Senator Goldwater tried again and introduced bill S.247. After years of building up public support as well as lobbying Capitol Hill, the WASP had a little more hope of achieving their goal during this session of Congress. By this time, they had gained the active involvement of Bruce Arnold, the son of General "Hap" Arnold who had run the Army Air Corps and authored the 1944 letter announcing the end of the WASP program. Several bills regarding the WASP were introduced in the House of Representatives during 1977. The first of these was H.R. 3277, introduced February 8, 1977. Sixteen other

---

[7] https://www.govtrack.us/congress/bills/94/s1345

78

identical bills were introduced throughout 1977.[8]

There was still controversy about the WASP, but by this point they had amassed strong public support for their cause despite the many veterans groups opposing the legislation. About a week shy of my first birthday, on September 20, 1977, the House of Representatives Committee on Veterans' Affairs held a hearing on "granting veterans' status to WASPS."

Senator Goldwater testified on behalf of the WASP. He pointed out that his bill to grant them veterans status had 27 cosponsors in the Senate, and the current House bill had 150 cosponsors. Senator Goldwater described the experience of the WASP, from the training to the types of aircraft they flew, and the fact that 38 WASP perished while serving.

"Now, here are women pilots who served in war time at very dangerous work and who are not entitled to veterans benefits because of a technicality they could not prevent, the fact that they were women."[9]

–Senator Barry Goldwater

John Sommer, Jr., The American Legion representative at the hearing said the organization opposed veteran status for the WASP because it

---

[8] Govtrack.us

[9] To Provide Recognition to the Women's Air Force Service Pilots for Their Service During World War II by Deeming Such Service to Have Been Active Duty in the Armed Forces of the United States for Purposes of Laws Administered by the Veterans Administration: Hearing before a Select Subcomm. of the Committee on Veterans' Affairs House of Representatives, 95th Cong. 245 (September 20, 1977) (statement of Sen. Barry Goldwater).

would "denigrate the term veteran."[10] He equated the WASP to other civilian groups who had provided services during the war.

Congresswoman Margaret Heckler of Massachusetts asked Mr. Sommer, "Do you believe wrongs should be righted by a government?"

Mr. Sommer replied that the government should right wrongs, but since the WASP had never been "sworn into the military" or "received a discharge from the Department of Defense," The American Legion's position was that the women of the WASP were not veterans.

"That was the wrong that this legislation proposes to right," Congresswoman Heckler replied. She pressed Mr. Sommer about his comparison between the WASP, a group expected to become militarized as confirmed by three generals on the record, with other civilian groups who had no such expectation. "These women were wronged by the Congress," she said, referring to the failed bill in 1944 which was based on gender discrimination, confirmed by the testimony of others such as Senator Barry Goldwater.

When I read this, I realized what a significant gesture our local post of The American Legion had made by presenting our family a certificate of posthumous honorary perpetual membership for Gammy.

Later in the year, the House Veterans' Affairs Committee also brought forth several additional opponents to the WASP veteran status. On the contrary, a letter from the Deputy Secretary of Defense dated October 21, 1977 explained that the position of the Department of Defense was to support the WASP legislation to "correct past inequities" and "represent a strong symbolic statement of this Administration's commitment to equality."[11]

Rather than pass the individual Senate bill into law, the language of the bill was added as an amendment to the G.I. Bill Improvement Act which passed the Senate on November 4, 1977. President Carter signed

[10] Ibid., 444 (statement of John Sommer, Jr., Chief of Claims Service, The American Legion).

[11] http://wingsacrossamerica.us/records_all/press_archive/sns2.pdf

that legislation into law a few weeks later, creating public law 95-202. Section 401 of that law declared, pursuant to approval by the Secretary of Defense, that service of the members of the WASP and similarly situated groups would be considered active military service "under all laws administered by the Veterans Administration." This very specific wording was the basis for the legal argument which underpinned the Army's decision to deny our family's request for Gammy at Arlington National Cemetery almost 40 years later.

The law was not the end of the requirement to gain veteran status for the WASP. They then had to apply for approval from the Department of Defense under the direction of the wording of the law. On March 8, 1979, the Secretary of Defense declared the service of the WASP as active duty service per the requirements of public law 95-202. Other groups could also apply for approval based on a factor test; eventually 37 more gained the same recognition under that procedure, including – after an additional legal fight – the Merchant Marines who served during World War II. It was 1979 – 35 years after the WASP program was discontinued – when Gammy received her Form DD-214, the official document showing her separation from active duty service in the military. This meant the WASP had spent roughly a decade lobbying for retroactive veteran status, which ended up being limited to one department of the federal government.

In September 1979, Gammy applied for a job with the federal government. With her crisp new DD-214 in hand, she marked "veteran" in the appropriate box on the job application, which related to receipt of veteran preference points in the hiring process. She received a letter in October 1979 from the Office of Personnel Management (OPM) which explained that her veteran preference points had been denied because her service was "not considered active duty in the Armed Forces

of the United States under the veteran preference laws."[12] Gammy
subsequently received a contradictory letter in November 1979 stating
that her veteran preference points had indeed been approved after
OPM had received instructions to credit five points for WASP service.[13]
In December 1979, a third letter arrived stating that OPM had been
correct the first time in not applying the veteran preference points
and to contact the General Counsel of OPM for further information.[14]
Gammy contacted the General Counsel, a woman named Margery
Waxman, who then explained in yet another letter that the WASP
service was not creditable based on the distinction in the law that the
WASP service applied only under the Veterans Administration.[15]

Based on this confusion in the interpretation of their newly acquired
status as veterans, Gammy went to Congress to give testimony about
her experience. On my fifth birthday, September 29, 1981, Gammy
spent the day on Capitol Hill talking to lawmakers and appearing
before the Subcommittee on Oversight and Investigations of the
Committee on Veterans' Affairs at the House of Representatives in
room 334 of the Cannon House office building. I found an old copy of
the official transcript among Gammy's documents. Of course, at the
time of Gammy's testimony I was too young to know what Gammy
was doing in her spare time. I did unknowingly support her efforts
by regularly sporting my "Gammy Flew Planes in WWII" T-shirt as a
child.

Gammy testified before the committee about her experience with
OPM in applying for a federal job. She mentioned that other WASP
also had problems with their veteran status as it related to the

---

[12] Implementation of Title IV of Public Law 95-202, Relating to WASPS and
Similarly Situated Groups: Hearing before the Subcommittee on Oversight and
Investigations of the Committee on Veterans' Affairs House of Representatives,
97th Cong. 9 (September 29, 1981) (statement of Elaine D. Harmon).

[13] Ibid.

[14] Ibid.

[15] Ibid.

federal government. Gammy relayed that her impression was that the purpose of the law granting them veteran status was for it to apply generally in the federal government. Gammy read aloud a portion of a letter written by Senator Barry Goldwater who explained how the intent of the original law was for the veteran status of the WASP to apply in all situations requiring clarification of the term 'veteran' as it related to the WASP within the context of federal law.

Gammy continued, "We have had several military funerals, and I have no absolute proof of this, but through the grapevine, I have heard that we have been told that this would never be allowed again. Now, this is one area that comes under the Veterans Administration, and it is our understanding that we are eligible for military funerals. If there is any question about it, we would like to have this clarified."[16]

The representatives at the committee hearing responded that they would follow up on this confusion about military funerals, but in Gammy's numerous boxes, I didn't find any documents or letters indicating that the promised follow-up ever occurred.

Since the WASP had been a part of the civil service during the war, the women who continued in civil service jobs after the war could apply their WASP service toward their time in government service for retirement calculation purposes. Ironically, once public law 95-202 passed and their service was finally declared as eligible for military status consideration, the federal government excluded their WASP service for civil service time calculations. Their WASP service was now considered military as it related to civil service and the calculation of their length of time in employment was reduced. So, the same employer that told Gammy that she could not have preference points for her military service because it only applied under one department also excluded other WASP from counting their war time work as a period of civil service because it was now considered *military service.*[17]

---

[16] Ibid., 28-29 (statement of Elaine D. Harmon).

[17] Ibid., 9 (statement of Elaine D. Harmon).

Despite the discussion about burial benefits at the congressional hearing, Gammy eventually attended several funerals at Arlington National Cemetery for fellow WASP who received no military honors. Funerals for service members typically have – at a minimum – an honor guard that presents a folded American flag to the next of kin. Arlington National Cemetery divides its services into different levels, one being full military honors for officers. This includes a caisson (horse drawn carriage) which pulls a wagon carrying the flag draped casket, an honor guard of up to 16 members, folding and presentation of the American flag, a 21 gun salute, a bugler to play taps, and a chaplain to lead the service. Generals in the Army, Air Force, and Marine Corps, and Admirals in the Navy and Coast Guard, may receive a flyover of military planes. A second level of honors at Arlington National Cemetery is standard honors for enlisted members. This level provides similar services minus the caisson. Spouses of service members are not provided any funeral honors. Almost all of the WASP at Arlington National Cemetery were buried with a spouse, and since their own service was not recognized, they received no military funeral honors. This policy changed in 2002 – but not without another fight.

On February 15, 2002, WASP Irene Kinne Englund passed away. She had trained with class 43-W-8. Her husband had been inurned at Arlington National Cemetery in 1996 based on his service in the United States Navy. Naturally, Irene wanted to be placed with her husband after she passed away. When her daughter Julie Englund began the paperwork for Irene's service at Arlington National Cemetery, she learned that Arlington would allow her mother's ashes to be placed beside her father's only under the designation of spouse, without the military funeral honors afforded to deceased service members.

Julie began a campaign to get the attention of the public by writing op-eds in newspapers like *The Washington Post*. Arlington National Cemetery assigned the date of June 14, 2002 for the funeral service and Julie hoped that the Army would change its policy before the funeral. Julie's argument was based on public law 106-65, which stated that the Secretary of Defense must provide funeral honors to any veteran who requested it.

After garnering enough attention from news outlets, the Army reversed its decision and sent a press release explaining the decision to provide military honors at Irene's funeral. Since the provision of military honors fell under the section of federal law relating to Veterans Affairs, the WASP were deemed eligible for honors at military cemeteries, if requested. The press release stated that the WASP and the other "active duty designee" groups granted veteran status under public law 95-202, "...already are eligible for inurnment at the Columbarium at Arlington as a result of the 1977 law."[18]

Irene Englund was inurned at Arlington National Cemetery on Flag Day: June 14, 2002. She received the level of military honors that the Army had assigned for active duty designees, which included "a military chaplain, and a detail of up to 16 service members to serve as body bearers, conduct a rifle salute, fold and present the United States flag to the family of the deceased, and play taps."[19]

Nine WASP attended the ceremony, including Gammy. When asked by a reporter from The Washington Post to compare Irene's funeral with a prior WASP funeral at Arlington National Cemetery, Gammy described the previous funeral she had attended as, "The worst funeral I'd ever been to. They put the urn in the Columbarium wall, and that was it. Even the chaplain couldn't believe it was happening."[20]

The news outlets reported that Arlington National Cemetery was now allowing WASP to be inurned and have military honors at their funerals, "After more than half a century, the WASPs have finally won

---

[18] United States Army, press release, June 10, 2002, accessed at: http://www.arlingtoncemetery.net/rules-altered.htm

[19] Ibid.

[20] Vogel, Steve. "A Pioneer's Honorable Rest." The Washington Post. June 15, 2002. https://www.washingtonpost.com/archive/local/2002/06/15/a-pioneers-honorable-rest/38b47fbb-1edd-4205-9972-bc467e761fda/

full recognition."[21]

The awareness of the role the WASP played in paving the way for women to serve in the armed forces continued to grow after the 2002 controversy at Arlington National Cemetery. In 2009 Gammy stood in the Oval Office with her pilot friends Bee Haydu and Lorraine Rodgers while President Obama signed a bill awarding the Congressional Gold Medal to the WASP. Members of Congress presented the award to the WASP in a ceremony at the United States Capitol in March 2010. Gammy, along with hundreds of her WASP colleagues and their families, attended the ceremony, necessitating televisions in other areas of the building to accommodate viewing for audience overflow. At this point, it seemed that the women of the WASP were widely recognized as part of the veteran community and considered as eligible to have their ashes placed at the Columbarium with military funeral honors.

So it was surprising that in 2014, Arlington National Cemetery started to deny military recognition for the WASP once again. On October 4, 2014, Ruth Glaser Wright Guhsé, WASP class 44-W-10 passed away. She was in the last graduating class of the WASP. After her training ended, she was transferred to Aloe Army Air Field in Victoria, Texas. Her duties included towing targets for anti-aircraft artillery training.

Ruth's son applied to have her ashes inurned at Arlington National Cemetery. Unexpectedly, the cemetery administration denied the application. He applied a second time in early 2015, and the administration again denied that Ruth's WASP service established eligibility for placement of her cremains at Arlington National Cemetery. Ruth's son decided not to pursue applying for an exception to policy because he felt his mother should be there on her own merit. Because he felt his family would be more likely to visit a grave located in the Washington, D.C., area, he opted to have Ruth's ashes placed at Alexandria National

[21] Serafin, Barry. "WWII Female Flier Gets Arlington Honors." *ABC News*. June 21, 2002. http://abcnews.go.com/WNT/story?id=130280&page=1

Cemetery, one of the cemeteries maintained by the National Cemetery Administration of the Department of Veterans Affairs. An Air Force Color Guard provided honors during her funeral.

I only learned about the denial to Ruth's family in the months after Gammy had already passed away. I wondered if the requests from Ruth's family had prompted the Army to write its official memorandum dated March 23, 2015 in which it explained that the Army had mistakenly granted inurnment rights to active duty designees and would no longer allow WASP to have their ashes placed at Arlington National Cemetery.

Whatever had been the impetus for the Army's decision was unimportant now. The Army had already successfully turned away at least one of my grandmother's fellow pilots – that I knew of – with the justification that the World War II service of the WASP was once again unrecognized by Arlington National Cemetery. I wanted to make sure the Army stopped offending and frustrating grieving families like Ruth's or my own.

Our family had the advantage of starting with well-placed team members: I had a law degree and lived in the Washington area, making visits to Capitol Hill easy; Whitney had experience as a lobbyist; Mom loved making those FOIA requests; Tiffany had majored in women's studies and had worked in public policy; and best of all, even though Gammy was no longer with us, she would have been proud to let her own ashes sit in a closet while she served as an example of necessary equality for her sister pilots.

I had always considered Gammy a veteran. Now I only needed to convince the public, the media, the United States Army, and maybe even Congress, that I was right.

8

Final Flight

Summer 2010

I moved back to Maryland from California, where I had been living off and on for some years after attending college in San Diego, to attend the University of Maryland School of Law. Even though my grandfather had been an attorney, or maybe *because* he had been an attorney, Gammy hated attorneys. She was disappointed in my decision and had no qualms about expressing it.

Whitney and I were both visiting her one day when Gammy stared at me and said, "I hate lawyers." Then she turned to Whitney (who was a lobbyist at the time) and said, "I also hate lobbyists." She added, "But Whitney gets a pass because she is also a veterinarian, which is a noble profession." Then she looked back at me and had nothing else to say. Whitney smiled at me; I rolled my eyes in return. However, Gammy was glad that we were living near her so we could see each other more often, probably in the hopes of enlightening us about our misguided career choices.

Gammy had been diagnosed with breast cancer about five years before I moved back to Maryland. Specifically, she was diagnosed with adenocarcinoma of the breast – intraductal type, ER+, PR-, Her2+.

Surgeons performed a mastectomy early on and Gammy followed up with multiple visits a week to the VA Medical Center on Irving Street in Washington, for chemotherapy treatments, laboratory tests, and other necessary health care. Mom had been taking Gammy to most of her appointments, with Uncle Rob and his wife trading off sometimes. Whitney filled in where she could and also acted as the medical interpreter. When I came back for law school, I started helping out too.

On chemotherapy days, I picked Gammy up in the morning at her white house on the hill. When I first returned for school, she was still getting around well by holding onto my arm for balance. Eventually she started using a cane. She carried her necessities in her WASP tote bag featuring the Fifinella logo. Gammy wore her VA identification card in her blue WASP badge holder around her neck. She always insisted that I drive her old car instead of my own, so I grabbed her keys and helped her into the passenger seat. Then we made the 45 minute drive to the VA hospital. I felt like I might be headed for certain death along with Gammy while driving her rattling old green compact, but she insisted that her mechanic had it all under control.

As we meandered down New Hampshire Avenue and North Capitol Street on these trips, the conversations ran the gamut from politics (according to Gammy, politicians were "worthless") to her experiences at the VA hospital ("people there are very friendly") to random family discussions (she loved to point out that my grandfather was buried "right over there" if we caught a red light by the graveyard on the way back from the hospital.)

"Gammy, how is chemo? Does it make you sick?" I asked early on.

"No. The first time I didn't feel that well, but since then I haven't had a problem. I like going to chemo at the VA. I get to visit with people. I get to see all the veterans. It's a nice place. At least I am not bored at home," Gammy replied.

"I'm sorry I couldn't make it to the Gold Medal ceremony. Did you enjoy it?" I asked.

"Oh, yes, it is always great to see the other WASP. I'm glad to see so many people learning about what we did in the war," she replied.

"Did the president come?"

"No, he wasn't there but quite a few senators and representatives were."

"You already met him at the White House for the gold medal bill signing anyway," I said.

"Honestly, I am still mad that I never got to meet Bo," she lamented about missing out on a visit with the White House's famous Portuguese Water dog.

Gammy was fun to converse with, even if I disagreed with a lot of what she said. At 91 years old she was sharp and witty and on rare occasion broke out into song, generally an old folk tune that I didn't know. I heard her sing a couple of the WASP songs from training as well. One was particularly racy and involved a woman and a man sharing a cockpit and then a baby arriving later on:

Zoot-Suits and Parachutes

Before I was a member of the AAFTD
I was a working girl in Washington, D.C.
My boss he was unkind to me, he worked me night and day
I always had the time to work but never the time to play.
(CHORUS)
Singing zootsuits and parachutes and wings of silver, too
He'll ferry airplanes as his mama used to do.
Along came a pilot, ferrying a plane,
He asked me to go fly with him down in lover's lane
And I, like a silly fool, thinking it no harm
Cuddled in the cockpit to keep the pilot warm.
(CHORUS)
Early in the morning before the break of day
He handed me a short-snort bill and this I heard him say

Take this, my darling, for the damage I have done,
For you may have a daughter or you may have a son;
If you have a daughter, teach her how to fly,
If you have a son, put the bastard in the sky.
(CHORUS)
The moral of this story as you can plainly see
Is never trust a pilot an inch above the knee,
He'll kiss you and caress you, and promise to be true
And have a girl at every field as all the pilots do.

In the earlier days when Gammy was still using a cane, I dropped her off at the front door of the VA hospital on chemotherapy days and she insisted on making her own way inside to treatment. Sometimes I went inside to see her nurse to find out how things were going. I picked Gammy up in the afternoon unless I had class, in which case Mom or my uncle would get her. On days when she had exams or other appointments, I went inside to attend the medical visits with her.

Whitney decided we needed a notebook to keep track of what the doctors told us since we had so many people helping Gammy out. Gammy couldn't always remember what the doctors told her and whoever had accompanied her would inevitably forget a lot of the doctor's discussion. So the WASP tote bag gained a notebook in which the doctors and nurses wrote about the day's medical discussions and upcoming appointments.

Gammy was a bit of a celebrity at the VA hospital. In June 2011, the Department of Veterans Affairs even wrote an online article about her and the struggle of the WASP to get recognition as veterans. She explained how the documents about the WASP were hidden away for 30 years and they had to fight to obtain the veteran status allowing Gammy to receive her current cancer treatment at the VA. Gammy didn't want the WASP to be forgotten, so the efforts were worth it.

As we slowly walked the long corridors of the busy facility, people saw her WASP logo bag and stopped us regularly to say hello or take photos.

"Excuse me, ma'am, but were you a WASP?" was the typical question from a passerby.

"Yes!" Gammy always replied enthusiastically.

"Ma'am, I am honored to meet you. Is this your granddaughter?"

"Yes, she is," Gammy would respond.

"You have quite a grandmother," her fan would remind me.

"Thank you, I know," I always replied. I knew it was true, that Gammy was an unusual grandmother who had been part of a historic group of pilots, but I had never seen Gammy the same way that these admirers did.

I helped Gammy continue down the wide hallway to the chemo room. "Gammy, we are going to have to start arriving earlier because you're too much of a celebrity here. I need to start handling your fans."

She chuckled.

9

Final Fight

December 2015 – January 2016

After the meeting with Mom and Albert, I spent the following few weeks continuing my obsessive social media blitz. Each morning before getting out of bed and each night after coming home from work, I spent hours combing through related materials online and reaching out to networks of people interested in our topic. People on social media began to actively share our petition and our story.

I had to continue to learn more about Gammy and the WASP to educate people (and myself) about why recognizing her as a complete veteran was crucial to our fight. I decided to visit the College Park Airport Museum for inspiration. Gammy had learned to fly at the College Park Airport when she completed the Civilian Pilot Training Program prior to the United States entering World War II. When I was a kid, she used to take me there to watch planes take off and land. Over the years, she donated a lot of her memorabilia to their museum, including her uniform and Congressional Gold Medal. I was hoping that by sharing some of this on social media, it would attract attention with news reporters. I took photos of her pilot's license, her log books, and other documents there. Our family has few photos of Gammy from her time during the war, so this visit was helpful. I felt guilty staring through the glass at her photos and memorabilia because I could not remember the last time I had visited the museum.

As I was contemplating our situation in front of the case that housed her WASP uniform and wondering if Gammy would think fighting with Arlington National Cemetery was even worth the trouble, a few people came by to look at the display about her. It was strange to stand there and watch people discuss Elaine Danforth Harmon, a historic figure whose memorabilia was valuable enough to be in a museum, while I was immersed in a fight with the US Army about Gammy, my grandmother whose ashes were deemed not valuable enough to be in Arlington National Cemetery.

"That's my grandmother's uniform," I told a family pointing into the glass case.

"Oh really? Wow," a young blond woman replied. She turned and spoke in Russian to her son and husband. As I had been staring at the case lost in thought, this young family had approached, chatting in Russian and pointing at Gammy's display. The young mother pointed at me and her son, about 7 years old, waved at me. "Your grandmother, she flew planes?" the woman asked.

"Yes, during World War II. This exhibit case and that one over there have her memorabilia," I replied and motioned with my hand to another glass case. "And over in that display is her Congressional Gold Medal."

"Is your grandmother still alive?" the woman asked.

"No, she passed away about nine months ago," I informed her.

"I am sorry to hear that. I am glad to meet you. Thank you for telling us about her." She chatted to her family as they strolled off through the museum. I thought about the time Gammy went to Russia to meet the women who had flown combat missions over Germany during the war, the ones nicknamed "Night Witches." She told me that even though she and the other WASP didn't speak Russian, and the Night

94

Witches didn't speak English, they had loads of fun together. I walked back to the museum entrance.

"Hi, I am Erin Miller. My grandmother was Elaine Harmon, the WASP whose uniform and things are here," I said to the young man wearing a collared shirt with the museum logo on it behind the front desk.

"Oh, yes, it's great to meet you!" he replied with a wide smile.

"I was wondering if it would be possible to see some of the things that aren't on display?" I inquired.

"Yes, but you should talk to the director of the museum, who isn't here today. Here, take this so you can call her and ask about it on Monday," he informed me as he handed over a business card.

"Thank you," I replied. "I also wanted to tell you about a petition our family has on the Change.org website. My grandmother wanted to be at Arlington National Cemetery after she died, but they denied our request, so we are trying to get the policy changed."

"Oh yes, the staff knows about it. I think we all signed it already," he reported.

"Really?! That's great! Thank you!" I gushed. His earlier enthusiasm suddenly made sense.

* * *

On December 20, 2015, the day after the museum visit, I tweeted a link to our petition to Andrea McCarren, a reporter at one of our local television channels in Washington. She often reported on stories about veterans and was also training a service dog on behalf of an organization, so I hoped that our story about Gammy being denied at Arlington National Cemetery would pique her interest.

Each day, I spent hours contacting people via email or phone, looking for relevant stories in the news, and searching through social media. Tiffany, Whitney, and Mom kept me updated on the reactions they received to the petition and the campaign. In the evenings, as I struggled to fall asleep, I tried to quell my anxiety by thinking about anything productive I had done during the day. I constantly wondered if I had done enough to move our story forward and get closer to our goal. This campaign had already taken on the hours of a part-time job, and was quickly approaching the time commitment of a second full-time job, along with a corresponding reduction in sleep.

The next morning Andrea sent me a message asking if I lived in the area and requesting an email from me. I was thrilled that after weeks of spreading the word on this, a reporter was interested in the story. I learned from Andrea's email that she had done some background research on Gammy and the situation with Arlington National Cemetery and wanted to do a television interview with me. She planned to pitch our story at a meeting with the news producers that morning and would let me know later on that day if it was accepted.

I was confident the news media would be interested in the story eventually, even before we had a petition going, but I waited anxiously to hear if our story was going to be included among the many competing stories out there in the world. I spent the rest of the day trying to keep my eyes from darting over to check my phone. Every time the little green alert light on my phone started blinking, I picked it up.

"Oh my gosh!" I quietly exclaimed to myself as I saw an email from Andrea confirming the story was going forward. I jumped up from my desk at work and popped into my co-worker and friend Gina's cubicle next door. She was concentrating on her computer screen and had her headphones in, oblivious to my presence. I brought Andrea's email up on my phone screen and startled Gina as I held it out over her keyboard.

Gina's eyes scanned across the phone screen reading the email's contents. She pulled out her headphones, stood up and hugged me.

"Tomorrow? Interview? This is great!" She exclaimed.

"I suggested the College Park Aviation Museum so we could have my grandmother's uniform or Congressional Gold Medal in the background," I told Gina.

"Good idea," Gina said.

I saw another friend named Brandy down the aisle of the cubicle farm and waved for her to come over. I held the phone out so she could read the email too. She jumped up and down with a big smile on her face and gave me a bear hug. Then her smile disappeared and she got serious.

"Okay, but this is the real problem. What are you going to wear?" Brandy asked.

"I think a suit. I should look serious right? Like I know what I'm talking about!" I joked.

Brandy and Gina laughed and jokingly offered to be my beauty and style squad for when I became famous and needed an entourage of assistants.

The next morning, I gathered some photos of my family and Gammy to take to the interview. While sifting through boxes of things from Gammy's house that now filled our basement, I found a blue scarf with the WASP name printed in a repeating pattern on it. These blue scarves were given to the WASP to identify them at public events. This was Gammy's scarf, so I decided it would be nice to wear it, to have something of hers with me. I decided I would wear it at any media function or anywhere I was talking about our situation, to make myself stand out as a representative of the WASP. Then I had to do my makeup, which was the most annoying part of this entire campaign. I would much rather be out hiking around in the woods or playing sports than worrying about makeup. But I wanted to project a professional image on television, so a little makeup was part of my job as the leader of this campaign.

I arrived at the museum for the interview and while checking myself one last time in the mirror, my ongoing feeling of anxiety intensified.

I didn't have a problem speaking in public or in front of cameras. I realized I was concerned about whether I would say something compelling enough to make people care about Gammy being denied a burial place at Arlington National Cemetery. I knew the issue inside and out; I had been dealing with it for months now. But spitting out legal justifications for things on camera would not make people feel a great deal of empathy. Viewers and the media loved drama – people crying and getting emotional about the problem at the center of a news story – and that wasn't my style. I was trying to solve a problem, not sit around crying about it.

I waited in the museum lobby area and chatted with the staff members, who were as excited as I was that Gammy's story was getting attention from a well-known and respected local reporter. As I was explaining to the staff how grateful I was for offering the museum space for the interview, I spotted a yellow Labrador dog whose presence in the parking lot alerted me to Andrea's arrival. All the posts I had seen on her Twitter feed about training a service dog named Bunce, who was slotted for eventual assignment to a military veteran, made me certain I would like Andrea before I had even met her.

Andrea wore her television station's logo jacket and she breezed through the front door with Bunce bouncing alongside. "Hi. Erin? Andrea McCarren. Nice to meet you. This is Bunce, as I am sure you've figured out! I try to take him on location as often as possible, so he gets used to being out in public." She greeted me cheerfully with a firm handshake and then turned to greet the museum staff.

Like most on-camera news reporters, Andrea was attractive, with big eyes and medium length brown hair, cut and styled in that magic television way so that it always looked nice, even during outdoor news stories in bad weather. She was accomplished in her media career, having received at least 20 Emmy awards, and had worked in Washington area local news for more than 20 years. Andrea expressed genuine interest in doing the story, which I appreciated.

She introduced me to the cameraman and we all walked back through the museum as they looked for a good place to shoot the interviews. I considered Andrea's agreement to do a news story about Gammy and Arlington National Cemetery to be an accomplishment in itself. Now I had to do my part – an effective interview.

"I've never been to this museum. It's great. How have I missed it? What a cool place!" Andrea exclaimed.

As we walked through, I pointed out Gammy's uniform, log books, photos, and the Congressional Gold Medal that she had donated to the museum. Andrea went upstairs to interview the museum's assistant director first. The balcony on the second level provided a view over the historic planes of the museum's interior out to the landing strip of the operational airport beyond the museum's floor-to-ceiling glass windows.

Then it was my turn. Andrea and the cameraman set themselves up in front of the display case featuring Gammy's uniform and filmed me while I pointed out Gammy's memorabilia before we started doing the formal interview.

"Tell me about your grandmother, Erin. What was she like?" Andrea asked me a mix of questions about Gammy's role in my life as well as the legal problem with Arlington National Cemetery.

"My grandmother was the most patriotic person I have ever known. She had an American flag flying on the front porch of her house every day." As I was talking, I felt like I had so much to say, but I knew that little of it would end up in the final cut. In that moment, facing the camera and rattling off facts about Gammy and the WASP, I realized how much trust I had to put in Andrea to choose the best snippets to create a compelling story. I hoped that my intuition about her was correct.

"I know my grandmother would be very disappointed to learn that, in a way, her country has let her down," I explained to Andrea when she asked what Gammy would think of the situation. At that moment, I held back some tears while thinking about how much this would mean to Gammy and how upset she would be if we were unsuccessful.

After we finished the interview, I thanked Andrea for doing the story. "Erin, you did a really good job with the interview," she told me. I took the compliment to heart, although I imagined that she said that often.

Andrea told me the story would be on that night at 5:45 p.m. I hoped that Andrea's report would generate some attention to our problem and get people to sign the petition. When I got home, I set the DVR to record our first news story! I texted everyone I knew in the area and told them to look out for the story about Arlington National Cemetery. I emailed our extended family to see if they could stream it online. Tiffany was in Mexico with her family visiting her in-laws, and Mom had gone along with her. I put the word out on social media. Then I went for a run.

"Our first official news story about Gammy and Arlington! Aren't you guys excited?" The dogs stared back at me from their beds in the living room while I stood on one leg, stretching in my running tights in front of the television. Rosco yawned. "Don't over exert yourself there, Rosco," I said to him as I changed stretching positions.

As the television news approached an advertising break, the anchors started reading clips for the upcoming segments.

"Coming up next, a local aviation legend being denied at Arlington National Cemetery? Our Andrea McCarren has the story!" one news anchor announced.

I let out a screech of joy. "Guys, that's our story! That's Gammy! The aviation legend!" The dogs perked up their vulpine ears at my screeching, but promptly went back to sleep.

As Andrea began her report, I still could not believe the reason for which I was about to be on television. The situation was surreal: having to fight with the Army about Gammy's status when she and the other WASP had fought about it more than once and had supposedly gained their recognition already. Andrea included some history on the WASP, courtesy of the interview with the assistant director at the museum, and then followed with my interview. She concluded the story with some of the touching comments on the petition, highlighting the one from a Marine Corps veteran who wrote, "She belongs there. She can have my spot."

I heard the video chat tone ringing from my cell phone and saw Tiffany's photo on the screen.

"Hi! Did you all watch?" I asked.

"Yes! That was great!" Tiffany and Mom replied in unison as they appeared from Mexico on the video screen.

"I'm glad we figured out how to stream it live on the smart TV here," Tiffany said.

"Andrea did such a good job," Mom said. "Please tell her we thought the story was great!"

"I will, I'm emailing her now!" I replied.

Mom continued, "I like how she put the story together with some old footage, and your interview, and information about Gammy. It was well done."

That night I was almost too energized to sleep. Instead of feeling relieved, I was even more anxious. The news story was a great step ahead, but to me also signified increased commitment to ensure Gammy got into Arlington National Cemetery... and greater disappointment if I couldn't make it happen.

* * *

The following weekend was Christmas. It was a strange Christmas, the first time away from Gammy's home and overstuffed tree. Instead, we spent the holiday discussing the mission to get her ashes into Arlington National Cemetery. I didn't know if people were sitting around surfing the internet while they were on holiday, but we got a lot of responses to our petition. Tiffany sent an update on the campaign to the petition signers with a link to our television news story. I think my focus on fulfilling Gammy's well-earned final request distracted me from the otherwise sad aspect of the holiday weekend.

A couple of days later, we got a message on our Facebook campaign page from a reporter named Matthew Barakat at Associated Press (AP), an international news organization whose reports are featured in media outlets worldwide. After driving home from work, I parked the car outside the house and saw the message from Matthew on my phone. I didn't want to get distracted by the dogs, so I sat outside in the car while he interviewed me. I was ecstatic about this because I knew that if AP did a story and it was compelling enough, then it would get disseminated widely and hopefully create enough buzz about our campaign to get the attention of the right people. We spoke for about 30 minutes about everything from my childhood growing up with a World War II pilot grandmother to the legal situation with Arlington.

"Why Arlington National Cemetery?" Matthew asked me.

"There are a few reasons," I replied. "My grandmother wanted to be there because it is a historic cemetery where members of the public, who may not even have grave sites of relatives to visit, go to learn about the history of the armed forces. She wanted to have WASP representation at Arlington as a learning tool and historic marker. Additionally, other members of our family are buried there since we are from the Washington area, so in a way it is a local cemetery for us."

Matthew also requested an interview with Mom, who wasn't home at the time. I thanked him for interviewing me and told him I would have Mom call as soon as she was available. I then dialed Mom's cell, hoping she would answer, which was a rare occurrence, since she often had her cell phone turned off or did not carry it with her.

"Mom! Where are you?" I asked while still sitting in my parked car in the driveway.

"Erin? Yes? I am on the Beltway," Mom barked at her car's audio system as she drove.

"Mom, I just did an interview with Associated Press! They want to do an interview with you too. When are you coming home?"

"Well, I am going to the high school basketball game. Can I call tomorrow?" she inquired.

"No! You have to talk to him right now!" I implored her. "Mom, this is really important, it could go in newspapers across the country. You have a cell phone. Can't you call when you get to the game? You have to come home and call or call him on your cell."

"Fine, I will come home and call him," Mom replied.

I hadn't been at this too long, but I had already realized that when the press was interested in our story we had to respond as soon as possible before something more newsworthy popped up on their radars. I wanted to make their jobs as easy as possible and ensure they got what they needed from our family quickly. Whitney and Tiffany understood this but getting Mom to comply required some persuasion.

A couple days later on New Year's Eve, I got an email from Matthew saying he had finished our story and it should show up soon on the news wires. As soon as I left work, I sat in my car in the parking garage and searched the news on my phone to see if our story had appeared.

"Yes!" I yelled at the phone as I saw that several news outlets had already picked up the story and more versions continued to appear. I was wondering if the fact that it was New Year's Eve would somehow lessen the impact of the story, but I was excited nonetheless. I messaged my sisters.

Me: You guys, go look for the AP article! I saw it already on some news sites!

Tiffany: I'm looking, I see some too!

I had to drive straight from work to Whitney's house in New Jersey for the holiday weekend. The entire three hours I was driving, my phone was beeping and I hoped it meant good news – that people were finding the story and sharing it.

Once I arrived, we all talked about how many articles we had found. I had received a lot of emails and messages about all the new stories too. Tiffany found the story in the Japanese news, which meant our campaign for Gammy had now gone from an online petition at Change.org and a local television news report with Andrea McCarren, to an internationally featured news story in the span of one week. I spent several hours sharing everything online on our social media platforms. We also updated our petition to share one of the news stories with those who had signed on.

The rest of the weekend became a flurry of activity. Mom wanted to contact as many WASP as possible to make sure they knew we were fighting with the Army about Arlington. I called a few of the WASP and their families. I spoke with WASP Dawn Seymour and her family, who lived in New York. The Senate had not announced a schedule of the confirmation hearing for their nominee for Army Secretary yet, but Mom wanted to have one of the senators on the Senate Armed Services Committee ask some questions about the denial of the WASP at Arlington National Cemetery at the hearing. Our senators from Maryland were not on that committee. Since Dawn Seymour lived in New York, we were hoping she would be willing to contact Senator Kirsten Gillibrand, who was a member of the committee, and see if she would ask some questions or bring the topic up at the confirmation hearing.

I realized when speaking with Dawn on the phone that weekend that speaking with these other WASP was like speaking with Gammy. They all had big personalities and the same matter-of-fact manner as Gammy. Even though they were all over 90 years of age, they were all willing to help in any way they could. I felt like Gammy's spirit was still around when I conversed with the other women of the WASP.

I also spoke with Dawn's children to explain the details about contacting Senator Gillibrand to request Arlington questions at the hearing. Dawn had met Senator Gillibrand before and was eager to make contact again to help with this situation. Since Whitney had been a legislative fellow at the Senate, she had some ideas about the types of questions that would be effective. After that and other conversations that weekend, our team expanded to officially include former WASP and their families. I also made a list of the WASP who agreed to chat with the media if we needed them.

Over the weekend we got more media requests. I found that people were writing blog posts about our situation. *NBC Nightly News* wanted to do a segment with us that week. The director at the WASP museum in Texas contacted me to say that MSNBC was interested in doing a story as well. Since I had no idea how long this media interest would last, I decided to ensure my sisters appeared on television at least once so everyone had a chance to speak for Gammy. As I made plans with various news producers, I scheduled Tiffany for a tentative live appearance on MSNBC the following weekend.

10

Final Flight

November 2011

O n Veterans Day, November 11th, Gammy held onto my arm as we walked through the parking lot with Mom at the Applebee's near the University of Maryland, Gammy's alma mater. Gammy loved the free Veterans Day meal offered by the restaurant and she wasn't going to miss out just because it was getting harder for her to get around. She wore her blue WASP patterned scarf, her blue blazer with a WASP patch, and her gold WASP wings necklace.

"It's such a nice thing they do for the veterans," Gammy commented.

"I agree, Gammy," I said.

A young brunette woman in an Army uniform came out the front door of the restaurant and approached us on the way to her car.

"Excuse me, ma'am, are you a WASP?" she asked.

We stopped walking so Gammy could respond. "Yes, I am."

Before she could start talking again, this young soldier's eyes filled with tears. "Ma'am, I am honored to meet you. I want you to know what it means to me and to all the women who serve that you all did what you did. I wouldn't be doing this job if it weren't for you all." She wiped away a tear and then offered her hand, which Gammy shook. At this point I was getting teary eyed too.

"Thank you," Gammy said. "Are you stationed around here?"

"No ma'am, I am in town for training for a little while," the soldier responded.

"I'm always glad to see the women serving now," Gammy offered.

The soldier smiled, "Thank you for paving the way for girls like me!"

The soldier continued on to her car. When Gammy was in WASP attire, these interactions were common for her. But I didn't get to witness them often when I was younger. I was seeing more of them now that I was taking her to appointments at the VA hospital. Conversations like those were the moments when I was proudest of what Gammy and the WASP had done because I could see the direct impact on the later generations of female service members.

Not too long after our Applebee's outing, I went to Gammy's house one morning to visit and anticipated that Gammy would hand me one of her famous newspaper cutouts – fun articles about dogs, or articles opining on the state of the nation. I bounded up the narrow and short staircase from the back door to the kitchen and saw Gammy sitting at the table in her breakfast nook by the kitchen window that overlooked the verdant front yard. She was hunched over a bowl of cereal.

"Hi Gammy," I greeted her as I walked past to the sink. I heard some mumbling in response and turned to look over at her.

When she lifted her head, I saw that the entire left side of her face was drooping and her mouth was half open, clearly involuntarily. Milk dribbled out of the corner of her mouth and fell on her shirt where moist cereal bits were already resting. She continued to eat despite half of the food missing the target.

"Gammy, what happened to your face?" I walked over to get a closer look.

"I don't know. It just started dl..oo..pping. When... I woke up... it was like that." Her mouth couldn't pronounce the word "drooping" anymore.

"Gammy, how long has it been like this? Did you go to the doctor?"

"Just a couple days. I don't... need the... doctor. It's not that important," she struggled to reply.

"Gammy! When half your face stops working, that is important!" I chastised her.

I dialed Mom's phone number on my cell as I watched Gammy continue to try to spoon cereal into her mouth.

"Mom, Gammy's face is drooping," I explained.

"What do you mean? What is wrong?" Mom asked from the other end of the line.

"I don't know. She says it has been a couple of days. Why hasn't anyone taken her to the doctor?" I demanded.

"I don't know. I can come take her later today when I get back," Mom explained.

"Okay. Bye." I hung up the phone. "Gammy, Mom is going to take you to the doctor."

The functioning side of Gammy's face grimaced with annoyance. She sighed and asked, "Is that really necessary?" as she continued to spoon cereal into her half-open mouth.

"Yes, Gammy," I told her.

Gammy ended up at the doctor in due course, where he diagnosed her condition as Bell's palsy, which caused her face to droop. The doctor conveyed the news in such a way that Mom felt it wasn't necessary to be concerned – a problem that normally resolved on its own.

11

Final Fight

January 2016

The Associated Press article, which had been used as the basis for several media stories in the previous few days, and had been reprinted in publications worldwide, provided a huge boost in the national and international profile of our campaign as the new year began. Two days after AP released its article, a friend from Texas messaged me that during her morning workout, she had glanced up to see Gammy's "beautiful face looking down" at her from the row of televisions mounted on the wall at her local gym. We received similar reports from across the country. Our campaign had momentum now, but we needed someone who could change the law to come forward and help us. Legislators who put their full support behind a proposed law – prioritize it in their legislative agenda, highlight it in media appearances, and encourage other legislators to vote for it – are referred to as "champions" in their legislative body, from a city council to Congress. There are legislators who introduce bills and don't follow through with supporting them. We didn't need someone like that, we needed a true champion.

Mom called me on Sunday afternoon to say that there were several messages on the answering machine at the house from "media people." She had no idea how they had found her number since she thought it was unlisted. When I returned from Whitney's New Jersey house on Sunday night, I returned calls to the producers at a local Washington television station and Greta Van Susteren's cable news television show.

The producer from the Greta Van Susteren show said she was excited to hear from us. She wanted Mom and me to be on the show Monday night. I carried the phone into Mom's room to make arrangements. Mom was watching television in bed. "Mom put it on mute," I whispered as I sat on her bed. She grabbed the remote control and silenced the television.

"Okay, let me ask Mom," I said into the phone. "Mom, they want us to be on tomorrow night," I cupped my hand over the phone as I waited for Mom's reply.

"I don't feel well. You did one TV news story, isn't that enough?" Mom scrunched her face as she replied.

"No! We have to do as many as possible, what are you talking about? I would do it alone but they want you to talk also," I admonished her.

"Fine." Mom sighed. "Can we at least do it on Tuesday then?"

"Mom is asking if we can do it on Tuesday?" I conveyed to the producer on the phone. "Okay, thanks so much!" I finished the conversation with her and hung up.

"She said it will be fine," I informed Mom.

The next morning, I got a call from the local news producer who wanted to interview Mom that day. I told her I would contact Mom and see what I could arrange. I knew Mom was still not feeling comfortable with all these potential television appearances, but I had to work and couldn't make time for an interview.

"Mom, I need you to go do an interview today," I informed her over the phone.

"Okay," she reluctantly agreed. "I am not dressed for interviewing. Maybe I can keep my coat on so people don't see what I wore today.

Where do I go?"

"I told the reporter you can meet at Arlington National Cemetery. It's with channel seven, so look for their news van. At noon," I instructed her.

Meanwhile I got an email from Kate Landdeck, the history professor in Texas, saying she was appearing on Huffington Post live online at noon and the show wanted a family member to talk as well. I messaged Whitney.

Me: Hey, can u do HuffPost live at noon? On video chat? I have to work.

Whitney: Yes, I am at home. Hopefully Isabella will be good.

Me: Thank u. Mom is talking to Channel 7 at noon too. I'll tell Kate, you will be with her

Whitney: Good work, ok. Oh, I also am writing up talking points for the NBC interview

Me: Ok, cool

The Huffington Post producer told Whitney her "jaw was on the floor" at learning this situation with Gammy and Arlington had come up. At noon, during lunch, my friends and I watched Whitney and Kate talk online on my cell phone on a live stream from *Huffington Post* while Mom was off at Arlington doing an interview for the local news. Everyone loved how Whitney did the whole interview holding her infant daughter. Great granddaughter Isabella made a news appearance for the WASP!

That evening we also waited for Mom's appearance on her segment for the local news.

"I hope they edited this. I felt like I was rambling when she asked me questions," Mom said as she sat on the sofa next to me.

"I'm sure it will be fine Mom," I reassured her.

"What's up with the Greta show tomorrow?" Mom asked me.

"The producer says we have to do it another day because they are having a congresswoman on to talk about our problem," I informed her.

"Who?" Mom asked.

"Her name is McSally. I don't know who she is. I texted Whitney but she didn't answer. I'm going to call her," I replied.

I dialed Whitney's number. It seemed logical to ask her if she had any experience working with this congresswoman's office when she had been a lobbyist.

"Hey, why aren't you responding to my message?" I asked over the phone.

"I'm driving," Whitney replied.

"Erin, it's on!" Mom exclaimed and pointed to the television.

"Hold on Whitney, Mom is on TV," I said over the phone.

Mom and I watched her interview from earlier in the day with the local news crew. They had filmed it at the Women In Military Service For America Memorial, which also had a display about the WASP. Mom crinkled her face at a couple points in reaction to something she had said in the interview.

"Was it okay?" Mom asked after the report ended.

"Yes, it was good Mom. But I can't believe you kept your coat on during the interview," I replied.

"I didn't like what I had worn to work," she explained.

"Helloooo," Whitney's voice carried through my phone.

"Sorry, we were watching Mom's interview," I explained.

"How was it?" Whitney asked.

"It was good. We need all the stories we can get, right?" I replied.

"Totally," Whitney said. "What was your question again?"

"The producer from the Greta show says this congresswoman is, I'm quoting, outraged, about this issue," I explained. "Who is Congresswoman McSally? Did you ever work with her office?"

"I don't know her. She must be a freshman. Look her up," Whitney instructed.

"Okay. Hold on. I'll read to you." I put the phone on speaker mode and set it next to me on the couch as I opened an internet search page on my laptop and started scanning through the results. "It says McSally represents district number two in Arizona, and yes it is her first term. Good job ex-lobbyist," I announced toward the telephone sitting nearby.

"Thanks my sister," Whitney's voice echoed from the phone's speaker.

"Oh my gosh, this is crazy!" I blurted out as I scanned the website.

"What? Tell me!"

"She graduated from the Air Force Academy then she was in the Air Force for twenty-two years and retired as a colonel. She sued the Pentagon because women service members were being forced to wear full-body covering attire, like Muslim women, when they were stationed in Saudi Arabia and eventually the law was changed." I continued to summarize the information from the website, "It says she was the first woman to fly a plane in combat for the United States and the first to command a fighter squadron. No wonder she's mad about this. How did I not know about her before? Maybe we should have called her last summer. I feel like an idiot!"

"The show should be good then!" Whitney exclaimed.

* * *

The next morning I responded to emails on my phone while I waited for the elevator at work, my mind drifting to what Congresswoman

113

McSally might say later that night on television. I glanced down the hall at the television monitor which rotated notifications about the office when a familiar face appeared on the flat screen.

"Hey did you guys see that Senator Mikulski is coming today?" I asked my coworkers when I got to my cubicle.

"Here?" Brandy and Gina replied almost in unison, as they had been doing often since our training class together.

"Yes, to give a speech. I saw an announcement on the monitor downstairs. I am going to go over there and try to talk to her. But it's in the other building. I don't have a parking permit for that one," I explained.

"There's a shuttle," said Brandy, who always knew what was going on at work. "What are you going to say to her?"

"I don't know. My grandmother died nine months ago and her ashes are still in the closet, so can you please help us?" I joked.

"I can picture you actually saying that, you know that right?" Gina pointed out.

"Yeah, maybe I won't say exactly that," I replied.

Brandy looked at her phone and then frantically said, "The shuttle leaves in one minute, go, go, go!" I ran to the elevator and sprinted out the front door to hop on the shuttle just in time. I texted my sisters on the ride over.

Me: I'm on Mission Mikulski this morning

Whitney: What?

Me: She is coming to our work to give a speech, I am going to tell her we still need help

Tiffany: Woo hoo! Mission Mikulski!

Whitney: Find a staffer when you get there

Fortunately the shuttle arrived much earlier than the scheduled speech time, so I was able to secure the first seat next to the podium. Eventually the room was packed with attendees. When the senator showed up, I watched the people around her and found one who looked to be a staff person.

"Excuse me," I said to the young woman in a blue blazer who appeared to be part of the senator's team.

"Yes," she replied.

"Hi, I will just take two seconds, I know you are preparing for this talk. I am Erin Miller. My grandmother was Elaine Harmon, the World War II pilot denied entry into Arlington National Cemetery. We contacted the senator's office already and got a response, but the problem is still not resolved. Can I get more assistance?"

"Yes, I didn't work on that issue, but I have seen the story. Here, take this, so you have my number, and meet me after the speech so we can have a talk." She wrote her cell phone number on the back of a business card and handed it to me.

Several people gave speeches that morning. The senator said she had secured a certain sum of money in the federal budget to refurbish the building we were sitting in because it was "a dump." I found this hilarious, as did most of the people in the room who started laughing when she said it. It was sad, but true. After the speech ended, tons of people were trying to talk to her. I managed to sidle my way to her and introduce myself.

"Senator, my grandmother was Elaine Harmon, the World War II pilot that was denied at Arlington Cemetery. We asked for help from your office but the problem still isn't fixed," I explained as we shook hands.

Senator Mikulski replied, "I remember meeting your grandmother and respected her service. Your grandmother was great and I know you have had a difficult fight."

"I wanted to say thank you for looking into this. I am going to talk with one of your aides now. Thank you." The senator continued to greet other attendees as she made her way out of the auditorium.

The senator's aide then brought me into a conference room down the hallway where we chatted about the problem at hand. "Tell me more about the background on this issue," the aide requested.

"My grandmother was one of the Women Airforce Service Pilots, there were thirteen from the state of Maryland. She wanted to be placed at Arlington National Cemetery, but we discovered that the Army, which runs Arlington, changed the regulations a month before my grandmother died, and she is no longer eligible to be there," I explained to the aide. "We sent documents to the senator's field office in our area back in August, and we received a reply from Arlington, but it was only a letter explaining what we had already been told. We would like to continue to fight this decision."

"Yes, I understand, thanks for bringing this up with me," the aide replied as she made some notes on a legal pad.

"We have an online petition with thousands of signatures, and we have gotten some international media for this story. I think we are getting a lot of traction," I said.

"The senator is traveling for the rest of the day, so I can't look into this until I get back to the office tonight," she explained. "But I will look into it tonight and get back to you and see what else we can do to resolve this."

"Thank you for listening, I appreciate it," I said to her as we parted ways.

While I sat in the hallway waiting for the next shuttle back to the other building, I messaged with Tiffany and Whitney.

Me: Mission Mikulski Accomplished!

Tiffany, Whitney: Woohoo!!

Me: Her aide said she will look into it and get back to us tonight or in the morning.

When I got home, Whitney and Isabella had already arrived. We had to go to Chicago in a couple days because Whitney would be attending a work conference and she had enlisted Auntie Erin to babysit Isabella.

"So what is going on with the Greta show?" Whitney asked as she changed Isabella's diaper.

"I got a text from the producer. She said she didn't want to ruin the surprise by telling me anything but we would not be disappointed. I cannot wait to see this. I am so freaking excited." I stood in the living room scrolling on my phone. "I did an interview with ABC national news on the way home from work. The reporter said it should be out by the time I get home. I want to email it out to everyone before this Greta piece starts." I had already emailed the whole family to tell them to watch Greta Van Susteren's show that night because something awesome was going to happen, but I didn't know what it was. "I found the article. At least ABC News got official statements from the Army and Arlington, even though they're total B.S."

"What did they say?" Whitney asked.

"The cemetery made a mistake by allowing the other WASP to be there!" I summarized from the article on my phone. "Ridiculous!"

"Come sit on the couch and set the DVR," Whitney requested and held out the remote control.

Mom arrived just before the segment with Representative McSally was about to start while Whitney, Isabella, and I were waiting on the couch.

"Is it on yet? Are you recording it?" Mom asked as she came in the door, discarded her giant purse on an empty chair, stood in the middle of the living room in her winter coat, and stared at the television.

"The show is on but our part isn't on yet, and yes, it is recording," I replied. The advertising ended and Greta appeared on the television screen.

"It's on! It's on!" Mom yelled.

Greta started out by explaining that the upcoming story would "make your blood boil!" I loved it. Everyone was mad about this! Then she introduced Representative McSally and promptly interrupted her by saying Gammy's ashes were in a closet in Silver Spring.

"Yes, that's our closet!" we all yelled in unison and cheered.

Representative McSally went on to explain the story and discuss her own experience in the military and her personal connection to the WASP. It was clear that she was passionate about this problem and thought this decision by the Army was as ridiculous as we did. Then she continued by saying that since the Army didn't seem to be interested in reversing its decision, she would do something about it.

"We are going to introduce legislation, probably this week to over-turn it," Representative McSally announced on national television.

Whitney's eyes grew wide as she processed what Representative McSally was committing to. Whitney and I looked at each other, paused for a moment and then we both yelled, "Woohoo!" and gave each other a high five.

Mom yelled, "All right!" as she continued to stand by the television, still wearing her long black winter coat.

Representative McSally explained, "They've been fighting since they served for the basic respect that is due to them – that they served in the military, and this is the last slap in their face."

Greta continued, "You and I will both show up at Arlington Cemetery when we get this one done."

At the end of the segment, Greta talked about the petition at Change.org and posted a link to it on her website and other social media.

"Oh my gosh! This is good right?" I asked Whitney.

"Yes!" Whitney exclaimed, "This is amazing!"

I pulled my phone out and brought up the Change.org website. "We already have thousands more signatures!"

"Rewind it! Play it again!" Mom requested. I grabbed the remote control and set up the video clip again. The house phone rang and I went to retrieve it since Mom was engrossed in watching Greta's segment again. I brought the phone out to Mom who had finally settled on a chair.

"Hello? I know! It was amazing," Mom said to her sister Chris over the phone. "I don't know what to say. They talked about the closet on television!" Mom laughed. "Okay, thank you. I have to make Erin play it again. Good night." Mom hung up the phone. "Erin, restart it!"

I reached over to take the remote control for the cable box to rewind the video a third time so it played in the background while we talked. As Mom heard the segment start again, she shouted, "Get 'em Greta!"

"Mom, pay attention or I have to turn off Greta. We need to talk about tomorrow's interview," I instructed.

"Okay, let's go over our talking points for the NBC interview tomorrow," Whitney said as she picked up the papers the two of us had discussed earlier and handed copies to Mom and me. We wanted everyone to be on the same page and it was also an effort to keep Mom focused and prevent her from going on a tangent about all the memos and decisions she kept talking about. "The most important thing is to be simple and not get into the weeds," Whitney advised.

"I don't know why you didn't mention here about how the Army is flip-flopping. They said one thing and now they are changing their minds," Mom complained as she looked at the talking points.

"Mom, we don't have time for all that. Stay focused. Gammy died. They said no, we need them to say yes. This is why the WASP were important. Here is how people can help us," I reminded her. "Stick to the talking points."

Mom pursed her lips but appeared to tacitly agree – or she didn't feel like arguing. "I have to go send some emails." She stood up to leave, carrying her laptop upstairs.

The living room looked like a media center. Whitney and I were both on our phones. Whitney's tablet, my laptop and tablet, and piles of WASP documents and books, along with printouts of the talking points Whitney had drafted for our NBC news interview were spread all over the coffee table. A couple of the boxes containing Gammy's disorganized photos and papers were sitting on the floor. Greta Van Susteren's news story with Congresswoman McSally played on a loop on the television in the background.

While I was updating the social media accounts, I sent a link of the Greta show clip to Tiffany so she could update the petition. Within an hour we had received over 13,000 additional signatures. Then I emailed the video clip of Greta's show to Senator Mikulski's aide and told her we would be on Capitol Hill the next day so we could meet if necessary.

"Do you think McSally would want to meet us?" I asked Whitney while I was responding to all the emails about the big development in our situation. I could not believe that a representative in Congress that I had never heard of had gone on national television and promised to introduce legislation to fix our problem.

"I don't see why not. I'll ask her office." Whitney sent an email to Representative McSally's office on Capitol Hill. It was almost midnight, but we hoped that someone would get back to us early the next day before we had to be at Arlington National Cemetery for the interview.

"We're going to have to update our talking points if this legislation actually happens before this interview tomorrow," I pointed out as I flipped through papers on the coffee table.

"Oh my gosh!" Whitney exclaimed as she stared at her cell phone.

"What?" I asked.

"McSally's chief of staff replied to my email in under two minutes! They're going to make time to see us in the morning before the interview," Whitney said in disbelief.

"This is awesome!" I exclaimed. "Okay, I have to encourage Mom to go to sleep now or she is going to stay up all night writing emails and be tired tomorrow." I closed my laptop and headed upstairs. After I brushed my teeth and checked my phone one last time for the night, I saw that Mom had copied me on her final email for the night: *I have been ordered to go to bed.*

* * *

I sat in the back of Whitney's car the next morning as she drove past the leaf-bare trees lining the Baltimore Washington Parkway on our way to Capitol Hill. I spent the entire ride with my phone in one hand, talking to people, emailing, and texting, and occasionally trying with the other hand to feed a bottle to five month-old Isabella who was beside me in her car seat. Mom was reviewing her copy of the talking points. Luckily there wasn't too much traffic since we had departed after rush hour.

"You need a driver," Whitney said to me from the front of the car.

"Good thing I have a sister in town to drive me everywhere," I retorted. My phone vibrated with a new email. "Mikulski's staffer is watching the Greta Van Susteren video from last night."

"Ha, I wish I could see them when they watch that!" Whitney exclaimed.

My phone rang. "Hi. Yes. Okay. No, I haven't seen it. What? That's ridiculous. We are on our way to Representative McSally's office right now. Oh? Okay, I will ask." I hung up the phone. "The NBC News people want to interview McSally. The producer said there's an announcement on the Arlington website about us."

"What?!" Whitney and Mom asked in unison from the front of the car.

"I don't know. I am looking for it right now." I scrolled through the phone looking for the Arlington National Cemetery website, but then it vibrated again to indicate a new email had arrived.

"I got another email from the Mikulski people." I summarized the email out loud as I read from my phone. "The aide says she is calling Representative McSally's office to coordinate on legislation with the Senate. Wait, I just got another one. She says they are going to see about getting all the women senators on board too! This is good right?!"

Whitney yelled from the driver's seat, "Yes! This is awesome!"

"WASPs have never been eligible for either inurnment or burial at Arlington," I read out loud to Mom and Whitney from the Arlington National Cemetery website, emphasizing the extra "s" that Gammy had never approved of. This statement directly contradicted the memorandum from 2002 in which Arlington officials confirmed that WASP had always been eligible for inurnment at the Columbarium. "The cemetery put this on their news page! They must have seen Representative McSally on TV last night. They're digging in their heels. You know this only makes me want to get Gammy into that cemetery even more! They're being ridiculous!"

"I'm sure the cemetery will be thrilled when we show up on their property for a national news interview today," Mom joked.

We arrived at Capitol Hill and I made my first official foray on behalf of Gammy in the halls of the congressional office buildings. There are three main office buildings for each chamber. The offices for the House of Representatives are in massive colonnaded stone buildings with wide marble floored hallways that occasionally open into rotundas. The three structures are connected by underground tunnels to each other and to the Capitol building itself, which sits between the House and Senate office buildings. Whitney had spent lots of time in her previous job walking through here and I had accompanied her on occasion. Now we had a personal mission to accomplish. I decided that I would walk to every one of the 535 offices of voting members of Congress if I had to.

"Representative Noem, hello," Whitney said to a sharply dressed brunette walking our direction in the hallway. In response, she looked over at us and locked her eyes on Isabella.

"Hellooooo... Who is this?" Representative Kristi Noem asked while reaching her arms out to squish Isabella's tummy.

"This is Isabella," Whitney replied.

"Isabella! What a beautiful name! Can I hold her?" Whitney freely gave up Isabella to her new admirer.

"Remind me how I know you again?" Representative Noem asked Whitney.

"I was at AVMA, animal welfare," Whitney explained.

"Oh, right. And this is your daughter?" she asked.

Whitney nodded.

"She is precious! What are you all doing here?" Congresswoman Noem asked while she continued to coo over Isabella.

"My grandmother was the World War II pilot denied at Arlington National Cemetery. Maybe you've seen it in the news? We are going to see Representative McSally. This is my mom and my sister Erin," Whitney explained. Representative Noem reached out to shake hands with us while holding Isabella in the crook of her elbow.

"That's your family? I'm sorry to hear about that. Good luck! Martha is great. She will be helpful," Representative Noem said. "Ugh, I have to run. I want to keep Isabella all day!" She reluctantly handed Isabella back to Whitney. "Nice to see you again Whitney and nice to meet you all." Then Representative Noem jogged away.

"I think that congresswoman wants to kidnap your baby," I joked as we walked down the hallway.

"She's my favorite. She's awesome." In her previous job, Whitney had worked with Representative Noem's office occasionally and was impressed with how the congresswoman regularly traveled 1,300 miles between Washington to work on Capitol Hill, and South Dakota, where she worked on the family ranch.

We made our way to Representative McSally's office where her staff greeted us and said their boss was eagerly anticipating our meeting.

Considering the lives of members of Congress seem to be scheduled down to the second, I felt lucky and grateful that this representative had made time for an impromptu meeting to talk about Gammy and the new legislation.

We settled on the couch in the waiting area where a staffer offered us water to drink. Whitney unbundled Isabella from her winter attire. Newspapers from Arizona dotted the coffee table. Among the expected office décor related to a congressional district in Southern Arizona, I spotted two unusual items: a photo of Representative McSally playing football, and a red, white, and blue star graphic depicting the values of "Team McSally."

We didn't wait long before the front door of the waiting room swung open and a bubbly petite brunette, who I recognized from the previous night's television appearance, strode in followed by a couple of staffers.

"Are they here?" she asked toward the staffers already present in the office, one of whom immediately pointed in our direction.

"Hey! I am so glad to see you. Martha McSally." A smile appeared on her face as she turned to introduce herself, shaking hands with each of us. "Come in, come in!" Representative McSally invited us back to her private office. Once there, she and a couple of staff members sat in chairs around the coffee table, and the four of us settled on the couch. A photo of a golden retriever sat on the windowsill. Air Force memorabilia and airplane photos decorated the walls.

Before becoming a member of Congress, Martha McSally had become the first female Air Force pilot to fly a combat mission, piloting an A-10 attack plane – an armored war bird with a massive 30mm cannon – as she helped enforce the no-fly zone in Iraq during the mid-1990s. In 2001, she won a lawsuit against the Department of Defense when she argued that female service members stationed in Saudi Arabia shouldn't have to wear a full-body covering while traveling off base. She eventually reached the rank of full colonel before retiring in 2010 and was elected to Congress in 2014. She was sworn into her first term in January 2015, only a few months before Gammy died.

"Thank you for meeting with us," I said.

"I'm glad to meet you all, thank you for coming in," Representative McSally replied. "First, I want to say that I think this is just B.S."

I liked her already.

She continued, "I cannot believe this is happening. We're going to fix it, okay? We already have the legislation drafted."

"That's efficient," I remarked.

Representative McSally laughed and said, "I don't like to waste time. Tell me about your grandmother. What's been happening so far? Tell me everything."

I pulled the folder containing Gammy's documents out of my bag and set it on the coffee table. I began passing things to Representative McSally and she inspected each one. "You already know the problem. The Army doesn't recognize her service because the law from 1977 says their status applies only under the VA. Here is the decision memo from the Army. Here is her honorable discharge certificate. Her DD-214. This is a photo of her from the war. We only have a few. And the letter she wrote requesting to be at Arlington."

"...I would like to be buried at Arlington National Cemetery..." Representative McSally read aloud from the letter. "Wow, this is great. Can we make a copy?"

"You can keep that. It's a copy of the original one," I told her.

"Now I am just curious, why Arlington?" she asked.

Mom chimed in, "It was important to my mother that the WASP have representation there. She thought of Arlington National Cemetery like a way to preserve history."

"You know, so many people visit Arlington, even people who don't have family buried there, so I think her idea was that people visit and they walk around and might see this grave with 'WASP' marked on it and think about looking up their history and learning something. A way to keep their history alive." Representative McSally listened and nodded as I explained. "It was important to her since they were forgotten after the war. She didn't want that to happen again."

"I get it, that's important," Representative McSally said.

I saw my phone screen light up. "Sorry, it's the NBC people texting, one second." I read the message on my phone. "They asked if you want to do an interview also."

Representative McSally looked at the staffers sitting next to her who nodded, and then she said, "I think we have time. It's great that the media is picking up on this. You have to keep going."

I looked over at Mom and waved my hand at the congresswoman, "See Mom? She gets it!" Mom raised her hands in defeat. I turned back to Representative McSally who had a confused look on her face and I explained. "Mom asked me the other day, 'You did one news story, isn't that enough?' and I told her that we had to do as much media as possible and I plan to get on every media outlet that will take me."

"That's exactly what you have to do. They say you have to reach out to people in at least three different ways to get the message across," Representative McSally advised.

I was glad to hear that despite this being the first time I had met her, we were already on the same page regarding how to resolve this problem. Finally, I pointed to the photo on the windowsill and I asked, "Is that your dog?"

"Yes! His name is Boomer." She retrieved the photo down from the windowsill and handed it to me.

Then I had to pull out my phone and show her photos of my dogs.

"So we're sharing dog photos now?" Representative McSally asked.

"I guess so," I replied with a smile.

Somewhere between discussing our mutual love of dogs and being told that I was right to jump on any media opportunity that arose, I decided I felt comfortable placing my faith in Representative McSally to help us achieve our goal, despite having just met her. I think Gammy would have agreed that trusting this politician with something as important as her final resting place solely because she was a pilot dedicated to her canine companion was a rational decision on my part. I did not have much of a choice, since I didn't have any control over who pounced on our story and decided to write legislation for it. I was glad it turned out to be someone who at least seemed genuinely interested in fixing the problem.

"We have to leave for the interview," I said as I stood up. "Oh, picture! We have to take a picture."

We gathered together and I handed my phone to Patrick, Representative McSally's communications director.

"What does her shirt say?" Representative McSally asked pointing at Isabella as we arranged ourselves for a photo.

"Gammy flew planes!" Whitney replied.

"I love it!" Representative McSally exclaimed and laughed.

We posed for a few photos and thanked everyone there.

"Great! I guess we will see you at Arlington," Representative McSally said as she reached to shake my hand.

I looked at her hand and said, "No. I have to give you a hug."

"Oh, Okay," she replied with a smile.

I had never in my life imagined getting sentimental about Congress. If I hadn't been so excited about the new bill and feeling like we were making a lot of progress, I probably would have cried. And I am not generally taken to tears. But in that embrace was nine months of anxiety and frustration being released, the importance of which was not possible to convey with mere words or a handshake.

Our champion had found us.

* * *

Whitney and I both get hangry (angry when hungry). Since the interview was scheduled during lunch time, we had to eat something quickly before we went over to the cemetery. Whitney took us by the convenience store inside the congressional offices on the way out to the car.

"I like this McSally. She's enthusiastic," I proclaimed from the back of Whitney's car as I stuffed sushi in my mouth with one hand and held a bottle for Isabella with the other hand. "What do you think Whitney? You've met more members of Congress than I have. She doesn't seem like a typical boring legislator."

"I think we're lucky that she ended up doing this," Whitney replied as she concentrated on navigating the streets of Capitol Hill.

"Maybe you'll end up thinking she's as great as Representative Noem," I joked.

"That's a pretty high standard," Whitney retorted.

Once we arrived at Arlington National Cemetery, we found Representative McSally in her car in the parking lot. I called the producer as I wasn't sure where they wanted us to go. The producer informed us to drive to the gate and an escort car would lead us to the interview location on the cemetery grounds. We drove through to the gate and Representative McSally followed behind. When our car connected with the escort at the gate, we noticed that Representative McSally's car behind us wasn't moving.

"Why is McSally's car stopped?" Whitney asked as she glanced in the rear-view mirror.

I turned around to see the police officer motioning at her car.

"I don't know," I replied.

I called the producer to ask what was going on.

After hanging up the phone, I conveyed what the producer had told me. "The producer says they just learned that there is a law prohibiting members of Congress from being interviewed on Arlington National Cemetery property. Representative McSally and her staff had to turn around and go back to the office. The producer arranged to interview them later."

"Ugh. Typical Arlington from what I have seen so far," Mom said.

"I feel bad for her wasting time to come over here," I responded.

Whitney drove behind the escort car to a location near the long outer wall of the cemetery. The wall and the Columbarium courtyards nearby held small chambers called niches in which urns of cremated remains are placed, a process I had recently learned to call "inurnment." The lights, cameras, and other media equipment were set up and there were three chairs for us and one facing those for Rehema Ellis, the NBC reporter. She was charming and lovely in her elegant long wool coat. She said she was hoping to meet Isabella, who was bundled in blankets and napping in the car carrier placed behind the cameras.

I think we were at the interview for over an hour, but it felt much longer. It wasn't too cold out, but sitting still in a chair outside in January with a breeze was making me shiver. I tried to stop shivering when I was responding to Rehema's questions. The interview ran even longer because every time an airplane flew by (which happened often since the cemetery is next to Reagan National Airport) or a large truck passed on the road adjacent to the other side of the wall, we had to stop the interview and wait until the noise died down. Whitney decided the cemetery administrators had intentionally suggested that loud place for the interview.

As expected, it seemed like some of the questions were meant to elicit emotional responses. I decided news people all hope their subjects will spontaneously burst into tears. Our family was so focused on resolving our problem that none of us had the inclination to cry about it. Plus, we had just left the office of Representative McSally who was going to introduce legislation to fix our problem, so we were all ecstatic in that moment. I only wanted to explain why Gammy and the WASP were important, and why this issue deserved to have a swift legal resolution.

"How long are you all prepared to fight this decision?" Rehema asked.

Whitney replied, "My daughter is sleeping right over there, so that makes three generations right here ready to fight for this." However, we were all hoping to get this resolved before Isabella had to take over.

Isabella conveniently slept through the whole interview but woke up at the end so Rehema did get to meet her. Then I got a text from Representative McSally's office asking if we wanted to come back and film some shots with her for the NBC story. So we drove back over to Capitol Hill and joined her for some more interview footage. We discussed having a press conference the next day to announce the legislation. Whitney and I were going to Chicago early the next morning but we said we would work around it if necessary.

We left Representative McSally's office and headed back to Arlington (the city, not the cemetery) to meet with my new friend Caroline. I hadn't met her in person yet. We had been conversing online and by phone about the WASP issue and she had recently arrived in Washington for a fellowship in the Senate. This was a break from her usual job as a fighter pilot. Caroline had flown F-16s in combat and was a pilot with the Thunderbirds, the Air Force demonstration squadron, for three years. Like all the female pilots I ended up meeting during this process, Caroline was a fan of the WASP.

We met at a restaurant in the late afternoon, so we were the only patrons. I recognized Caroline from our social media photo exchanges. She was tall with long blond hair, probably not what anyone imagined a typical fighter pilot to look like. I gave Caroline a hug and then introduced her to Mom and Whitney. "I'm sorry, I am about to be very rude because I have to answer a ton of phone calls and emails, I've been missing them all day," I told her as my phone rang with a call from BBC news. I stepped outside to do an interview with a radio program.

When I got back in the restaurant, I was sitting for maybe a minute before my phone rang again. "Sorry, sorry," I whispered as I answered the phone and stood up to go outside again. Whitney held up a menu and I pointed out something for her to order for me. The Associated Press wanted to chat with me for a few minutes to follow up on what had happened in the past week or so since their previous story.

"I think that's it for phone calls. Maybe one more," I said as I returned to eat the food that had arrived with a fork in one hand and my phone in the other.

"It's okay, don't worry," Caroline replied.

"Actually," I said, looking at my phone, "I think no more phone calls, I have received emails from NPR all day but I haven't had a chance to call and now they say they don't need to talk anymore. I feel like I let them down, but I was so busy. How are you?"

"I'm good, your mom and sister were just filling me in on the day. Sounds exciting! I'm so glad this is happening. I love the WASP!" Caroline exclaimed.

"I'm glad to finally see you in person. Finding people who aren't related to the WASP but still love them is making me realize how important this is, how much support we have," I told her.

"There is a lot of support, trust me. You don't even understand how much I love the WASP, a lot of us do. I've been to the reunions and so many events with them." As Caroline continued to reminisce, her eyes lit up and she smiled. "When I was flying with the Thunderbirds, after the shows, a lot of people would come up afterwards to the pilots to talk to us. After this one air show, I had a crowd of people around and I spotted a WASP behind everyone. And I yelled out 'Hey, everyone, move aside, move aside!' and everyone looked around confused. I cut through the crowd and then escorted this WASP to the front with us Thunderbird pilots with everyone staring, probably wondering who this elderly lady was. Then I yelled, 'This woman is a WASP! They are amazing pilots! Do you all know who the WASP are?' And I started telling the whole crowd who the WASP were and everyone started cheering. I can't wait until this all gets done. You all shouldn't even have to be doing this. We are totally going to do a flyover at the funeral."

"I love that story! Let's not get ahead of ourselves and start planning the funeral yet," I replied. "But I appreciate your enthusiasm."

Later that evening after our long day, including a long drive home in rush hour traffic on the Beltway, I received an email from Senator Mikulski's office while I was packing my suitcase.

"Whitney!" I whispered as I slowly opened the door, knowing that Isabella was already asleep in the room where Whitney was staying. Isabella had been such a trooper as we carted her around all day in her "Gammy Flew Planes" onesie, our youngest lobbyist.

"What?" Whitney asked while she was arranging her and Isabella's things for the trip to Chicago the next morning.

"Listen to what's in this email!" I read quietly from my phone. "The senator will be introducing companion legislation in the Senate. We will also be sending a letter to the Department of Defense and offering it to the other senators to sign."

"All right!" Whitney exclaimed in a hushed voice. "This is great news."

"Yes, now we have the Senate too!" I said in a loud whisper.

12

Final Flight

May 2012

"I would call this rare and unique," one of Gammy's doctors opined as he pointed at a recent scan of her head. "This is something we've noticed in smokers or people with exposure to secondhand smoking. I know your grandmother doesn't smoke."

I looked at Gammy, who was sitting in a chair against the wall in the doctor's office at the VA medical center and staring straight ahead. I waited for a sassy comment from her about how smoking was a most disgusting habit, but it never came. She had lost hearing in the ear near the tumor and the other ear didn't work that well either. Her hearing aids "didn't work," even though we went to the audiology department regularly to confirm they were indeed functioning. I thought about my grandfather who had been a smoker and wondered if that was related somehow, although he had died over 40 years prior to this tumor growing.

The doctors did a scan of Gammy's head when it became obvious that the condition they had thought was Bell's palsy was not clearing up on its own. They discovered a sizable tumor growing out of the bone near her left ear, which was crushing the nerve that controls the facial muscles. The breast cancer that she had successfully been fighting off for almost a decade had spread through her bones into the area of her brain near the left ear. The doctors changed the dosage and frequency of her chemotherapy medicine to see if it would inhibit the growth of the tumor, which meant more frequent visits to the VA hospital.

Finally, the doctors ordered a biopsy to get a more detailed report about the tumor. I took Gammy to the VA hospital one morning for the procedure. The doctors showed me the scans and where they wanted to insert the needle into the side of her skull. I stayed with her during the biopsy. After it was over, I walked alongside as a VA attendant wheeled her on a gurney up to the recovery area. Then Gammy and I waited in the recovery area together for a few hours.

"Do you ever put that phone down?" she asked, stirring awake from her anesthesia.

"I really don't use it as much as you think I do," I replied with a smile, putting the phone on the end of her bed. "How was that Gammy? Are you okay?" I asked.

"Let's just say it was not fun," she replied.

"Are you going to eat this sandwich they brought you?" I asked.

"No, do you want it?"

"No, I think you need to eat," I informed her.

She sighed. "Bring it home, I will eat it later. Put it in my WASP bag," she instructed me. I rolled the top of the brown paper bag up and stuffed it in her tote.

Gammy climbed out of bed and I helped to dress her. She was getting thinner and clothes sagged on her now. Based on her frugal nature, I figured she thought buying new clothes was a waste of money, especially at this juncture of her life.

Later that night at her house, Gammy was sitting at the table with her head propped on her hands. Gammy was not the type to ever say she was in pain. Whenever the doctors or nurses at the VA asked "what is your pain level?" and referenced the numbered chart from one, represented by a huge smiley face (no pain), to ten, represented by an angry frowning face (excruciating pain), Gammy would usually say "oh, about two." So when we asked how she felt and she replied that her head hurt, we knew it must be bad. Mom, Whitney and I drove her back down to the VA hospital's emergency room around midnight. We sat together in the mostly empty waiting room. Gammy was slumped over half asleep at one end of our row of chairs.

"Now I don't know if we can go to Texas this weekend," Mom relayed as she stared at Gammy. With a tissue, Whitney wiped away some spittle that had dripped from the involuntarily opened corner of Gammy's mouth.

"What? Texas? Look at her, she can't go on a plane, what are you talking about?" I asked.

"The WASP homecoming is this weekend. She doesn't want to miss it. Then I am taking her up to the Reading air show in Pennsylvania," Mom replied.

"On the other hand, it's not like it will make her sicker, she will probably be exhausted," I rationalized. "Don't tell the doctor, he'll probably tell you not to take her."

"Good point," Mom said.

The doctor concluded the pain in Gammy's head was related to the biopsy from earlier in the day, so he prescribed a massive quantity of Percocet pills. She took several immediately. By the time we got back to her house, she said she was still in pain and then complained that the pills they gave her never helped. But she was exhausted and promptly fell asleep.

Over the next few weeks into the heart of the summer, Gammy scooted around the house with the walker I had located in her garage. I had gone looking for it after I recalled that the VA personnel had delivered it a few years earlier and how Gammy had objected to its presence in her house. Fortunately someone had stored the walker in the garage. The walker had a little tray attached to it where her giant brown prescription bottle of Percocet pills traveled around the house with her. She repeatedly said that the pills did nothing, yet she seemed to be in better spirits, so they must have had some positive effects.

Gammy didn't want to eat much anymore. She and I were about the same height once I had finished growing, but her slightly husky build had always outweighed my lithe frame. I had observed her rapid weight loss after her face started drooping and now I outweighed her by many pounds. In addition to having difficulty eating because food would fall out of the side of her mouth, she also said she couldn't taste anything, thus making the act of eating pointless.

In order to try to get her to maintain weight, the VA hospital prescribed her cases of nutrition drinks. I didn't like the idea of her relying on those, which were full of high fructose corn syrup and sugar. I brought over some protein powder and yogurt one day.

"I'm going to make you a protein shake. If you will drink it, I will come and make one every day," I informed Gammy while I hunted for the blender among the kitchen cabinets.

"What's wrong with the bottles from the hospital?" Gammy lamented.

"Gammy, those are all processed and full of sugar, you should eat other things too." I packed the blender with protein powder, yogurt, fruit, and juice and hit the blend button.

"I like sugar," Gammy reminded me. This was true. I recalled how when I was young she seemed to live off only Hershey's kisses and York Peppermint Patties. She often called me a "particular eater" for choosing salad over piles of candy.

I sat at the breakfast table with her and presented my creation. She sipped it through the straw, which she needed to use now to prevent liquid from streaming out of her mouth.

"I don't see the difference between this and the other ones," she grumbled.

"I told you, this isn't full of processed sugar," I replied.

I could tell she was unimpressed with my protein shake, but I asked if she liked it anyway. She cocked her head and replied, "It's nothing special." She drank the whole thing. Then she promptly requested another bottle of her hospital-provided nutrition drink.

Whitney and I also made her a two week supply of prepared food. We cut it up into tiny pieces and put it in her refrigerator so she only needed to microwave it. But after a while Gammy didn't want to eat that either.

13

Final Fight

January - March 2016

When most people think of lobbying, they probably imagine the representatives of big corporations or industries – those entities often referred to as "special interests." What I learned was that when there are ten thousand pieces of legislation sitting on a legislator's desk, someone needs to go make a case for why a particular bill is worthy of attention and a vote, whether yes or no. That makes each bill a special interest to somebody. Now that we had bills in both the House of Representatives and the Senate, my focus turned to making sure we had "yes" votes in both chambers.

We were fortunate to have someone as enthusiastic as Representative McSally championing our fight in the House of Representatives, but she was one vote out of 435 in the House. And there were another 100 votes in the Senate to consider. I thought we should take advantage of the forward momentum to make sure the legislation was passed. I knew there were bills that were introduced more than one time in more than one form in multiple sessions of Congress, like the WASP bills in the 1970s. I didn't know if it was a combination of bad timing, lack of support, or poor media coverage that ultimately doomed these bills to repeat tries in Congress, but I didn't want to find out. I looked at this as a one-time opportunity to get Gammy's ashes into Arlington National Cemetery and it required all the support we could gather.

The morning after our big day on Capitol Hill, Whitney and I woke up along with Isabella at 3:30 a.m. to go to the airport. I had gotten an email during the night from the BBC in England saying that my radio interview would be on around 5:15 a.m. After we checked the bags in at the kiosk, we found an application on Whitney's cell phone that streamed BBC radio international news service. While standing in the middle of the check-in area at the airport with one ear bud each, we listened with absolute excitement as the BBC broadcasted Gammy's story to radio stations all over the planet.

When we arrived in Chicago, we collected our bags, made a stop to change Isabella's diaper, and then proceeded to the train so we could go to the city and check in to the hotel for Whitney's conference. Whitney sat across from me with a sleeping Isabella strapped to her chest. I nodded off intermittently as the train rumbled along towards the city, awakening to respond when my phone vibrated to announce emails, texts, and phone calls regarding the Arlington problem. As the train filled with passengers commuting in the morning rush hour, I made arrangements to do an interview with BBC America radio.

As soon as we settled into our hotel room, Whitney took Isabella downstairs to greet friends at the conference while I stayed in the room to do the interview. I talked about how Gammy was a great patriot and an adventurous woman who encouraged us to be the same. I explained how she loved her service as a WASP and would be deeply disappointed to know about the Army's decision.

Whitney returned from mingling with her veterinary associates and said she was exhausted. The three of us napped for a while before I continued on with Gammy's public relations campaign. I sat in my pajama pants propped up against a pile of hotel pillows with my phone in hand and a notebook and pen resting beside me. I had begun to make notes of the contacts from different media organizations, times for interviews and air dates, and ideas for talking points. It became a record of our family's journey to get Gammy into Arlington National Cemetery.

"Now who are you emailing?" Whitney asked from the under the covers of the other bed, still groggy from her nap.

"NBC says they're moving the interview to Monday, supposedly because the audience is larger. Mom has her interview tonight with FOX Baltimore, so I am getting photos to that reporter. There is a reporter from a website who wants to talk to Mom. And I have a message from a lady who works at *The Examiner*, wherever that is." My phone vibrated again. "Oh, a guy named Ben from Change.org just messaged me on Twitter. He says he wants to help our campaign."

"That sounds promising," Whitney said.

"I didn't know there were people there. You know what I mean, people who would talk to us. I thought we would make an online petition and share it, the end," I explained.

"I thought the same thing," Whitney responded.

I dialed the phone number appearing in the online message. I went into the hallway because Isabella had started to fuss. Our room was at the end of the corridor on an upper level floor where an exterior window provided a view of the light rain falling over other high rise buildings in downtown Chicago.

"Hello, Ben? This is Erin Miller, from the WASP Arlington petition," I said.

"Erin, hi, so nice to connect with you," Ben replied from the other end of the line.

"I'm glad you contacted me. I didn't realize I would ever speak with anyone from Change. I thought it was only an online tool," I explained.

I heard Ben laugh before replying, "Yes, I have heard that before. We actually have people here too. On certain petitions, we devote staff resources to assist the petitioners in strengthening their efforts and we hope to help them ultimately succeed in their petition goals. We have been watching the WASP petition take off and we think it could benefit from some personal assistance."

"Oh, that's great, thank you," I replied. "What sort of things would you do?"

"I've seen your petition getting some media attention and growing with signatures, which is excellent. What we can do is reach out to more media people, share the petition with more users, and assist in any way possible depending on how the campaign evolves. Basically we can enhance what you're already doing with a different network of users," Ben explained.

"This sounds amazing. I appreciate the offer of help!" I gushed.

"Of course! That is what we are here for. What this would entail is paring down the petition a bit to appeal to more users. Now, Tiffany Miller, on the petition, who is that?" Ben inquired.

"That's one of my sisters, the petition is on her account, she lives in California," I replied.

"Ah okay," Ben replied. "And, what is your role?"

"I guess I am the campaign leader." I summarized what had happened already and explained how Tiffany and I had a simultaneous idea to do a petition online. "I've been coordinating media stories. Now that we have legislation in the House, I am starting to lobby for that bill. I just learned that the Senate will have a bill out next week. I am here in Chicago for a few days with my other sister Whitney who used to be a lobbyist, so we have been discussing strategy moving forward."

Ben replied, "Wow, I am impressed with how everything has gone so far and listening to you talk about your campaign strategy. I'm curious, do you have a background in public relations or media?"

I laughed and replied, "No, I'm just a lawyer who learned how to use Twitter."

Ben laughed as we finished our conversation and he let me know what he planned to send my way via email and a conference call with some other staff.

It was already mid-afternoon by that point, so Whitney and I went to a restaurant nearby. Ben, Tiffany, and I emailed back and forth several times during our late lunch to edit the petition so Change.org could send it out to more users.

"I think it is convenient that I have taken these days off work to come to the conference since I think I will be spending the whole trip dealing with this Arlington issue," I told Whitney as I consumed a large salad with a fork in one hand and my cell phone in the other.

"What's the deal with Change?" Whitney asked over a bowl of tomato soup while Isabella sat on her lap.

"I think it will be useful. He said they'll contact more media. They will share the petition with millions of their users too," I explained. "They're giving us a shorter website address for the petition. We have to edit the petition, make it more succinct, that's what we're emailing about now."

"Does this cost money?" Whitney inquired.

"No, I asked. I was suspicious about what they wanted. Ben said it is part of their job. I guess if someone starts a petition and they achieve the goal, it makes Change look good, so that must be their angle," I surmised.

Later that evening, there was a casual reception at the hotel bar for the conference attendees. Whitney and I made the rounds with Isabella in tow. Of course the Arlington issue kept coming up and I was surprised by the number of people who knew about it.

"Wait, that's your grandmother, Whitney?" guests who knew Whitney asked repeatedly in disbelief. "I saw that on the news!"

I requested that they all sign and share the petition. With smart phones in everyone's pockets or purses, it was easy to do.

When we returned to the hotel room, we called Mom to ask how her interviews had gone. She said they went well and she had learned that one reporter had a family connection to the WASP. According to Mom, her interview with the Baltimore television station was better than the others because the reporter spoke to her for a while before they started the official interview and that had made her feel more comfortable. We watched Mom's interview on the news station's website on Whitney's tablet while Isabella slept in the crib.

The next day, Whitney was at her conference while I watched Isabella and continued working on our campaign. Senator Mikulski's office called to say that she would introduce legislation in the Senate in the next week for us. I emailed Senator Cardin's office, our second senator from Maryland, to explain that I was Elaine Harmon's granddaughter and to ask if they were aware of Senator Mikulski's upcoming legislation. I expressed our family's hope that Senator Cardin would also be sponsoring it. About two hours later, a staffer from his office called to tell me that Senator Cardin had spoken with Senator Mikulski and that he would be signing onto the new Senate bill.

Tiffany emailed to tell us she was frustrated with her congressman. I had no idea until she emailed that she had been trying to get him to do something about this problem since October. She had called and emailed on several occasions and finally this week had pushed a staffer in the local office to give her the name of the legislative director in the DC office. Tiffany said the office had called back again to say they would try to get the congressman to cosponsor the bill.

Whitney and I got on speakerphone with Tiffany. I told her, "Tiffany, this is what you need to do: call the office and say, 'I am going to be on MSNBC live on Sunday. I would certainly like to be able to say that my own congressman is a cosponsor of this legislation to help us bury our grandmother.'"

"Are you sure that will work?" Tiffany asked.

"Definitely!" I replied. Whitney nodded in agreement from the other bed. I continued, "Can you imagine if you are on live national television and the news anchor asks if you have contacted your congressperson and you say, 'yes, but he doesn't seem interested in helping me.' He would look so bad!"

We hung up so Tiffany could call her representative's office. A short while later, she emailed us to say that her congressman's office confirmed he would cosponsor the bill.

"Good job, one more to check off the list!" I responded to Tiffany's email. "Now you get on Senators Boxer and Feinstein when the Senate bill gets a number!"

Later on, Whitney came back from a session at the conference while I was finishing a phone call. I held Isabella with one hand and the phone with the other. "Who was that?" she asked, putting down her conference paperwork and taking Isabella from me.

"A public relations person who found me on Twitter," I replied.

"Did she want you to hire her?" Whitney asked.

"She didn't directly ask that. She was talking about all these television shows we should be on," I explained. "I guess if PR people are calling me, then we must be doing something right. Right?"

"Yes!" Whitney exclaimed.

"I have an interview with an Arizona newspaper today too," I said.

Whitney's phone beeped. As she read the message on the phone screen, she said, "My friend in Colorado heard you on NPR!"

"Mom's neighbor emailed me, she heard it too!" I said. "Oh, guess what else?"

"What?" Whitney replied.

"Martina Navratilova tweeted about us!"

"Really?" Whitney asked.

"Yes, look at this," I said as I held up my phone open to the screen where Martina had sent out a link to the story about Arlington and Gammy.

"You're welcome, such an unfair policy!" Whitney read from the reply Martina had sent to me thanking her for sharing the story.

"How funny is that? Gammy loved tennis and a tennis legend is tweeting about her!" I said. "And she has over one hundred thousand followers, so that's a plus."

Whitney gave a thumbs up.

The next morning, we talked strategy in our pajamas on the hotel beds as we waited for Tiffany and WASP Bee Haydu to appear live on MSNBC. Our story also appeared on the front page of the *Arizona Daily Star*, a newspaper from the home state of Representative McSally.

"At this point I am not concerned anymore about whether or not the Army changes its mind. Because even if they change their regulation, they could reverse it again next year. If this bill passes, then they have to follow the law. I know Mom is still obsessing about questions at the Senate confirmation hearing, but I don't care about that anymore. Am I wrong?" I asked Whitney.

"No. We should focus on the legislation now. Here, you can look at the bills on this website." Whitney opened an internet page on my tablet to a website address for Govtrack.us.

"It says two percent chance of passing! That's depressing," I said after searching the website for our bill number, H.R. 4336.

"It's better than zero!" Whitney shot back.

"You're hilarious," I replied with an eye roll.

"See how it feels?" she joked.

"It says 79 cosponsors. Is that good?" I asked. "It seems good."

"Yes, that's good," Whitney replied. "It's great that we have a Republican and Democrat lead on the House bill. Hopefully Senator Mikulski will have a Republican on the Senate bill."

"I have to go to the bathroom." I left Whitney and Isabella on the bed. "This might be a dumb question, but why do we need a bill in the House and the Senate? Does that mean they're competing with each other?" I yelled through the bathroom door to Whitney.

"It's called a companion bill. Congress does it all the time. It shows support in both chambers," Whitney explained. "Either one could pass and ultimately become the law."

I came back out and told Whitney, "It feels like a competition to me. If there is a choice, I want McSally's bill to win."

"Why?" Whitney asked. "Isn't the important thing to get the law done?"

"Of course, I want the law to pass. But it makes a better story," I explained as I stood by the foot of the bed. "Come on, this female pilot happens to be in Congress when we need to get a law passed to bury our trailblazing pilot grandmother! How do we make that happen? Get lots of cosponsors?" I asked.

Whitney laughed and replied, "I don't know if we have any control over that. Some bills get lot of cosponsors and then nothing happens anyway."

"A lot is better though, right? It doesn't hurt to get a lot?" I asked.

"No," Whitney replied.

"Okay, then that's what we'll do." I pulled up the cosponsor list on my phone and started checking whose names were not on it. I saw that my own congressman wasn't on the list yet, so I called and emailed his office. I set up news alerts on social media for keywords WASP, Arlington, and Martha McSally. I started following the social media feeds for other members who were supporting the bill already like Representative Susan Davis, the lead Democrat cosponsor of the House bill.

Tiffany made a spreadsheet with all the members of Congress on it. When someone cosponsored, we marked them on the list. I looked at the remaining people on the list and tried to think of who I knew that was a constituent in each of these districts. Whitney and Tiffany did the same. Fortunately, we had a large network of extended family and friends throughout the United States in a variety of congressional districts. I wrote up a sample email to send to Congress and emailed it to people in districts where there was not a cosponsor yet. I told people to call as well. Tiffany told me I was turning into Annette Bening's lobbyist character from the movie *The American President*; all I needed was a giant map on the wall to mark off votes. We turned our extended family and WASP network into a lobbying firm.

Even though Representative McSally was obviously passionate about ensuring this was resolved, there were many other factors that affect passing a bill. Whitney was a lobbyist for four years and none of the bills she worked on ever passed. Sometimes there was a lot of support, but a bill never moved forward for a vote. Bills were sent to a committee and then never left. News events can suddenly change people's views on the underlying issue or take attention away from it entirely. I didn't even know if we needed to do anything. Representative McSally and her staff were engaged and competent, but I thought it was important to do anything and everything we could to support the legislation.

The group of lawmakers serving in the 113th Congress from 2012-2014, barely avoided the title of "least productive Congress" in history by passing several bills after the 2014 elections had ended. Of the bills that became law, 84 were "ceremonial," doing things like renaming a building or issuing a commemorative coin.[22] Overall, the 113th Congress introduced 9,089 bills and joint resolutions to get to 296 laws, a passing rate of 3.26%.[23] So the website wasn't too far off when it estimated a two percent chance that this bill to let us place Gammy's cremains in Arlington National Cemetery would pass.

* * *

The day after returning from Chicago, the campaign to get Gammy into Arlington National Cemetery continued to accelerate. I wanted to continue working all day and night, like I had been in Chicago, on the new mission to help get the legislation passed. If I could have taken two months of leave to focus solely on this legislation, I would have. But I didn't have that luxury, so I had to find time to campaign for Gammy and the WASP while working at a full time job.

All day I was fielding emails related to media stories and the bill.

---

[22] Quinn, Melissa. "Turns out the 113th Congress Wasn't the Least Productive." *The Daily Signal.* December 30, 2014. http://dailysignal.com/2014/12/30/turns-113th-congress-wasnt-least-productive/

[23] Congress.gov

Senator Mikulski was going to officially announce the companion Senate bill. Her aide asked me to write a statement for the related press release. She connected me with a reporter named John Fritze at *The Baltimore Sun* to interview for a story about Senator Mikulski's bill.

Tiffany composed an update to the petition to send out regarding the legislation and how the petition signers could help get the legislation moved in Congress. Whitney and I helped with editing, but we wanted to wait to send it out until the Senate bill number was assigned so that people had a reference number when requesting support from their Senators.

I received an email from another member of Congress in Maryland informing me that she would be cosponsoring the bill. Because of the way the districts in Maryland were drawn, I lived within a few minutes' drive of several congressional districts, so I contacted all of them. I also asked friends or relatives in each congressional district to contact their respective representative's office.

The producer from *NBC Nightly News* emailed to say that our story was moved again because David Bowie had passed away so they were airing a segment on him instead. She said they would likely have it on Thursday instead. At this point I stopped telling anyone when it might be on. I thanked the producer for keeping me updated.

My phone beeped as I made my way home from work that afternoon. I pulled the car into the parking spot and checked the messages. I saw that Patrick from Representative McSally's office had sent one.

Patrick: Erin, I wanted to let you know that Martha will be leading a special order session tonight, starts at 7pm.

Me: Thanks Patrick! How exciting! Will it be on C-SPAN? Can we watch?

Patrick: It should be on television, yes

I had no idea what Patrick was talking about. The first thing I did when I walked into the house that night was look up "special order session" on the internet. I learned that in a special order session, a representative can request time to talk for up to an hour after the House of Representatives is done with business for the day. Votes, speeches, and other activities of Congress usually air on C-SPAN, a channel dedicated to showing government proceedings.

"You guys! Representative McSally is going to talk about our bill for an hour!" I exclaimed to the dogs, who were waiting for me to get off my phone and take them outside. With the dog leashes in one hand, I emailed the family from my phone in the other hand as we walked around the neighborhood. I told everyone to watch television that night because members of the House of Representatives were going to be talking about the WASP, and maybe Gammy, for an hour. After returning with the dogs, I went out for a run.

I stood in the living room in my running tights pointing the remote control at the television trying to find the right channel while texting with Whitney and Tiffany on my phone.

"Since when are there so many channels of C-SPAN?" I shouted.

Prior to the special order session, representatives had the opportunity to give one minute speeches about a variety of topics. A few of them spoke about the WASP and the new bill, H.R. 4336. Whitney messaged that one member was already speaking on the floor about the WASP bill.

Whitney: Ashford giving speech about WASP!

Me: Where???????????????

Whitney: C-SPAN Floor of House

Me: What channel is that??????

Whitney: Mine is 109

Me: 109 is not C-SPAN here ugh

Whitney: McSally is getting on for 60 minutes!!

Me: Ok I found it, I rewound it!

Tiffany: Watching on C-SPAN website!

Representative McSally came to the front of the chamber with a large poster board print of the famous photo of four WASP walking away from a B-17 and set it on an easel. Then she began her speech. Watching Representative McSally on the floor of the House of Representatives discuss my deceased grandmother by name was easily one of the most surreal experiences of my life. My sisters and I texted with each other throughout the hour.

"That is not the way we treat our heroes," Representative McSally implored her colleagues after explaining that, because she had been denied entry at Arlington National Cemetery, Gammy's ashes were now sitting in a closet. She continued on with more history about the WASP and background on the situation with Arlington, saying, "Let's be clear, the only reason they were not active duty at the time was because of gender discrimination."

Me: @$$^^# awesome! Talking about Gammy by name!!*

Tiffany: Aaah! I had to pause it because my child was pulling knives out of the dishwasher and now the playback isn't working!!!!

Me: Do you want to video chat and watch the tv here?

Tiffany: I restarted my computer, it is working now. She is doing awesome! Love the sarcasm. So excited to see this!

Me: I know! I have to watch it again!

Then Representative McSally yielded the floor to the cosponsor of H.R. 4336, and coincidentally, my former representative in Congress when I had lived in San Diego, Representative Susan Davis. She recalled meeting several of the WASP in previous years, especially at the Congressional Gold Medal Ceremony in 2010 at the Capitol. Representative Davis commented on how feisty and spirited the WASP were, and that one from her congressional district said she would have been the best fighter pilot if they had been allowed to fly in combat.

"I'm delighted to join in this effort and right this injustice," Representative Davis said in closing.

Several more members of Congress stood to pay tribute to the WASP and support the bill advanced by Representative McSally. An especially enthusiastic supporter was Representative Ileana Ros-Lehtinen from southern Florida, home of WASP Bee Haydu and Shirley Kruse, who she mentioned in her speech. As the author of the Congressional Gold Medal bill for the WASP, Representative Ros-Lehtinen had been present with Gammy in the Oval Office when the president had signed it. She said she was honored to support Representative McSally in her new "mission" to recognize the WASP at Arlington National Cemetery.

I never imagined that I would be enraptured by watching members of Congress give speeches. Having grown up in the Washington area,

I was accustomed to seeing my local news stations cover Congress regularly; it was a daily discussion which over the decades had lost its novelty. Additionally, throughout grade school, teachers had occasionally subjected us to watching sessions of C-SPAN in lieu of normal classroom work. Suddenly, when the members of Congress were discussing something directly affecting my life, it was fascinating. I had only met Representative McSally five days before this and she had already done something I never thought would happen: she had made me excited to watch C-SPAN.

Knowing how hard Gammy and the WASP had fought in the 1970s to be recognized as veterans, it was nice to see so many people in Congress standing up for them without hesitation. When it was over, I immediately sent a message to Patrick.

Me: Patrick, tell your boss that was AWESOME!

Patrick: Will do!

Me: Tell her our whole family says thank you and sends a big hug!

Then I watched the entire special order session again for a second time. Not only was I now voluntarily watching C-SPAN programming, I was enthusiastically watching a rerun of C-SPAN programming.

* * *

The next day, the Senate bill was assigned number S.2437. We officially had bills in both the Senate and the House of Representatives, each with both a Republican and Democrat lead. In theory, the process ran more smoothly with bipartisan support and a bill in each chamber of Congress. The next challenge was getting Congress to hold a vote on at least one of the WASP bills –and ensuring the senators and representatives voted yes.

After bills are introduced they are assigned to a committee or committees to study them and propose changes before they are voted on by the full legislative body. H.R. 4336 had been assigned to the House Committee on Veterans' Affairs. While the VA committee was holding the bill, I continued to promote Gammy's story in the media and through the petition, and our network of supporters continued to grow.

To add a more personal touch, the Change staff sent a producer to Tiffany's house to create a video about the story behind the petition. A reporter from Gammy's alma mater, the University of Maryland, called to write a feature story in its alumni magazine. Mom's sister-in-law, Linda, had announced to her local meeting of the American Association of University Women (AAUW) that our family was seeking supporters and now the national organization was endorsing our legislation in Congress – meaning the leadership asked their hundreds of thousands of members to sign the petition and contact their individual members of Congress. Along with other organizations who had endorsed the legislation, like Women in Aviation International and the National Women's Law Center, AAUW's support added legitimacy and a growing number of voices to our campaign for Gammy and the WASP.

After work one day that week, I placed my bag down on the dining room chair, took off my winter coat, and hit the play button on Mom's answering machine. The dogs ran over to greet me and I bent over to pet them. I almost hit my head on the counter as I reacted to the message on the machine starting up.

"*Hey there!*" A man's voice shouted in a thick accent reminiscent of a used car sales person from a television commercial, "*I am looking for the Terry Harmon having to do with the woman pilot denied at Arlington*

Cemetery! Hope this is the right number. I want to tell y'all, well I am down here in Texas, I don't know what your politics are, but you should call Donald Trump for help! Trump would really help! I hope y'all have a nice day and get this sorted out."

I heard the front door open and shut. "Mom, come listen to this message!"

"What message?" she asked, leaning over to the pet the dogs who were whining with excitement at her arrival.

I pushed play on the answering machine again and the message from the stranger in Texas started up.

Mom was startled by the voice coming from the machine and laughed a little. After it ended she said, "That is what you would call random."

I laughed and replied, "Yes, I would say that."

"I don't understand how people keep finding my phone number. It is supposed to be unlisted," Mom complained.

"I like that people are supporting us, but it is a little creepy when strangers find us like that," I agreed. "So are you going to do it?" I asked Mom.

"Do what?" Mom asked.

"Call Donald Trump," I said.

"I guess I would if I had his number," Mom replied.

"It's probably not as easy to find his number as your supposedly unlisted number," I joked.

Mom went and turned on the television to watch the news, which was also covering Donald Trump because he was campaigning to be elected as President of the United States. The media was focused, to me it seemed even more so than in prior years, on covering the campaign and the numerous candidates as much as possible before the November election, still nine months away. There were about 17 candidates on the Republican side, a couple of candidates from non-mainstream parties, and the Democrats had Bernie Sanders and Hillary Clinton as front-runners. To me, all that those candidates represented in that period of time was competition for media attention about Gammy's story and the bills in Congress.

Mom clicked through the channels on the television, all featuring news pieces about the election or the candidates, and said, "Doesn't the media realize we don't want to watch political news all the time? Sometimes we want normal news. Can't they go back to reporting about murders?"

Fortunately there were still reporters interested in something besides the election. The next day at work I received a phone call and had to excuse myself during a meeting.

"Erin, hey, I know we said we would do this interview tomorrow or later in the week, but I am in town now. Would it be okay to do it today? How about in an hour or so?" the reporter from CBS News asked.

I looked at the clock on the wall showing 11:30 a.m. "How about at one at the College Park Aviation Museum?" I asked.

"Sounds good, see you then, thanks again. Sorry for the rush!" I heard from the other end of the phone line.

"Erin, everything okay?" I heard my manager say as I turned around to see the meeting breaking up.

"Oh fine, fine. I have to leave though," I informed him.

"Now?" he asked.

"Yes, I'll go type it in the time sheet before I go, thank you." I saw he still looked befuddled. "She'll explain," I nodded to my coworker standing nearby who laughed and nodded back.

I stopped at home to get my blue scarf and pick up Gammy's ashes, which rode in their black box in the passenger seat. On the drive to the museum, I practiced lines for the interview.

"Now why do you think the Army has refused to recognize the women like your grandmother at Arlington cemetery, Erin?" I said, imitating the news reporter. "Well, because they're misogynist ass..." I looked over at Gammy's box of ashes. "Because they are narrowly interpreting a law from the 1970s intended to give them full veterans benefits, including the right to be placed in national military cemeteries." I looked over at the box. "Better? Yes, okay. Thanks, Gammy."

Once I arrived, the reporter and cameraman set up near one of the old airplanes in the museum. I stood with the blue WASP scarf around my neck and Gammy's box of ashes in the crook of one arm to answer questions. After some basic questions about me, Gammy, and the WASP, the reporter asked, "If you had to explain the crux of this problem in one sentence, what would you say?"

Without hesitation, I repeated one of the talking points from the car ride earlier, "According to the Army, the rights granted in the 1970s to the WASP do not extend to the Department of the Army which runs Arlington cemetery." And with that, another interview was ready for the news cycle.

Our network of supporters also continued to push stories in the media. Kate had her op-ed, "The Women Excluded from Arlington National Cemetery," published in *The Atlantic*. The editorial board at Gammy's hometown newspaper, *The Baltimore Sun*, wrote a piece in favor of our position.

We began the next week on a high note, having reached 50,000 signatures on the petition. The eastern coast of the United States was bracing for an impending blizzard due to reach the Washington area around Friday, which meant the press conference would likely be put off another couple of weeks. Washington had shut down in the past with even the threat of a few flakes of snow, but an actual blizzard would mean days of closures.

Patrick from Representative McSally's office called to let me know there was still progress being made even if the blizzard was interfering with the plans for a press conference.

"Erin, I wanted to talk to you about something that came up this morning. Martha was in a meeting this morning with the Acting Secretary of the Army. She brought up your family's situation and the Acting Secretary said that your family had not applied for an exception, is that correct?"

"Yes, that is correct. We don't think she should be admitted as an exception to policy, she should be there on her own merit," I explained over the phone.

"Okay, good, that's what Martha thought. She said the Acting Secretary then implied that if your family applied for an exception, it would be approved and you could have the funeral for your grandmother at Arlington as soon as a date is available," Patrick continued. "So she told him that as far as she understood, your family wanted to wait and make sure that there was a law in place for all of the WASP and you were not interested in an exception. I am just calling to make sure this is accurate."

"Yes, she understands perfectly," I explained. "Even if we wanted an exception, I think going ahead with one would diminish the attention on the legislation. Since there is the possibility to fix this for all of the WASP, I think that's what we should focus on. Our family can wait. Thank you for calling, Patrick, and tell your boss she can speak for our family anytime. She understands our position."

"Thank you, I will let her know," he replied.

Hopefully this offer by the Army meant it was annoyed by the negative publicity and would change the position it had taken.

The number of supporters in Congress continued to increase, which generated more local media coverage across the country. Senator Amy Klobuchar from Minnesota became a cosponsor of the Senate bill and was featured in a news story with WASP Betty Strohfus. Betty was from Faribault, a small town in Minnesota which claimed her as one of its most famous residents. Born in the same year as Gammy, 1919, Betty had entered the WASP earlier as a member of class 44-1. After the war, she tried to become a pilot for a commercial airline, but it didn't accept her. The local news channel had gotten Senator Klobuchar and Betty together at Betty's home for a news story about the Arlington National Cemetery situation.

Betty, one of the more petite women of the WASP, had on a blue blazer with her WASP pins and service ribbons attached. Senator Klobuchar and Betty flipped through photos from the WASP days. The reporter asked if it was important to Betty to have the WASP recognized as eligible to be at Arlington National Cemetery. Betty replied, "It would mean a lot to me." She paused for a moment, getting choked up, before continuing, "we haven't been treated like the other veterans, and I think it's too bad... if they needed us they'd come and get us, but otherwise, they really didn't want women to fly," Betty explained to the reporter.

"She's someone who answered the call to duty, but she was also a pioneer and she should be honored for that," Senator Klobuchar explained.

* * *

"Erin!" Mom yelled to me from her bedroom upstairs.

"Yes," I replied after coming up the stairs and poking my head around the open door.

"I just got off the phone with Ruth Guhsé's son," she informed me.

"The WASP that was denied burial at Arlington before Gammy died?" I asked.

"Yes," Mom replied. "I learned that the application for Ruth was denied not once, but twice."

"Oh, really? That's interesting," I said.

"Her son didn't want to apply for an exception either. Like us, he wanted her to be in Arlington on her own merit. After he was denied the first time, he applied again and was denied. And the Army told him about the exception but he didn't think it was the right thing to do," Mom explained.

"So where is Ruth? Are her ashes in a closet too?" I asked.

"No," Mom responded. "He said Arlington wouldn't even return his phone calls and they never sent him a letter. He got frustrated and decided to have her laid to rest at Alexandria National Cemetery because, even though their family is scattered across the country, he thought more people would be able to visit if her grave was in the Washington area."

"That's sad that she didn't get to be where her family wanted her," I said.

"Yes," Mom agreed. "Oh, one other thing."

"What?" I asked.

"I went to the Senate confirmation hearing for the Secretary of the Army nominee today," Mom said.

"How did that go?"

"I thought he did a good job. They didn't ask any questions about the Arlington situation though," Mom explained.

"It's okay, Mom," I consoled her. "I'm focused on this legislation. I am not worried about the Army anymore. The Army is wrong and if this law passes then they have to follow it and can't keep changing the rules whenever they want." I stopped at the doorway of her bedroom and turned back to say, "Don't stay up late, we have an interview in the morning."

"Okay, okay," Mom replied with a smile. At least now she found my regular instructions entertaining.

Friday morning, with a blizzard looming, a black SUV picked up Mom and me at 4:30 to take us to the television studio to do an interview with Fox News. The federal government had closed for the day to prepare for the blizzard, so there were even fewer cars on the road than usual at that early hour.

After the professionals at the studio did our hair and makeup, they put us in the green room to wait for our time slot on camera. Mom and I sat on the sofa together underneath a wall full of framed photos of celebrities who had appeared on the network shows. I pulled out my bag of lobbying stuff and handed Mom the talking points sheet.

"Okay, Mom. Remember the talking points. The producer said we'll only be on camera for two minutes. Gammy died, she wanted to be at Arlington National Cemetery, the Army said no, we're fighting to overturn the rule, and now Representative McSally has a bill in the House to fix the problem," I said.

"Yes, Erin," Mom replied as she stared at the talking points sheet.

After a few more minutes an assistant arrived. "We're ready for you two," he said and led us down the hallway to a small room with one camera and a scenic backdrop photo of Washington, D.C. He arranged two chairs next to each other in front of the camera. "Make sure you look at the camera. Some people look at the wall and it looks strange on television, like they're staring into space," he explained. "This earpiece lets you hear what the television host is saying, when she starts talking to you, talk back," he said as he fit one earpiece on each of us. "Okay, come sit down. Make sure you stay close together," he instructed as we sat in the chairs. "This is a tight shot for two people, you might go off camera if you don't sit close. Are you all okay?"

"Yes," Mom and I replied in unison.

"I will be out here waiting!" the assistant said and closed the door behind him as he left the room.

We sat in silence for a few minutes while advertising streamed through the earpieces. Then the host's voice returned and I could hear her introducing Gammy's story. Mom was startled when the reporter in New York started asking questions through the earpiece.

Mom began rambling off a long response that didn't answer the question from the reporter. I could tell she was getting off track and I wanted to kick her leg to signal her to stop talking but I knew it would look bad on television. Then the reporter asked me about the motivation behind denying Gammy a burial at Arlington to which I replied that we had no idea what the motivation was, but lack of space was the excuse they gave. The reporter thanked us for being on the show and our segment was over. The assistant came in the room to take the earpieces and show us out.

On the car ride home, as I searched for a video clip of the show to share on social media, Mom looked concerned.

"What's wrong?" I asked.

"I wish I hadn't wasted our time on the air with such a long-winded answer," Mom replied.

"Don't worry about it, Mom. The show has millions of viewers, the important thing is to get the story out there," I said. "Look, I found a video clip!" I held my phone up so we could watch together as the car drove back through the city toward home.

Since work was cancelled, I spent the day following up on items related to Arlington. A reporter from the *Los Angeles Times* wanted to interview a WASP in Southern California to make the connection from our family's situation to the other women in the group. I took out Gammy's WASP directory book and searched the California section. We had been trying to keep updated on the WASP who had passed away, so many of the names were crossed out in pen with "deceased" written nearby. I dialed the number of one WASP named Jean Landis who, from the book, and from a quick internet search of obituaries, appeared to still be alive.

"Hi, I am looking for Jean Landis," I said over the phone to the woman who answered.

"This is she! How can I help you?" Jean asked.

"My name is Erin Miller, my grandmother was Elaine Harmon. I think you knew each other? Anyway, have you seen any of the stories about the situation with Arlington National Cemetery not allowing my family to bury my grandmother there?" I inquired.

"I have and I think that situation is absolutely horrible!" she exclaimed. "I can't believe what they're doing."

"Yes, it is horrible," I agreed. "I am calling because I need help from a WASP in Southern California. I have a reporter from the *LA Times* who is doing a story about the Arlington problem. Would you be willing to talk with her?"

"I am willing, but I am very busy," she replied. Jean listed off a plethora of events she needed to attend in the next few days. "I still drive, you know! I have to drive to several places in the next few days."

"Wow, you are busier than I am!" I was taken aback by how much this ninety-seven year old woman had going on in her life. I should not have been surprised – the WASP all seemed to be in demand for speaking engagements and media appearances. "This will just take fifteen minutes or so. You can do this over the phone. I don't think it will be too inconvenient," I pleaded.

"Of course, I want to help. If the reporter calls me, I will do my best," Jean responded.

The snow began Friday evening. On Saturday morning, the dogs and I were up at our usual time around 5:30 a.m. The wind was blowing, the snow was falling hard, and it was cold. I trudged through the dark in my full length down coat. I had to wear my tall rain boots because the snow was so deep, but my toes were freezing despite the thick wool socks I had on. The dogs hopped through the snow behind me like bunny rabbits, tiring quickly.

I am not sure if it was because of the blizzard, which had trapped about 80 million people on the East Coast inside all day, or if Change had emailed our petition out to more people, but we got over 35,000 signatures that weekend. The Senate bill had 13 cosponsors. Snow continued to fall and signatures continued to appear. By Sunday evening, there were more than 24 inches of snow outside and more than 94,000 signatures on the petition.

* * *

By the next morning when the *Los Angeles Times* article that Jean had interviewed for was published, we had 118,000 signatures and 37 inches of snow. Ben had encouraged me to start thinking about writing an op-ed to shop around at news outlets. Since work had been cancelled again and I had to wait for the snow plow, I had time to write.

In addition to competing with the upcoming election for media time, news about the blizzard named Jonas now monopolized the airwaves. Fortunately, reporters were still interviewing WASP supporters and people were still signing and sharing the petition online. Mom called WASP Shutsy Reynolds to thank her for interviewing for the article that had come out in the *Uniontown Standard*, from Shutsy's hometown in Pennsylvania. While I spent more than five hours shoveling snow, we arrived at 133,000 signatures. By the end of the week there were 109 cosponsors on Representative McSally's bill.

That Sunday Mom and I visited Arlington National Cemetery with Katherine, an Air Force photojournalist. There was still snow on the ground, but the sun had been out for a few days, so it was no longer 37 inches deep. The pathways and the roads around the cemetery had been cleared off. I appreciated the thick layer of snow and the sense of peace which accompanied the snow when it blanketed the cemetery. If the purpose of a cemetery is solemn reflection, then winter assisted with its fresh air and the type of weather that often kept many visitors away. The snow brought a heightened sense of tranquility and stillness.

We visited the Columbarium area where we hoped Gammy's ashes would eventually be placed, assuming the legislation worked out. Over the course of four hours, Katherine took photos and short video clips as we meandered through the cemetery. Mom stopped us for a moment at the grave of one of her colleagues who had been killed in an explosion in Afghanistan. The gravestones peeked out of the snow in neat rows across the grounds toward the hill where the Air Force Memorial reached out over the trees. Gammy absolutely had a place among these fallen heroes.

* * *

Tiffany delivered some good news as we headed into February: Senator Boxer's office had emailed to say she would be cosponsoring the Senate bill. The total number of senators cosponsoring was up to 17, and we got three more on the House bill for a total of 121. Tiffany continued to hammer away at her other senator. I continued with my long distance lobbying efforts and sent several people whose member of Congress was not on the cosponsor list a sample email to use to contact their representative or senator. We were all receiving sporadic emails and phone calls from friends and extended family reporting what their representatives in Congress had done or not done. Strangers commented on social media wondering where their members of Congress stood on the bills.

Although the media continued to feature the story, like *The Chicago Tribune*, which had published a supportive editorial that week, I had begun to feel like the campaign needed another push forward. Thinking back to the promise I had made to myself on the day when we had first visited Representative McSally's office, I decided it was time to go down to Capitol Hill myself and talk to Congress.

My phone rang that afternoon and the number on the screen looked like one from the switchboard at the offices for Congress.

"Hello," I responded.

"Hey, Erin. It's Patrick," the voice on the other end said.

"Patrick! How are you? Good to hear from you."

"Good, good," he replied. "I wanted to update you on a few things. Martha wrote a letter to the Acting Secretary of the Army requesting a reversal of policy, and we have about fifty members of Congress that have signed on. Hopefully we will get a few more before we send it over."

"That's great," I said.

"We are still working to coordinate a press conference, but with all the people involved, the scheduling is difficult. Don't worry. We are working on it," he assured me.

"Okay, thanks for letting me know," I told him. "I am going to start coming down to the Hill in person to talk to the reps and senators this week."

"That's great, I think that will help move things along," Patrick replied. "Stop in and say hello if you have a chance!"

"Of course! And thank you so much for keeping me updated on everything, I appreciate it," I told him.

"No problem, have a good day!"

After I hung my phone up, I noticed I had a text message waiting.

Ben: Erin, I will be in DC this week, would you like to meet in person

Me: Absolutely!

Almost as soon as I had hit the send button, the phone rang.

"Erin, it's Ben. I thought it would be easier to coordinate on the phone than through lots of messages," he explained from the other end of the phone line.

"Ben! What great timing. I just got off the phone with Patrick to tell him I was coming down to the Hill myself this week to lobby in person!"

"Great minds think alike," Ben retorted. "I made some leave-behinds with the bill and petition info. I am arranging a couple meetings for Thursday, so let's meet early in the morning and see what else we can set up."

"Sounds good, see you then," I said.

* * *

In mid-February, Caroline and I had planned a visit with Lorraine Rodgers, who was a WASP pilot in class 44-W-2 and friend of

Gammy's. Although they were not in the same training class, they became good friends in the 1970s while the WASP were lobbying Congress to get veterans benefits. Since Lorraine and Gammy both lived in the Washington area, they attended a lot of events together. After becoming aware of how much of Gammy's life I had missed hearing about, I decided I should get to know the other WASP. I agreed with Mom that it was important to talk to the WASP about Arlington since the legislation was affecting their rights. I knew Caroline would want to join in since she loved hearing the WASP flying stories. If Lorraine was anything like Gammy, she would be excited to meet Caroline too.

Lorraine's house reminded me of Gammy's house: a stately single family home, adorned with family mementos, where she had lived for many years. We sat in the living room among the keepsakes, Lorraine in an arm chair and Caroline and I on the adjacent sofa. Lorraine's blond hair was well-coiffed and she sported a dark velour track suit. Unlike Gammy, Lorraine had large scrapbooks filled with photos from her WASP training time. I was lucky to have stumbled upon one loose old black and white photo of Gammy sitting on a plane, in a box of jumbled documents.

"You have so many photos, Lorraine," I commented.

"I was fortunate to have a camera during training," Lorraine said. "Most women didn't. I even have photos of when my brother came to visit Sweetwater!"

As the conversation progressed, I learned that not only had Lorraine been a trailblazing pilot herself, but also that she had married a Navy fighter pilot. She spoke of him with a twinkle in her eye and I got the impression they were both daredevils back in the day. Lorraine said her husband didn't even know she could fly when they first started dating. She told me about her kids and her grandkids.

Then Lorraine pointed to a framed photo on the mantle and said, "There, see that photo? That is my granddaughter." I stood up and walked to the fireplace to get a better view of the indicated photo. "I think that bearded man she is with does the news," Lorraine said.

"Yes, he does. His name is Wolf Blitzer," I replied.

Lorraine shrugged and then asked me, "Tell me more about what you are doing, I didn't quite understand."

"Well, as you know, my grandmother Elaine passed away last year and..." I began.

"I loved your grandmother, she was a terrific lady," Lorraine interrupted.

"Thank you, that is so nice of you to say. My grandmother wanted to be in Arlington National Cemetery, but they told us she wasn't allowed. So we are fighting the Army. And we have a bill in Congress to make a law that WASP will be recognized for inurnment at Arlington National Cemetery if they want to be there." I couldn't tell if Lorraine was following what I was explaining as she pursed her lips and made a concerned face while I spoke. "That's why we've been doing news stories, to support this bill and make sure it gets passed so we can have a funeral for her there."

At that point Lorraine paused for a moment, took my hand, cocked her head and asked, "Didn't we already do this?"

I laughed and said, "Yes. You did." I realized her earlier look of consternation was not because I was confusing her with my explanation, but because the story was exactly like what they had done in the 1970s. It was confusing!

"I think Congress will be more helpful this time. In fact, Representative McSally, the one who introduced this bill was an Air Force pilot," I explained further.

"You don't say!" Lorraine exclaimed.

"Here, let me see if I can find a picture for you." I picked my phone up and searched the internet for a photo. "Here she is with the plane she flew, the A-10."

"I know that's an A-10," Lorraine said.

"Sorry, forgot I was talking to a pilot!" I apologized and looked over at Caroline who laughed along with me.

"Lorraine, do you have any favorite flying stories?" Caroline asked.

"Oh yes, dear." Lorraine was overjoyed to oblige. "I will tell you about one time that I crashed. The plane was going along fine, and then I ended up in a spin, an inverted spin at that. And for no apparent reason. I saw the ground coming at me from upside down. I was trying to get out of it but it wouldn't straighten up. I knew I had to use the parachute. We were supposed to count to ten. I said, one-two-ten!" Lorraine gestured as if jumping from a plane. "After I made it to the ground, I was lying on my back out in the middle of nowhere. I heard horses coming. I heard two men confirming their suspicions about seeing a plane crash. Then I sat up and took off my helmet. When they saw my blond hair spill out, their eyes got so big, and they said, 'Well, it's a little lady!'" Lorraine smiled as if this had just happened yesterday and she was still ecstatic to have interrupted the preconceptions of these two men. We all laughed. Even from the brief time I had known Caroline, I knew she could relate to being underestimated as a blonde female fighter pilot.

Mom had mentioned this story to me earlier in the day when I told her I was going to visit Lorraine. Mom had explained that in the past Lorraine had said that the Army determined there was sabotage on her plane and she had been told that the wires had been sliced causing them to break while airborne. Lorraine didn't always mention the sabotage because, according to Mom, people said it was never proven with documents.

"You know what else the Army did? Or didn't do?" Lorraine asked. "The Army didn't pay to send the bodies home when the women in the WASP died!"

"My grandmother mentioned that to me before," I told Lorraine.

She continued, "You know the telegrams they sent? All it said was 'Your daughter died in an accident. Where do we send the body?'" Lorraine scowled in disgust.

I stood up and left Caroline and Lorraine to exchange flying tales while I leafed through Lorraine's photos and memorabilia on the dining table behind them. Through the pages of black and white or sepia toned photographs, I got a sense of the dusty and adventurous period of WASP training that Lorraine and Gammy had gone through. There were several photographs of Lorraine showing off her oversized zoot suit or posing with one of the many airplanes she flew during training. I looked over at Caroline and Lorraine who, despite the fifty-odd years separating their careers as pilots, laughed as they shared stories filled with aviation lingo. As much as Caroline revered Lorraine and the WASP for blazing a trail for pilots of her own generation, Lorraine was eager to hear from Caroline about what she had never been permitted to do – fly in combat.

With more than 200 hours of combat flying, Caroline had plenty of stories to share, but one in particular mirrored the story Lorraine had told us earlier. Lorraine listened intently as Caroline told it.

"I was out with one other F-16 and the control was talking to us on the radio, telling us what heading we should take," Caroline began. "He told me to take one sector, so I replied, 'Roger that.' He told the other pilot to take a certain sector, so that pilot replied, 'Roger.' Then the control said back to me, 'No, I told you to take the first sector.' I replied, 'Roger.' Then the control asked if we could hear his radio instructions, and again instructed the other pilot to take the assigned sector, to which the other pilot replied, 'Roger.' The control replied, 'No, not you.' I finally understood the problem and said over the radio, 'I think I understand the confusion. You have two female pilots up here.' There was a moment of silence, and then the control guy came on the radio and said, 'Roger that. Two females. So you know your sectors then?'"

They both burst out laughing.

"Imagine that!" Lorraine exclaimed.

As Caroline and I prepared to leave, we each gave Lorraine a hug and thanked her for her time.

"Can I ask you something? Do you want to be buried in Arlington National Cemetery?" I inquired of Lorraine.

She replied, "Oh, most likely, since my husband is there."

I liked her indication that the decision was not finalized yet, ever the independent WASP.

* * *

Thursday, February 11, 2016 was a frigid and windy day. Walking from the Union Station Metro stop to the House of Representatives office buildings took about 15 minutes. As I stood on the corner in front of the Senate office buildings waiting to cross Constitution Avenue, my legs started to go numb from the cold. I had tights on and wore a down coat, which was warm enough when I was moving, but standing still on the corner trying not to blow away in the strong wind, I wanted to wrap myself in a heavy comforter. Compared to many parts of the United States, the winter in Washington is relatively mild, but this day was especially cold.

One thing I knew from wandering the office buildings of Congress a few times with Whitney was to wear good shoes. I had my running shoes on to walk from the Metro but I exchanged them for flat dress shoes in the bathroom when I got to the office building. I also put on Gammy's blue WASP scarf, my personal trademark of this campaign. Then I went to meet Ben.

I already knew what Ben looked like from our social media conversations, but when I saw him in person, I realized how much he looked like so many other young professional men in Washington. His well-fitted blue suit, classic black glasses, and beard were almost a uniform in this town.

"Ben, nice to meet you," I said and shook Ben's hand.

"Likewise," he responded. "Ready for some lobbying?"

"Yes! Let's do it!" I replied.

Ben laughed. "I only have one appointment lined up. We can walk around to some others and see if we can get meetings. I am focusing on the VA committee members right now since the bill is in that committee." Ben handed me a copy of the list of representatives on the House of Representatives Committee on Veterans' Affairs, which had to review the bill, offer any amendments, and vote to move the bill along before the full House chamber could vote on it. "There are representatives who have already cosponsored the bill, so we can hopefully meet with them or their staff to thank them for supporting the bill."

"And the ones who haven't cosponsored we are going to convince to cosponsor," I said.

"That's the idea," Ben replied.

Since it wasn't time for the one scheduled appointment we had yet, we started by walking to a few other offices on the list to see who was around to chat.

"Can I help you?" a young man asked from behind the front desk in the first office we walked into.

"We are here about H.R. 4336, the WASP Arlington Cemetery bill," Ben said, and pulled out one of the info packets he had put together.

"What is your name?" the staffer asked.

"Ben, I am from Change.org."

"My name is Erin Miller."

"Do you have a business card?" the staffer inquired.

"No," I replied.

He took Ben's business card and then pulled out a small piece of paper and a pen. "Can you write your name on here, and the bill number you are here about and I will see who is available for a meeting," he instructed me. I wrote my name and "H.R. 4336." The young man disappeared for a few minutes.

"I guess I will be ordering business cards tonight," I joked with Ben.

"I'm sorry, nobody is available at the moment," the young man said as he returned from the back of the office. He reached over the counter and grabbed a business card from the tray nearby. "This is the person who does the veteran issues, if you get in touch with her, you can set up a meeting," he informed us.

"Thank you," I said. I took out my phone and started typing while still standing in front of the counter. Ben headed for the door and then paused when he realized I wasn't behind him.

"What are you doing?" Ben asked.

"I am emailing the person on the card," I informed him. I started reading what I was typing, "I will be in the building all day... if you have time to talk about H.R. 4336... let me know. Thank you, Erin Miller."

We stepped back into the hallway and continued to the next office on the list.

"You have some fast email skills," Ben commented as we walked down a corridor with a row of interior courtyard windows where the sun shone onto the marble floor.

"What's the point of having a cell phone if I am not going to make good use of it and email these people immediately?" I replied. "I need to bury my grandmother. I don't have time to wait around for these people."

At the next office, we repeated the routine at the front desk with a little scrap of paper upon which I wrote, "H.R. 4336." We took a seat in the waiting area until a staffer came to get us. He led us to the congressman's office where Ben and I sat on the sofa and the staffer took a seat across from us.

"How can we help you today?" the young man in his late twenties with slicked-back dark hair and a crisp suit asked.

"My name is Ben, from Change.org, this is Erin Miller. We are here today about the WASP Arlington Cemetery bill, H.R. 4336. My role here is to discuss the petition Erin and her family have on our website which has over one hundred and fifty thousand signatures and is one of our top petitions worldwide. I know your boss is already a cosponsor but we hoped to thank him for the support and ask him to help push it through with his colleagues on the VA committee." Ben placed the information from his packet on the coffee table and the staffer leafed through it.

"And what is your role, Erin?" the staffer asked.

"To get my grandmother buried in Arlington National Cemetery," I replied.

The staffer looked up from the info sheets.

"Well, okay then," he said. "If I may ask, if this is not too crude, where is she now?"

"In our closet at home," I replied. The staffer's face showed concern. "Her ashes, her ashes are in the closet," I reassured him.

"Okay. I am sorry about this. What is the situation and what is this legislation going to do?" he asked.

I knew from Whitney's guidance that some staffers would want detailed information and some would only want a succinct argument and good reason to get on board with the legislation. Fortunately, our situation was easy to explain, and I thought there was good reason for members of Congress to sponsor it. I pulled out Gammy's DD-214, her honorable discharge certificate, the letter asking to be in Arlington National Cemetery, and the black and white photo of Gammy on the plane.

"My grandmother was Elaine Harmon. She served in World War II with the Women Airforce Service Pilots. They were not officially part of the military due to gender discrimination during the war, although militarizing them was the plan. In the 1970s, their group lobbied for recognition as veterans, and they were successful in getting Congress to pass a law to that end. Unfortunately, that law was written very narrowly to apply only under the Veterans Administration, as the Department of Veterans Affairs used to be called."

I pointed to the letter sitting on the coffee table. "My grandmother passed away last year in April and left us this letter asking to have her ashes placed at Arlington National Cemetery. The Army told us no, because her service is only recognized at the Department of Veterans Affairs which runs more than one hundred cemeteries across the country, but not Arlington. Arlington, as I am sure you know, is run by the Department of the Army. The requirements to have ashes placed at Arlington are: one day of active duty service, an honorable discharge, cremation certificate, and paperwork to support these requirements." As I recited these requirements, I pointed to the documents on the table. "Here is my grandmother's D.D. two fourteen, showing her record of active service. Here is her honorable discharge certificate. We have her certificate of cremation at home. The only thing missing is for her service to be equally recognized as active duty at the Department of the Army like it already is at the Department of Veterans Affairs. This legislation will ensure that she and the other women who served with her will have the option of having their ashes placed at Arlington National Cemetery. I need this bill, H.R. 4336, to pass into law so that I can bury my grandmother."

"I'll be honest, that is hard to say no to," the staffer said.

"I'd say so," Ben agreed.

"My boss served in the Marines, he is very supportive of this," the staffer explained.

"That's why we're here," Ben replied. "The bill isn't controversial, won't cost much to implement, has bipartisan support, and positive media attention. I think this is one of those cases where there are people who support this bill and people who haven't heard of it yet."

"I will talk to the boss right away, and keep you updated," the staffer said. "Thank you for coming by."

We thanked him and exchanged contact information. Once we were back out in the hallway, we pulled our sheets out to plan for the next office visit.

"I think you should do all the talking from now on," Ben said.

I laughed. "Thanks."

We arrived at Representative Kathleen Rice's office and after the front desk routine, including another little piece of paper with "H.R. 4336" written on it, we stood in the waiting area to see if anyone was available to talk. Most of the representatives and senators had maps on their walls showing their district or state. As I stood there staring at the map of Long Island, New York on the wall, I remembered a few emails I had received via our WASP network from a museum collections manager. I asked the young man at the front desk, "Is the Cradle of Aviation museum in this district?" Before he could answer, another staffer peeped his head out from behind the doorway of a back room and replied in the affirmative.

"Yes, it is! I was listening to you explain your situation and the bill earlier," the staffer in the back room said.

"With that museum in your district, your boss definitely needs to cosponsor this bill," I told him.

He emerged from the back room and came to the front counter. He picked up a business card from the tray and said, "Email her."

"Thank you!" I replied. I pulled my phone out and typed out a message to the staffer named on the card.

I clicked away on my phone as Ben and I walked to the next meeting.

"Now what are you doing?" Ben asked.

"I remembered that last year at an event with my sister I met a guy who works for a representative that hasn't cosponsored yet. I am emailing to see if he is around to chat," I replied.

"And to think I was a little concerned about having only one appointment this morning," Ben joked as he held the door open to the next office.

After we emerged from that meeting, I saw the blue light blinking on my phone.

"We got an email back from Representative Rice's office, the aide can meet with us now," I informed Ben.

"Back upstairs we go!" Ben joked and spun around toward the staircase.

Ben and I were sitting at a table in the waiting area of Representative Rice's office when a young woman came out and introduced herself as the aide who works on veterans issues.

"Sorry, but all the offices are full right now, we have a lot of meetings going on. Do you mind if we sit out here?" the aide asked.

"No, not at all. And thank you for getting back to me so quickly," I replied.

I pulled out Gammy's documents and photos and Ben handed over the information packet to the aide while the two of us gave our rundown on why Representative Rice should sponsor the bill.

"Plus, I noticed that your district is where the Cradle of Aviation Museum is located," I said while I pointed to the map on the wall that I had noticed earlier in the day. "Seems like a bill you should definitely sponsor!"

"Trust me, this is something the congresswoman will support," the aide said. "Can I just say, I am so excited that you came in here today?"

"Really? Thank you," I replied.

"Were you on television the other day? On MSNBC?" she asked.

"That was my sister Tiffany," I replied.

"Oh, okay, but I have seen you also on other news, right?"

"Yes, I have done a few interviews," I informed her.

"I'm glad to see this issue getting traction. I will make sure to have the congresswoman look at this right away, especially since she is on the Veterans' Affairs committee," the aide said.

"We appreciate it, thank you," Ben said.

Ben and I headed to lunch at the cafeteria in the basement of the office building. After paying for my lunch, I waited on the other side of the cash registers for Ben. I had lost him in a sea of bearded men in blue suits between the salad bar and the hamburger venue. Ben spotted me first and we found an empty table, also not an easy task in a lunch spot crowded with a mix of congressional staffers and people lobbying on behalf of a variety of organizations.

"Ben, do you do this with a lot of the people behind the petitions?" I asked in between bites of salad.

"Yes, this is part of my job. I coordinate campaigns that involve legislation on a federal level like yours. I try to help the petitioners interact with the members of Congress who can help," Ben replied.

"I imagine you have met some interesting people," I said.

"Yes, I have accompanied people to support a wide variety of actions," Ben informed me. "A lot of the people don't live near DC. They may only get here one time so I try to help them be efficient, target the right people quickly to make the most of their visit. The staff always gets excited when a petition starts doing well like the petition for your grandmother has."

"I am excited too," I replied. "I can't believe how much support we have been getting. I am grateful for all of it – the media, you all at Change, the members of Congress. It's been overwhelming."

"It must be somewhat difficult emotionally," Ben said. "This is a very personal issue for you and your family."

"It feels strange to be excited about everything that has happened," I replied. "Because the reason behind it all is sad. I think my grandmother would be glad that we are fighting back. But I feel like I have to win or I will disappoint her. It has made me anxious. I am on my phone twenty-four hours a day. I think about this campaign for her twenty-four hours a day. Part of the anxiety is that even with lots of support, including Congress, there is no guarantee of anything. I feel like it could all fall apart in an instant."

I saw the light on my phone blinking and picked it up to check the email.

"You are on top of things with that phone," Ben said.

"Thanks," I replied. "My grandmother hated my cell phone. But look how handy it is now! See, we have a meeting in ten minutes and another meeting set up at two o'clock." I smiled and waved the phone around.

We finished lunch and hurried upstairs to another meeting with a representative from the Veterans' Affairs committee. The staffer who met with us, like all the staffers so far that day, was enthusiastic and optimistic that her boss would end up cosponsoring H.R. 4336.

Our next office was in one of the other House office buildings, so we got on the elevator to go downstairs to the underground tunnels that connect the buildings. The elevator was crowded and I noticed one congressman in the back corner.

"Nice scarf," he remarked. "Why are you wearing that?"

"I am here to advocate for H.R. 4336, so that my family can bury my grandmother at Arlington National Cemetery. She was a pilot for the Women Airforce Service Pilots in World War II and the Army recently decided that they are no longer recognized at Arlington."

The congressman's face changed from jovial to serious, "I thought you were going to say something about advocating for fashionable neckwear. Tell me more about the bill," he said.

Since the elevators in the office buildings are slow, there was plenty of time to talk. As we collected passengers on the way down to the basement, yet another congressman got on and started chatting with the one who was already speaking with me.

"Hey, this young lady was telling me about her grandmother not being allowed in Arlington National Cemetery! She flew planes during World War II!" the first congressman shouted over the heads of the passengers packed in the full elevator to the second congressman.

"Actually, I lived in your district for a while," I said.

"You don't say!" The elevator doors opened and the second congressman slung his backpack over his shoulder as he stepped out. He turned and asked me, "What is the number of the bill again?"

"H.R. Four, three, three, six!" I shouted over several people in the elevator. "Four! Three! Three! Six!"

As the congressman jogged off, I heard him repeating to himself, "Four, three, three, six. Four, three, three, six."

The elevator arrived at the basement level. Ben and I exited through the narrow doors with the rest of the passengers. When the remaining congressman learned he was headed to the same building as us, he offered himself as an escort. We took his route through the parking garage and eventually the tunnels. He charged ahead as Ben and I gave chase. He waved at the security guards and others who recognized him along the way while he and I talked more about Gammy. Once he heard more about the story behind the attractive neckwear, he agreed to cosponsor the bill. "Contact my staff and tell them what you just told me," he instructed me, accompanied by a firm handshake. When we arrived in the other building, he sped off down the hallway joined by a couple aides.

"That was amazing!" Ben exclaimed.

"Maybe we should spend the day riding up and down the elevators. Even though they go slowly, it seems to be an efficient way to get votes," I joked.

While Ben and I repeated our routine in the building next door, I received an email from the first staffer we had met with that day explaining that his boss wanted to meet us in person that afternoon. He was already a cosponsor but I wanted to thank people like him who were already supporting us.

After squeezing in one more meeting with a staffer in a hallway alcove due his boss's office being full, Ben and I made our way back to the office we had visited earlier that day. The staffer then escorted us to a hearing room so we could chat when there was a break during the meeting that the congressman was attending.

The door to the hearing room opened and people poured into the hallway. The staffer got the attention of the congressman. As we spoke, his staff took photos.

"It is an honor to meet you, Erin," he said with a smile as we shook hands.

"Nice to meet you," I replied. "I wanted to thank you for cosponsoring this bill for the WASP."

"Absolutely, when my staff brought me this information, I was on board immediately, this is a terrible situation," he replied. "Tell me about your grandmother."

"She was patriotic and enthusiastic. We played tennis together when I was a kid. She loved her friends from the WASP and was honored to be a part of that group and be able to fly and serve this country," I replied.

"And we should honor her and all those women properly," he remarked.

I noticed a Marine Corps pin on his lapel. "My dad served in the Marines too, in Vietnam," I said.

"Semper Fi!" the congressman shouted.

The staffer collected the congressman to return to the meeting that was reconvening.

"Can we post these photos on social media?" the staffer asked me.

"Of course! Please do!" I replied.

Ben and I thanked the staff for coordinating the meeting. We went down the hall to a quiet area to check our email and messages.

"Hey, good news. Tiffany says Senator Feinstein will cosponsor the Senate bill," I read from my phone. "The senators are sending a group letter to the Army too."

"Great!" Ben replied.

"I also received an email from the staffer we met with in the alcove earlier, his boss will cosponsor as well!" I announced.

"This has been a productive day, I am sad that I have to go," Ben said. "It was nice to meet in person. We'll have to do another day of meetings together!"

"Of course, thank you for being here. It was good to have support," I replied. Ben and I shook hands and he headed for the elevator.

I continued alone for the remainder of the day to one more meeting with a congressman from the House VA committee who was also a cosponsor, followed by a few impromptu stops, including the offices of the four Maryland representatives who had not cosponsored yet. As I walked down the corridors, I spotted a familiar name on an office identification plaque. I recalled that representative giving nice remarks about our bill on the House floor a few weeks back.

I opened the office door and explained my situation to the staffer at the front desk. "I wanted to stop in and say thanks." The congressman was not in the office, but the staffer offered me a blank card to write a thank you note. I left it on the congressman's desk.

At this point it was after 5 p.m. and most offices were closing. But I decided to keep going until all the doors were locked. My final visit of the day was to the office for the representative from my own district of Maryland. I explained why I was there to a staffer at the front desk, but she informed me that the congressman had already gone home. I gave her my contact information and turned to leave.

"Why Representative McSally? What is her interest in this?" the staffer asked me as I reached for the door handle.

"She was in the Air Force, I think she feels a personal connection with this issue," I replied as I held the front door to the office open.

"Oh, that makes sense. Is that why you went to her?" she inquired.

I smiled and replied, "I didn't go to her, she came to me."

I wished the staffer a good evening and walked out the door.

* * *

Since the response had been positive the prior week at the House of Representatives, I decided to make a similar trip to the Senate. To cut down on the number of hours of leave I was taking at work, I planned to work for half the day and then head to the Hill. By working from 6 a.m. to 10 a.m., I would only miss a couple hours in the morning when Senate offices were open, but it meant getting up at 4:15 a.m. to walk the dogs in the dark, cold winter morning.

"Hey lady," Caroline greeted me in the hallway of one of the Senate office buildings after I arrived.

"Hey there," I replied and gave her a hug. "I don't want to distract you from work, I just wanted to let you know I would be around if you have any free time."

"Come with me," she replied. "I'm going to give a talk."

"I don't know if I should. I came down to visit these offices." I held up the printed list in my hand. "Where are you doing the talk?"

"Senator Isakson's office," she replied.

"That's a coincidence," I said. "He's the first office on my list." Senator Isakson was the Chairman of the Senate Veterans' Affairs Committee.

"Perfect!" Caroline said and we chatted some more as she led me down the hall.

When we arrived at the Senator's office, one of his staff members took us back to a conference room where at least twenty people waited for Caroline. I took a seat at the large table in the middle of the room and Caroline stood at the head of the table facing everyone.

"They asked me to come speak today about my experiences. I have been fortunate to have a career as a pilot within different areas of the Air Force," Caroline began. "I have flown F-16s in combat and was honored to be the right wing for the Thunderbirds, and I also graduated from the Air Force Academy, so if you all have any questions about that, I can answer them at the end. I was interested in being a fighter pilot as a young girl, maybe about thirteen years old. My dad used to take me to air shows, and one time I mentioned to him that I wanted to be a fighter pilot. He never told me girls weren't flying fighter planes, so I assumed I would be able to do it. Fortunately, as I was moving through high school and eventually to the Air Force Academy, that restriction against women being fighter pilots was lifted and I was able to pursue my dreams. But I do have to acknowledge what my dad told me when I was young. He said, 'You know, there were these women called the WASP and they flew planes during World War II, so if they can do it, then you can too.' I took that to heart and I learned all about the WASP and they became my inspiration. They have a mascot, who is a little gremlin named Fifinella. I have a patch with Fifinella on it and I have it with me every time I fly. And I want to point out that my friend Erin, right here," she gestured toward me as she spoke, "is the granddaughter of one of those WASP. She is fighting to make sure the WASP are recognized at

Arlington National Cemetery so that her grandmother can be buried there." I waved to the audience.

After Caroline finished her talk, the Senator's staff member approached me. "Erin, great to see you. Thank you for coming by," he told me. "I want you to know that the Senator is fully supportive of this bill for your grandmother and the WASP, we are hoping to move it quickly."

"That's great news. Thank you for working on that," I responded.

"I want to introduce you to one of Senator Perdue's staff," he said and gestured for another young man who had been watching Caroline's talk to come over.

"Nice to meet you," I said and reached to shake his hand.

"You as well. Do you have any info sheets about the bill? I think Senator Perdue should be cosponsoring as well," he informed me.

I pulled out the paperwork from my bag and handed it over.

"I am going to make some copies, if that's okay, so we can have them available for the other members of the committee," Senator Isakson's staffer informed me.

"Absolutely, that would be a great help, thank you," I replied.

Caroline and I stepped back out into the hallway.

"I have to get back to work," she said. "It was so good to see you. Want to get food later after you're done?"

"Definitely, I'll text you," I replied. I gave her a hug and said, "Thank you for that. What a coincidence. I am glad I happened to be here today! And your talk was great."

"Thank you, see you after work!" Caroline headed down the hall.

I spent the rest of the day walking around talking to staffers of senators on the Senate Committee on Veterans' Affairs, colloquially referred to as "SVAC," while the House committee was called "HVAC." In between meetings, I was helping an editor at *The New York Times* fact-check Sarah Rickman's op-ed, which would be coming out over the weekend. Sarah had written several books on the women pilots of the World War II era, so her article would be more detailed than most others with reference to the historical aspects of the overall fight for the WASP to gain recognition.

I stopped in at Senator Jon Tester's office, another member of the SVAC. I didn't have an appointment and I had to repeat the routine with the little slip of paper at the front desk.

"I took your information to the back. Everyone is busy, but if you want to wait for a bit, someone might be free soon," the front office staffer told me. I took a seat in the waiting area and checked my phone for updates. I got word from Representative McSally's office that a couple more representatives had signed on to the House bill. I also received an email from Representative Walz's office (of the Minnesota district where WASP Betty Strohfus lived) informing me that they were finalizing the work to cosponsor the House bill.

"Erin," a voice called from the doorway.

I looked up to see a young man with a beard who had emerged from the back of the office.

"Yes," I stood up to shake hands with him.

"Would you like to come back and talk?" he asked.

"Yes, thank you," I said and followed him back through the interior halls of the office to a small conference room.

"I'm glad you stopped by. I can't usually take walk-in appointments because we are so busy, but when they told me who was here, I knew I had to speak with you," he said.

"Thank you, that's kind. I appreciate you making time to talk," I replied. "I assume you know about the legislation then?"

"Yes, actually the senator is supportive and I'm sure the other senator from Montana will support it too. Montana had a role during the WASP service and we want to acknowledge that," he informed me.

"I hadn't even thought about that!" I replied.

"But tell me more about your grandmother and the bill," he said. I gave my quick speech about Gammy and the WASP being denied as veterans early on and how it had continued to the current situation with Arlington National Cemetery.

"We've been doing some research about the WASP and the Montana connection. Montana was involved in the WASP program as well as some other World War II aviation programs. WASP flew repaired planes or new planes from the factories, many of them staffed by female riveters, to Montana, where they were then transported via Alaska to Russia."

"Here, let me leave you our info sheet, so you know where we are with the bills." I handed over the papers.

"Thank you for coming by, it was great to meet you and talk about this, I hope we can get this done for your family and the WASP," he said as we stood to leave the conference room.

"Thank you, I am grateful for and overwhelmed by the support," I replied as we shook hands.

That evening, the editor at *The New York Times* called to follow-up for Sarah's op-ed.

"Erin, I have a question about where you crossed out 'WASPs' and wrote 'WASP,' in the copy I emailed to you," the editor asked over the phone.

"My grandmother always told me that we were supposed to say 'WASP.' And if we ever said 'WASPs' with the 's' on the end, she would get mad and tell us not to do that. I never questioned whether it was grammatically correct, I did what my grandmother told me to do," I informed the editor. "I know a lot of the other women feel the same way."

"Thank you for explaining. I think our newspaper's editing style is to use 'WASPs,' but I wanted to make sure and ask you about it first," she explained.

"I know it seems trivial, but I can't bring myself to add the 's' even now. Thank you for asking about it." I wondered if Gammy would have argued over one letter of the alphabet with the editing division of *The New York Times* if she were here. That Sunday, Sarah's op-ed appeared in the print edition, featuring the famous 's' that Gammy hated.

* * *

On a rainy morning the following week, I stood outside under an awning to speak with a reporter by phone at *The New York Times*. After Sarah's op-ed, the newspaper now wanted to do a feature piece. Ben had helped set it up, so he was on the call too.

"Ben, before you dial the reporter into our call, I have to tell you that Tiffany is obsessed with *The New York Times*," I told him. "I don't want to say anything about this to her until they agree to do the story because it will be a great surprise, and if they don't write it, she'll be disappointed and probably mad."

Ben laughed, "Okay, sounds good." He connected the reporter into our call and gave a basic overview of the situation and how Change fit in. "There are one hundred and forty-one cosponsors on the House bill. This petition already has enough signatures to be in the top zero point zero seven percent of all petitions on the site, but the story is really about Erin's family and the WASP, so I'll let you two go from here."

* * *

On Wednesday morning when I arrived at Senator Joni Ernst's office, it was filled with Iowans awaiting her arrival. I struck up a conversation with her staff while I was waiting. Senator Ernst walked in and greeted the room in her chipper Midwestern manner, which contradicted what one might imagine from the first female combat veteran elected to the Senate.

Senator Ernst spotted my blue WASP scarf and walked right over after she was finished with her introduction to the room.

"Erin, it is so nice to meet you in person," she said with smile as we shook hands.

"I wanted to thank you for being a leader on this legislation here in the Senate and for being supportive in general," I told her. "My family and I appreciate it, as do the other women of the WASP who are still here."

"Of course," she gushed. "This is important, we are going to move this as quickly as we can so you can have that funeral for your grandmother."

"Thank you for that. I'm sure we'll see each other soon, I'll let you get back to your visitors," I said. I turned back to the staffer I had been speaking with earlier. "Thank you for setting this up, I appreciate it."

"It is my pleasure," she replied.

Then Senator Chuck Grassley appeared in the office. The senior senator from Iowa, he was both distinguished and personable and exactly what one would imagine from someone who had been in Congress for more than forty years.

"Senator Grassley," the staffer I had been speaking with called out to him. He turned and came over to us. "Let me introduce to you Erin Miller, granddaughter of Elaine Harmon, the WASP who was denied burial at Arlington National Cemetery. Erin has a bill that Senator Ernst is leading on to get the WASP recognized at Arlington."

"It is an honor to meet you Erin," Senator Grassley said and shook hands with me.

"Thank you sir, I am honored to meet you as well," I replied. "Like she said, I am here to gather support for this bill to get equal recognition for my grandmother and the WASP at Arlington National Cemetery. They were granted veterans status by law in the 1970s, but the Department of the Army doesn't recognize their service for purposes of having their ashes placed in Arlington because it says their service is only recognized within the Department of Veterans Affairs. I need to get this law passed so I can bury my grandmother."

"So what's the controversy with the bill?" Senator Grassley inquired.

"It is not controversial. It has a lot of support," I said.

"Well, it sounds like something I should cosponsor. Contact my office and tell them I want to cosponsor it," he instructed me. He pointed to the staffer with whom I had been speaking earlier and said, "She knows who you can coordinate with."

"Yes, I will do that. Thank you so much Senator," I replied and reached out to shake his hand.

"You are welcome," he said before wandering off to chat with the other visitors.

I turned back to the staffer who I had been speaking with earlier and said, "Thank you, that was great!"

"Of course, no problem," she said. She pulled her phone out and started tapping away on the screen. "Here let me give you the email for the right person at his office. I think you should go talk to Senator Daines's office too, let me connect you with them."

"Thank you, this has been such a productive meeting this morning," I said.

She laughed and said, "Glad to help, I know this is important to the senator, and there are a lot of people supporting this."

On the Metro ride back to Silver Spring later on in the morning, I had my phone out to send follow-up emails and texts to the people I had met with that morning. I got an email from a friend who worked in another representative's office.

Erin, turn on C-SPAN right now!

I opened a tab on my phone's internet to the C-SPAN website with live streaming from the House floor. As the subway train rumbled back toward home, I watched Representative Ileana Ros-Lehtinen giving a floor speech about the WASP.

At home, I put down my bag of lobbying stuff and prepared to go to the office for the rest of the day. I heard my phone ringing and I fished it out of my bag.

"Hello," I responded.

"Erin, it's Dave from *The New York Times*, we spoke yesterday," I heard on the other end of the phone line.

"Good morning, how are you?" I asked.

"Great. I wanted to let you know that you did a great job on the interview yesterday and the editors have decided to run a full story on your situation," he told me.

"That's amazing. Thank you for letting me know!" I said.

"We are transferring it to one of our reporters down in the Washington office, so you'll have to do another interview," he informed me. "They also want to come by and take some photos, if possible, of the ashes in the closet."

"Yes, that is not a problem, I can do that," I replied. "I already received an email from the reporter saying he has been assigned the story, but it didn't seem clear when he wanted to interview me."

"They want to do it as soon as possible, today if that works for you."

I looked around at the somewhat messy house and said, "Sure, I can make that happen."

"Great, I imagine they will give you a call shortly to set things up," he told me.

"Thank you! Have a great day!" I said before ending the call.

After further coordination with the reporter and photographer, we scheduled an interview and photo session for that afternoon, so I never made it to the office. We talked at the dining room table for about an hour as I flipped through Gammy's scrapbook and told them about her life. The photographer took shots of some of the scrapbook and her documents. The reporter perked up when I mentioned that Gammy's father had played professional baseball.

"My sister Tiffany, in California, whose name is on the petition, she loves *The New York Times*," I explained to the reporter. "It is a running joke between us, anytime she starts talking about some topic, she'll say, 'I was reading this article in *The New York Times*...'" The reporter didn't seem impressed, but I continued on. "Anyway, my point of saying this is if you happen to quote anyone in the story, I was hoping you could talk to Tiffany and get a quote from her because she would be so excited to see herself quoted in her favorite newspaper."

The reporter continued to jot things down in his note pad and didn't give me a definitive answer to my request. I moved on to chat more about Gammy and the bill.

"I think we have enough, do you want to go take some photos?" the reporter asked the photographer.

The photographer set up his tripod and camera to face the closet. The reporter and I stood in the doorway and chatted more about my grandfather's baseball career. My phone vibrated and I saw an email from Senator Grassley's office confirming he would cosponsor the Senate bill.

The next morning on February 25th, I commuted down to Capitol Hill again. The House Veterans' Affairs committee had H.R. 4336 on its agenda. First, I had an appointment to meet with Senator Amy Klobuchar from Minnesota, who had done the news interview with WASP Betty Strohfus.

"Good morning," the staffer at the front desk greeted me.

"Morning, I have an appointment with the senator," I informed her, and I handed over one of my freshly printed business cards that had arrived the day before.

"Yes, I see you here on the list, she'll be out in a moment," the staffer informed me.

The senator was meeting with several people that morning, so when my turn came, I tried to be efficient.

"Good morning, Erin, so nice to meet you," Senator Klobuchar said.

"Thank you for taking the time to meet with me, I see you have a lot of people to speak with. I wanted to thank you for supporting the bill for the WASP so I can bury my grandmother at Arlington. I have seen the news stories you've been doing too, I appreciate it and I want you to know that."

We discussed that the ideal solution was to have legislation passed so that the Army couldn't continue to arbitrarily change its policies. Senator Klobuchar agreed this was the best resolution to the problem.

"I wanted to give you this to thank you for helping our family and the WASP," I handed over one of the printed thank you cards I had ordered featuring a photo of Gammy in her bomber jacket.

"What a beautiful photo of your grandmother!" Senator Klobuchar exclaimed. "Thank you for this. Let's hold it up and take a photo!"

I handed my phone over to one of her staff members to take a photo of us.

"Can I give you a hug?" I asked the Senator as I was leaving. She put her arms up and we embraced. "Thank you, I am grateful for all the support from Congress. It's weird, I want to hug everyone," I said and laughed.

"Thank you for coming by. I hope we can get this worked out soon," the senator replied.

Outside it was sunny and not as cold as it had been in the previous weeks. I walked from the Senate office buildings, passing in front of the Supreme Court and the Library of Congress on one side of the street, and the Capitol building on the other, to the Cannon office building, for the mark-up hearing for the House VA Committee.

I made my way to room 334 for the hearing – the same room where Gammy had testified in 1981 when she had asked the committee members about burial benefits for the WASP. And now here I sat, 35 years later, to watch the latest members of the House of Representatives Committee on Veterans' Affairs provide the promised follow-up that Gammy had never received.

When a bill is "marked-up," the committee debates it, offers and votes on amendments, and then votes on the final updated version of the bill. After I arrived, I greeted several staffers who were preparing for the hearing for their respective bosses. A few came over to speak with me. One suggested I go say hello to his boss on the committee before the hearing started as he would probably like to know I was there to watch. I went over and shook hands with the representative.

A photographer took a photo of the committee members as the hearing began. The audience seating section was almost filled to capacity. There were more people watching than I had anticipated. I thought (and hoped) that this would be a routine formality in the process of getting the bill passed. Yet, I was also nervous that an unexpected argument over an amendment would arise, not be resolved, and then delay or prevent this bill from progressing forward. I kept thinking about how it took years for the WASP to get veterans benefits passed into law in the 1970s and I tried to avoid thinking about the possibility of waiting a decade to bury Gammy. I knew we had a lot of support and I focused on that to convince myself it would all work out.

There were seven bills on the schedule that day and H.R. 4336 was not first. The debate on the prior bill turned out to be entertaining. Two committee members got into an argument over what constituted requirements that patients be advised of some provision regarding healthcare in a medical office. One representative said the requirements were too stringent because they would necessitate hanging a sign with an explanation of the rules. So the other representative replied with something along the lines of "Are you telling me that hanging a sign is too demanding?" The audience actually laughed out loud at this.

"I now call up H.R. forty-three thirty-six," announced Representative Jeff Miller, the Chairman of the House Committee on Veterans' Affairs. My heart skipped a beat. *Everything will be fine.* The clerk began to read the text of the bill, but Chairman Miller quickly dispensed with that formality and recognized Representative Ralph Abraham from Louisiana for an amendment in the nature of a substitute.

In his Louisiana accent, Representative Abraham stated that he was proud to be a cosponsor of H.R. 4336, introduced by Representative "Mac-Sally." He explained that his amendment included all the groups who had already been granted active duty designee status under public law 95-202. I expected someone to bring this up because one of the only objections I had heard so far to the legislation was that it was limited to the WASP and there were 37 other groups who should have been included. Back in the 1970s, the same problem had presented itself: there were other groups who felt they should be recognized as veterans as well, although for reasons other than gender discrimination. So back then, the legislation got "messy" (as Kate said) because it needed to be drafted in a way to allow for other groups to make their concerns heard.

After Representative Abraham finished explaining his amendment, nobody blinked an eye.

Another representative added an amendment requiring Arlington National Cemetery to file a report explaining its capacity limits and requiring a plan to regulate the entry of veterans into the cemetery in the future. Nobody objected to this amendment either.

Chairman Miller took a vote on each amendment and proceeded to a vote for the bill. "The question now occurs on passage of H.R. forty-three thirty-six as amended, all those..." He stopped talking and turned his head.

Why are they stopping the vote? My mind raced over numerous possibilities – none of them positive. Representative Abraham's amendment was essentially replacing the original bill, so any objection was senseless.

Chairman Miller looked over at Representative Dina Titus from Nevada who had spoken up.

"I'm sorry. I just wanted to comment a little about the details of the WASPs who are included in the bill," Representative Titus said. "I was pleased to partner with Ms. McSally to introduce it. We forget about the WASP... they trained just like the men, they flew the flights in World War II... over sixty million miles in twelve thousand aircraft, thirty-eight actually died servin' our country...unfortunately their right to be buried at Arlington National Cemetery was taken away... I thank my colleagues for considering this, for viewing it positively, I

193

FINAL FLIGHT FINAL FIGHT

support it strongly..."

When I realized Representative Titus was presenting positive remarks on the WASP and not objecting to the bill in any way, I calmed down again. I didn't know if Representative Titus knew I was sitting there watching, but it meant a lot to me to have her read comments on the record about what Gammy and the other women of the WASP had done for the country during World War II. As I listened to Representative Titus commend the WASP for their contribution to the war effort, I recalled that one of Gammy's good WASP friends had lived in Representative Titus's district for decades.

I met WASP Helen Cannon in Las Vegas shortly after I had finished college when Mom and I went on vacation there together. Helen was as feisty as any other WASP that I have met. After Helen finished her time in the WASP she continued to fly recreationally, worked in education, and played a lot of golf, among many other pursuits. Helen was president of the Clark County School Board and was inducted into the Las Vegas Golf Hall of Fame. She drove Mom and me around in her large sedan to dinner at a local casino, holding her lit cigarette out the driver's side window as we rode through town. After we ate she made us stay at the table until the waitress collected the tip because, as she informed me, "people steal cash tips all the time."

Helen drove us by the middle school named in her honor in the year I was born. She showed me her woodworking shop behind the house. I stood in awe at the 85 year old woman showing off her band saw skills while a cigarette hung from her mouth. I watched the cigarette ashes drop onto the floor covered with sawdust as she explained woodworking to me in her husky smoker's voice. When Mom and I were driving back to our hotel, I asked if she thought Helen's family had ever told Helen not to smoke in the wood shop. Mom speculated that Helen's family had likely told her many times that smoking in a small area filled with wood and flammable liquids was a bad idea and that it had obviously been a futile instruction. Unfortunately, Helen Cannon died in 2009 so I could only imagine the colorful words she would have used to describe the Army's decision to deny the WASP at Arlington National Cemetery.

Chairman Miller continued with the vote, "Ms. Titus and Ms. McSally have worked together diligently on the issue and it has been expanded from just the WASP issue to the thirty-five [sic] groups out there that are negatively impacted by the current ruling. So I think this is an excellent bill for each and every one of us to support. All those in favor will say 'Aye'..."

The members of the committee spoke up almost in unison, "Aye."

"...the 'Ayes' have it...H.R. forty-three thirty-six as amended is agreed to," Chairman Miller closed the committee discussion, and then announced the bill should be reported favorably to the full House of Representatives, where it could be scheduled for a full vote. One more hurdle in this process was behind us. There were more bills up for discussion at the committee, so although I wanted to run up and hug all the representatives, I quietly thanked some of their staffers and then I left the hearing room.

Heading home on the Metro, I was elated as I replayed the morning's events in my head. I stopped at home to let the dogs out and then drove to the office to work for the rest of the day. Later that evening, I updated the fact sheets that I had been taking around to the offices to reflect that the bill was now out of the House VA Committee and we had new endorsements from more organizations.

The next morning began as usual by walking the dogs at 5:30, followed by updating social media, connecting with people, and searching for news stories. Ben and I had an appointment with Representative Ros-Lehtinen at 10:30, so I thought it would be a leisurely morning. Then I received an unexpected email from Representative Kathleen Rice's office that she would be available at 9:35 if I wanted to meet her. Without realizing it was already close to 8:30, I replied that I would be there.

I looked at the clock and realized that I had five minutes to get ready to have a chance to be on time, but I was still in my pajamas. I threw yesterday's clothes back on, put some makeup in my purse so I could apply it while on the Metro, grabbed the bag full of stuff I normally carried to the Hill, and ran out the door.

The road to the Metro station was almost completely free of traffic. Every light was green. After I parked, I ran to the station from the garage (that's why it's good to wear running shoes to go lobbying) and caught the train as it pulled up to the platform. On the train, I tried to make myself presentable before arriving at Union Station. I was able to walk briskly across Capitol Hill, arriving at Representative Rice's office at 9:33. Two minutes to spare!

Representative Rice was enthralled to discuss Gammy, the WASP, and the legislation.

"Tell me all about your grandmother!" she insisted with a big grin as we sat around a table in her private office.

I did not imagine before I started this campaign that I would meet so many enthusiastic members of Congress. Maybe they were excited to talk about something other than budgets and the mundane things they must have typically discussed. Representative Rice smiled as I pulled out photos and documents and began to talk about my patriotic grandmother and how this problem would have disappointed her beyond comprehension.

"Everyone needs to be sponsoring this bill! I am going to talk to everyone about this," Representative Rice exclaimed.

"That would be great," I replied.

"Kathleen, you have a meeting," the scheduler said after opening the door to the office. Representative Rice must have been enjoying our chat because her scheduler came in multiple times to tell her that she had to stop talking and do other things, but she continued to talk.

"I wish we could talk about this all day!" Representative Rice said.

"I appreciate your support and your enthusiasm!" I replied.

"Kathleen, you have to go," her scheduler chided her again.

"I don't want to hold you up anymore, thank you for talking with me," I said.

"Okay, okay. I know. I have to go. I am so glad you came to visit," she said with a smile.

Finally, we stood up from the table and I gave her a hug. "Thank you for supporting this. It means so much to my family," I told her.

Ben and I arrived for our meeting with Representative Ros-Lehtinen of Florida, who had been a lead on the bill for the Congressional Gold Medal for the WASP in 2009. She was once again supporting the WASP with the current Arlington bill. I wanted to thank her and Ben wanted to chat about Change.org. When we arrived at her office, we saw on the television hanging high near the front door that she was presently speaking on the House floor in the Capitol. Her aides offered us coffee. Not any coffee, but a *cafecito*, for which I learned her office was famous. Ben accepted the offer immediately, but not being a coffee drinker, I declined. It smelled amazing; it made me wish I liked coffee. After Ben finished drinking, we headed over to the Capitol building.

One of the representative's friendly and efficient aides led us all the way to the Capitol building wearing high heels of at least three inches, an impressive feat given the distance, stairs, and marble floors. We did get a small break from walking while on the tram between the House offices and the Capitol building. Then we made our way up the stairs to the Rayburn Room, a large meeting area adjacent to the floor of the House featuring high ceilings, walnut-covered walls, and a few couches and tables. A large painting of George Washington watched over the discussions taking place. We sat at an open table to await the representative.

Representative Ros-Lehtinen bounded across the room with a smile on her face. A petite blonde who had escaped from Cuba at age eight, she had been representing the state of Florida in Congress since 1989.

"Good morning!" she exclaimed and held her hand up to give me an unexpected high five rather than a handshake. "Isn't this so exciting to see this legislation moving ahead?!"

"Yes, it is!" I returned her high five with a smile.

As we sat and discussed Gammy, I showed the representative some photos. I knew she was already familiar with the WASP since she had worked on the Gold Medal bill and several of the WASP lived in Florida. She became engrossed with Ben's explanations on the technical aspects of the petition website which could be used to discover what her constituents were concerned about.

"I know you already support this bill, I wanted to thank you. And for the Gold Medal bill," I told her, handing her one of the thank you cards featuring Gammy's photo.

She took my hand in her hands, looked me in the eyes, and said, "It is my honor and my pleasure to support this."

* * *

"Representatives in Congress are beyond enthusiastic," I said to Ben as we lunched together again in the House cafeteria. "I did not expect this level of energy from these people."

"People love this issue. I'm telling you," Ben replied after finishing off his drink.

"Ready for the Senate?" I asked.

"Let's do it," Ben said as he rose from the table and grabbed his tray.

We arrived at the Senate office building early for our appointment, so we decided to drop in on some offices. While waiting for our next unscheduled meeting, I talked on the phone in the hallway with *The New York Times* reporter to confirm the details of the article he was finalizing. As I finished up, a legislative assistant motioned for us to join him in the office. He led us to a back room and cleared off some space on a round table covered with file folders and invited us to sit down.

Unlike most of the legislative assistants I had been meeting with so far who tended to be under thirty years old, this aide was a tall gentleman with glasses and grey hair, and closer to retirement age.

"Thanks for meeting with us today, especially without an appointment," Ben offered.

"Of course, no problem," the aide replied. "I want you to know, first off, that I have several veterans in my family and I think I understand why you are seeking to amend this law. What more can you tell me about your story?"

"My grandmother, Elaine Harmon, died last year. She was a member of the Women Airforce Service Pilots, or WASP," I explained. "They were not made an official part of the military during World War II, despite training in the same way and on the same planes as the men who were doing the same flying missions domestically. And despite other groups like the SPARS, WACs, and other women's units that were formally made a part of their respective service branches, the WASP were not made part of the Army because they were women flying planes – a man's job. In the nineteen-seventies, the WASP successfully lobbied Congress to pass a law granting them retroactive veteran status. My grandmother left this note explaining that she wanted to be at Arlington National Cemetery." I pulled out the photocopy of Gammy's letter and passed it over to the aide. "Now I have learned that the Army won't let her be there because it doesn't recognize the law that granted the WASP retroactive military status in nineteen-seventy-seven. The Army says the law is only valid at VA cemeteries, and as you know, the Army runs Arlington."

"This is all impressive," the aide said as he looked through the photos and documents I had placed on the table. "What kind of support do you have in Congress? Is there pushback?"

"The House bill just passed out of VA committee, and I have spoken with several Senate offices that are supportive," I replied. "A few were concerned that the bills didn't cover all the groups, that they were tailored only for the WASP. But the House VA committee amended its bill to include all the groups, so that issue is moot now."

"I understand," the aide continued. "Like I said, I have many family members who are veterans, many who are buried in military cemeteries. But Arlington is filling up. They are running out of space. You're from Maryland, right?" he asked.

I nodded. I had a feeling where this was headed.

"One of my family members was buried at the Crownsville military cemetery. It's really nice. Like you mentioned, your grandmother is eligible for placement at a VA cemetery. If you are not successful with this effort, I think you should bury your grandmother out at Crownsville."

I paused for a moment before responding. "I am sure Crownsville is a nice cemetery, however my grandmother specifically requested to be in Arlington National Cemetery. That is where I plan on putting her ashes."

"I understand. Our office can't cosponsor this legislation though. Arlington is getting too full," he replied.

I looked over at Ben, who was seething. The aide stood up and showed us out of the office. As we made our way down the hallway to the elevators, Ben spouted off idea after idea of how to get that senator's office to come on board.

"Mad?" I asked with a smile.

"How are you so calm? I wanted to punch that guy," Ben replied.

"So did I," I explained. "But you know, this is the first office that has flat out refused to support us, and they don't even have a good reason. I've already been to at least a hundred offices on the Hill. We have a lot of support. And now that the VA bill has added on the other groups, the offices that were reluctant before should support us."

"If you want we can start a specialized petition targeted at only that senator's state. I will go all out, I swear," Ben said as we got on the elevator to head downstairs.

"I appreciate that," I replied with a smile. "I'm optimistic that our bill will pass despite the rejection from this one office. There are ninety-nine other senators in here, and I already know at least half are supporting this, so I don't think this one vote will be a big deal. I mean, he isn't going to want to be the one person not supporting this in the end, right?"

"I suppose so," Ben replied. "But we will keep the special petition in our back pocket, okay?"

"Sounds good," I replied. "Thank you."

"I have to go catch the train. Sorry I have to leave you here on that sour note," Ben said.

"It will be okay," I told him as we shook hands and he headed out the door.

* * *

On Sunday morning I bought several copies of *The New York Times* featuring a full page article about Gammy and the fight for Arlington National Cemetery. The famous photo of Gammy in her bomber jacket took up a large portion of the page. As I stood at the breakfast counter sipping hot tea and reading the article again, the phone rang. I assumed it was another family member who had spotted the article that morning.

"Hello," I answered.

"Hi, I am looking for Erin Miller," said a woman's voice on the other end.

"That's me," I replied.

"Oh great! I was hoping to reach you. Do you live in Silver Spring?" she asked.

"Yes," I responded with some hesitation. It was still unnerving how many strangers had found our phone number and home address.

"I saw the article about you in the newspaper today. I think it's great what your family is doing. I work at a middle school. The kids are doing projects on World War II and I wanted to know if you would be interested in coming to speak with the kids about your grandmother and the WASP?" she asked.

I thought about all the times I had seen Gammy go off to a school to talk about the WASP. Educating people – especially kids – about the history of the Women Airforce Service Pilots was one of her passions. On those many days years earlier when I watched Gammy adjust her blue WASP beret on her head as she headed off to a lecture, I never thought about who would continue her story once she was gone.

"Erin?" I heard the voice on the phone say.

"Sorry, yes. I would be honored to come speak. Why don't you email me the details?" I responded.

"I will, thank you. I'm glad you'll be able to speak. The kids will enjoy it," she told me.

I glanced back down at the newspaper article open on the counter with Gammy's smiling face looking back at me. I wondered how many of its millions of subscribers were teachers who would now share the WASP history with their students.

* * *

A couple of days later, I stood in the makeup aisle of the local pharmacy wiping drips of foundation on my arm. Another thing I had never envisioned happening after Gammy died was an emergency trip to acquire makeup at seven o'clock in the morning. I had been getting away with minimal effort on my presentation for local interviews, but in a couple of hours I had to be at CBS studios to appear for their national news show and I figured I should prepare accordingly. I had been busy, but could also blame procrastination for ending up here at this early hour for this chore. After choosing a few items based on a vague recollection of getting makeup done with friends a few years earlier, I went home to apply it.

I rode the elevator at the studio with the producer who was organizing the new piece about our situation with Arlington. "I've been wanting to do this story for a while, since I first saw it come out with AP. I saw that *New York Times* story and realized I had to make it happen," she relayed to me.

"Thank you for doing the story. I appreciate all the news coverage. It helps a lot," I replied.

"David is excited to meet you," she said as we stepped off the elevator.

"Really?" I asked.

She nodded.

I recognized the slim man with grey hair and glasses who arrived at the studio door just as we did as David Martin, the network's national security correspondent for more than twenty years.

"Erin." David reached his hand out to greet me. I found it difficult to believe that a reporter with years of experience telling war stories was excited to meet me. It was difficult to discern any excitement through his professional demeanor.

I shook his hand. "David, nice to meet you. Thank you for doing this."

He gestured for me to follow him to one of the two seats arranged under the studio lights and in front of the cameras. On a small table nearby sat a glass of water and a box of tissues, reaffirming my theory that news people want everyone to burst into tears during interviews. Once again I did not feel like crying. I was thrilled to be able to tell Gammy's story to millions of this program's viewers. It kept our situation in the public eye and the pressure on Congress to vote on the legislation – another tool to achieve the goal of getting Gammy's ashes into Arlington National Cemetery.

After the interview, I sat downstairs with the producer while she scanned in photos and documents to add into the news story. "Would it be all right if the camera crew came to your house to film the closet?" she asked.

"Yes, it's no problem," I replied.

The New York Times had already photographed the container of

Gammy's cremains in the closet, and now here was CBS News filming it. I had given them permission, although I knew Mom would be annoyed about it. After Gammy died, I never imagined that one day a major news organization would be in the house filming a box of her cremated remains in the closet because we had gotten in a fight with the cemetery.

After the news crews left, I tried to arrange Mom's room as it had been when I left the house that morning, and then I went to the office. When I returned home, I had to finish preparing for the school talk the next day. I was sitting on the sofa and working on my laptop when Mom arrived home from work.

"Are you working on your presentation for the school?" she asked as she walked to the dining room to set her things down and remove her coat.

"Yes," I replied without looking up from the computer screen.

Mom made her way upstairs. I heard Mom open the door and take a couple steps and turn around down the stairs. I knew what was coming next.

Mom stopped on the landing of the stairs. "Was someone filming my closet today?"

I looked up and smiled. "Maybe."

"I don't like all these news people filming the closet," Mom said.

"Mom, look." I tried to explain my thinking. "I know it's invasive, but it is a part of the story. It makes people connect with what is happening. Only the major news people have even asked to come here. They've been very respectful. They know it's a sensitive request."

Mom was quiet for a moment before replying. "Okay. I hope that was the last one though."

"I don't anticipate anyone else asking."

She turned to go back up the stairs, but paused. "Good luck with your talk at the school tomorrow."

"Thank you," I replied. "I need it. I don't know that I have ever given a talk to middle schoolers. I hope they aren't bored."

Mom laughed.

I was up until 1 a.m. creating slides for the talk and thinking about what to say. Gammy spoke from personal experience at her lectures. All I could do was show photos, repeat the few things she had told me about her time with the WASP, and talk about what I had learned fighting for her to be laid to rest at Arlington National Cemetery. I was a poor substitute.

At 5 a.m. I was awake again to walk the dogs in order to make it to work early enough to spend a few hours there before going to speak at the middle school. I stopped at home first to collect some documents that I thought the librarian might want as reference material for the kids. It occurred to me how useful it was for Gammy to have left behind so many documents. It was almost like she was anticipating this problem with Arlington.

When I arrived at the middle school, the exuberant principal met me at the front door and escorted me to the library. They had set up a projector and chairs and I saw that my first presentation slide featuring Fifinella, the WASP mascot, was already showing on the screen at the front of the room. I tied Gammy's blue WASP scarf around my neck and awaited the students.

An electronic beep sounded over the school's loudspeaker system. A couple minutes passed before the doors to the library opened and students started streaming in. I smiled at the ones who made eye contact as they sat down. One or two waved at me and I waved back. Soon students occupied all the chairs and fixed their eyes on me with looks of great expectation.

The librarian came up to introduce me. "Okay, settle down, everyone. Today we are lucky to have Erin Miller here to speak about her grandmother who flew planes in World War II. Those of you who chose your project topic about women in the war, this will be especially useful for you. You can ask questions at the end. Please welcome Erin."

"Thank you for having me here today. My name is Erin Miller, I am going to talk to you about the Women Airforce Service Pilots of

World War II, and my grandmother who flew planes as part of that program. I will start out with a basic overview of the program, how it got started and what the pilots did." I moved through about the first ten slides, which had a lot of photos with captions, assuming that was more interesting to kids than slides replete with lists of bullet-pointed information.

I clicked the pointer and the next slide appeared. I hesitated. Staring back at me was the reason I was here talking to these kids – Gammy, smiling away in her bomber jacket. "This is my grandmother, Elaine Danforth Harmon." I hesitated again. I took a deep breath. "Unfortunately she passed away almost one year ago." *She used to give talks to students. I hope I do even half as well as she would have done if she were here.*

The students clapped as I finished my presentation.

"Does anyone have questions for Erin?" the librarian asked the room.

The cynic inside me who expected to stand in awkward silence until the school bell rang was put to shame as every student in the audience thrust a hand in the air. The librarian stepped in to take control of the first questioner who wanted specific details about what happens when people are cremated. Fortunately the rest of the questions were not so complex.

"Did your grandmother have WASP friends of a different race?"

"My grandmother's best friend in the WASP was a woman named Maggie Gee, one of only two WASP of Chinese descent," I explained.

"Were there any African American WASP?"

"I know there was at least one African American woman who applied but she was turned away. From what I understand, Jackie Cochran said the program was already under scrutiny for training women so adding African American women would have complicated things even more."

"How did the involvement with the WASP affect the career opportunities for these women later in life?"

"Being part of the WASP didn't affect my grandmother's later career, although some of the women did join the military after their WASP service. Some fought hard to make their way in commercial aviation careers. But many went home and returned to their normal lives like others who had served in World War II."

"Was your grandmother scared when she went to be in the WASP?"

"What a coincidence that you bring that up. My grandmother never told me how she felt when she entered the WASP program. But recently I found a diary she kept while she was in training. There is an entry from the first day she arrived in Texas to train with the WASP. She wrote that she felt inferior to the other women because she assumed they all knew more than she did. But she went through with the training despite her feelings. Then she became friends with the other women and realized they all had a lot to learn," I informed the young lady in the middle of the crowd. "I brought her diary with me. Maybe your librarian will make a copy of that part for you." The girl's eyes widened with glee and I saw the librarian nod to indicate that she would photocopy the diary's relevant pages.

I pulled out a copy of Amy Nathan's book, *Yankee Doodle Gals: Women Pilots of World War II.* Then I held the book up. "This was my grandmother's favorite book about the WASP and the author sent me a few copies. I am donating this book to your library." The kids cheered and applauded.

The school bell rang and the kids gathered their things and scampered out of the library to their next classes. I had made it through the presentation. I had not seen any kids sleeping, they asked a lot of questions, and they clapped at the end. The talk was a success.

* * *

A few days later, the death of Betty Strohfus, the WASP who had interviewed with Senator Klobuchar, revived the urgency of achieving our goal sooner rather than later. That evening's broadcast of the *CBS Evening News* story we had filmed the prior week opened by reporting about Betty's final flight.

David Martin then explained a brief history of the WASP program and how the Department of Defense had deemed the WASP service as not eligible for Arlington National Cemetery.

Mom and I watched together as I announced to millions of television viewers, "The Army said no to the wrong family."

"Haha, yes!" Mom cheered from the other end of the sofa.

"I thought you would like that." I laughed.

Then David moved on to the interview with Representative McSally who explained how gender discrimination in the 1940s prevented the WASP from being integrated as Army pilots.

"What did you think about it, Mom?" No reply. "Mom?" I looked over at the end of the sofa and saw that she was clacking away on the keyboard of her laptop. "What are you doing?"

"I'm Googling you." Mom replied.

I laughed. "What? Why?"

"You're doing all this work, I thought it would be interesting to see if you come up on Google now." She said as she scanned the results page.

"That's a phrase I never imagined hearing you say to me. Find anything?"

"Yes! This is very cool Erin."

"Thank you Mom."

I hoped that the *CBS Evening News* story would continue to bring attention to the situation with Arlington National Cemetery. I received notice that the Ninety-Nines, an international organization of women pilots started by 99 women pilots in 1929, and AOPA, the Aircraft Owners and Pilots Association, had officially endorsed the legislation, meaning thousands of more people would hear about and hopefully would contact their members of Congress. Tiffany finished the

Spanish version of the petition, so I sent it to Representative Ros-Lehtinen's office which shared it on their social media. Change.org published the video story of the petition featuring Tiffany. National Public Radio broadcasted a story featuring WASP Nell Bright, who was a tow target pilot during her service.

My available leave from work was dwindling, but having worked on several Saturdays over the prior few months had compensated for some of the time. I planned to take advantage of any available time to continue to promote the legislation in the media or on Capitol Hill. The press conference was coming up the following week and a vote on the bill was likely not long off. I headed down to spend another afternoon lobbying for Gammy. At times, it felt unnecessary to spend so much time down there when people were generally supportive. However, I was compelled to do everything possible to make sure the bill became a law, because if I slacked off and for some reason it didn't pass, I would never have forgiven myself.

That day in the House offices, I didn't have a predetermined list. My plan was to walk door to door and if the nameplate on the door did not show a name on the cosponsor list, then I would have a talk with that office. I had my cell phone out while I wandered down the hallways comparing names on the doors with those on the cosponsor list online. I had my speech down to a tee and had heard all the questions before.

At Representative Mark Takai's office, the staffer at the front desk showed me into the congressman's office right away and told me an aide would be there shortly. I took a seat on the sofa.

"Erin Miller? Hi, it's so nice to meet you." A young woman in dress skirt and button up top entered the congressman's office and reached to shake my hand.

"Thank you so much. I appreciate you meeting with me so quickly," I replied.

"To be honest, I was hoping you would come into the office," she said. "We've all been following your story, I'm so glad to meet you."

"Really? That's so nice. I guess I don't have to give you my speech about my grandmother then."

"No, but I would love to hear about what's been going on," she said with a smile.

I filled her in on the latest activity. Then I asked, "Out of curiosity, why isn't your boss's name on the cosponsor list?"

"We're working on it. Don't worry, we'll cosponsor," she assured me.

"Thank you! I figured Representative Takai would have supported us since he served in the Hawaii National Guard. I'm glad I stopped by, it was nice to meet you."

As I continued my rounds, a few offices agreed to cosponsor on the spot. After four hours, I had visited 31 offices. I spent the evening emailing aides who had either promised that their bosses would cosponsor or who had been away from the office. At 11 p.m. one aide replied to say that his boss would be cosponsoring. The next morning, the cosponsor list had grown to 173 representatives with several new names on it.

After spending another Saturday at my paying job, I dedicated Sunday to Gammy's legislation. Several students had contacted me since the campaign started making headlines. Because of them, I learned about a competition called National History Day, involving hundreds of thousands of kids across the nation as well as a few foreign countries. Competitors researched a topic of history and presented it in one of the available formats. The students moved through local, regional, and state competitions, and ultimately the winners traveled to Maryland, just outside the boundaries of Washington, D.C., for the national finals.

The first two students who contacted me were Avery and Jessee, from Michigan. We had set up an appointment to do a video interview that afternoon. I sat at the dining table with my laptop open and my phone in hand.

A ring came from the laptop's speakers. "Hello," I answered to the two young ladies who had appeared on screen.

"Hi," they responded together and waved at the screen.

"Thank you for agreeing to be interviewed Miss Miller," said Avery.

"First off, call me Erin. And I want to thank you," I told them. "My grandmother used to give talks to students all the time. She would be proud to know you are studying the history of the WASP. I am happy to help in any way I can. Also, I had never heard of National History Day. I looked at the website to learn about it. What kind of project are you two doing?"

"We are producing a documentary," Avery replied.

"Cool. I doubt I would have been able to make a documentary in junior high school, that's impressive."

Avery and Jessee laughed.

"I apologize, I have to take a break in the middle of our interview. I have an interview with a radio show in a few minutes. It's live, otherwise I would have scheduled it at a different time. If you want, you can stay on video and hit mute," I said.

"That's fine," Jessee replied.

We only got through a few of their questions before my phone started to ring.

"Hi, this is Erin," I said into the phone. I waved to the girls on the video chat as they stayed on the line to listen to the radio interview.

"Joining me on the program right now is Erin Miller, the grand-daughter of one of the Women Airforce Service Pilots in World War II," the host announced to the radio audience. "Tell us about what is going on with Arlington Cemetery."

I gave an overview of the events leading up to the situation with Arlington, starting in 1944 with the failure of Congress to militarize the WASP because of gender discrimination.

"I see your grandmother's photo. We have it up on our website. She has the helmet, the real Amelia Earhart aviatrix look. Tell us about your grandmother," the host requested.

"My grandmother was adventurous and independent," I began. I described Gammy's upbringing and her path to the WASP. "I say my grandmother was a feminist, but not intentionally, she just thought flying would be interesting. She ended up representing some of the feminist goals of the 1940s," I explained to the radio host.

"We want you to get on the phone and email to your congresspeople and senators," the host announced to the radio audience. "What was that bill number again?"

"H.R. Four. Three. Three. Six!" I replied.

I hung up the phone after finishing the radio interview and went back to speaking with Avery and Jessee. When they had exhausted their questions, they informed me that the Michigan state competition was in April, about a month away.

"If you all win, we definitely have to meet in person! I don't know if you all are interested, but we can see if we can meet your members of Congress. Make sure to let me know how you all do in your competition."

"We will," Avery said.

"Thank you for talking with us," they said in unison.

* * *

It was mid-March, and the beginning of another busy week for our campaign for Gammy. The day started with a milestone: our petition reached 170,000 signatures. The press conference was going ahead on Wednesday. I continued to receive emails from congressional offices wanting to cosponsor the bills. The media continued to feature Gammy's story in the news with pieces like Petula Dvorak's column in *The Washington Post.*

The biggest news of the week was that not only had the Army officially decided to support the legislation as the most expedient way to solve the problem, but also H.R. 4336 would likely be voted on the following week. I was ecstatic about the news regarding the Army, but at the same time, I didn't want to tell people because I thought they would misinterpret it as meaning that the problem was resolved.

On Wednesday morning as I walked the dogs at 5:30 a.m., I envisioned the events of the day: interview at a local news station, meetings with members of Congress, a press conference for the bill, interview with the staff at Change.org, and somewhere in there, finding time to eat. Since the entire Metro subway system had been shut down for the day for maintenance, I assumed traffic would be terrible and planned on leaving the house with Mom earlier than would usually be necessary.

In the green room at FOX5 news studios, I checked my makeup in the mirror and took some photos with Mom while I waited to interview with the news anchor.

"Have more congresspeople said they will cosponsor?" Mom asked.

"Yes, we have over one hundred and eighty now," I told Mom.

"Great," she replied.

"Excuse me," a young man on the sofa on the other side of the room stood up and approached me. "What legislation are you discussing?"

"H.R. 4336, the WASP AIR Act," I told him and proceeded to explain.

"I work in Representative Connolly's office," he said, referring to Representative Gerry Connolly of Northern Virginia.

"I assume he is here to talk about the Metro shutdown," Mom said to the staffer, knowing that his boss represented a district full of Washington area commuters.

"Yes, you got it," the aide replied.

"I see here Connolly is not a cosponsor of this bill," I informed him as I scrolled through the list on my phone.

"I will work on it later today, we should be cosponsoring this," he handed me his business card. "Email me later."

Representative Connolly, a grey haired gentleman with matching grey mustache, came into the green room.

"Congressman, I want you to meet these people, they have a bill we need to cosponsor," the aide said as we shook hands with the congressman.

"Nice to meet you," Representative Connolly said with a smile. "Tell me more."

As we took photos together, I briefed him on H.R. 4336.

Then the producer came to get me for the filming. Mom followed behind with my phone to take photos. They put the microphone on and had me sit on the couches while they checked the sound and cameras.

"Erin Miller?" the well-coiffed news anchor asked as she approached me, having just come from the news desk into the studio.

I reached out to shake her hand. "Yes, nice to meet you."

"My name is Allison Seymour, I'll be interviewing you today," she said as she took a seat across from me and flipped through a few note cards in her lap. "I'm going to ask about your grandmother, then go into the situation with Arlington, and then what is going on with Congress. This is live, so the cameraman is going to let us know when the previous segment switches over to us."

"Sounds good," I replied. I looked over to the side of the studio to see a photo of Gammy in her uniform projected on a wall-sized television monitor.

"We're going to show the photos you sent us while you and I talk," Allison said. "What great photos!"

"Thank you."

The cameraman indicated it was almost our turn and then pointed to Allison.

"Second lieutenant Elaine Danforth Harmon served with the Women Airforce Service Pilots, also known as WASPs," Allison began. "When she passed away recently, her family was not allowed to bury her at Arlington National Cemetery. Now they're trying to change that. Joining us this morning is Harmon's granddaughter, Erin Miller."

After talking about Gammy and the WASP history, we moved on to the Arlington situation. "Before I was born, she was lobbying for these rights. Now she has passed away and I am still lobbying for her," I told Allison.

"You're going to the Hill today. Tell us about what you're going to do," Allison said.

"We have a press conference today at one thirty with Representative McSally who has introduced H.R. 4336, the legislation that would amend the original law to include inurnment rights at Arlington Cemetery for all these women," I explained.

"I can tell from the pictures that you were very close to your grandmother," Allison said. "I'm trying to find the right words to say this, but in the meantime, what are you doing with her remains? Are you waiting, hopeful that she will have a place at Arlington?"

"Absolutely. I plan on winning," I replied. "Her ashes are currently in our family's closet."

"Waiting for their proper home," Allison said. "Good luck to you."

While we drove from the news studio to Capitol Hill, Mom and I found all the traffic we had been expecting earlier. The news anchor on the radio announced that President Obama was going to make his Supreme Court nomination that day right before our press conference.

"Good grief, the Metro closes and the Supreme Court pick happens on the same day as our news conference?" Mom lamented.

"Goes along with everything else," I said.

We got to the Hill in plenty of time despite the traffic. Unlike most of the other days I had spent there on Gammy's behalf, the sun was out and the air was warm enough to need only a sweater, if that. After a few minutes of walking from the parking garage at Union Station, Mom asked how much farther we had to go.

I pointed to the Capitol building a few blocks ahead and said, "To the other side."

Mom grimaced.

"That's why I wear running shoes around here," I told her.

After taking Mom to meet with one member of Congress and a few staffers at other offices, I said we had to eat something before the press conference started. We went to the easiest spot: the Longworth cafeteria in the basement of one of the House office buildings. I managed to find a table back in the corner even though it was a busy day. Mom had gotten soup and I watched her holding it awkwardly while balancing her giant heavy purse hanging off one shoulder as she made her way through the crowded cafeteria. I imagined her dumping the entire thing down the front of her business suit. Fortunately she made it to the table without issue.

"The Army has written a letter supporting the legislation," I told her as we ate.

"Does that mean they're changing their mind?" Mom asked.

"The Army is not changing its policy, it is supporting the bill," I said. "I'm telling you in case someone brings it up at the press conference, but I don't want people to be confused and think the problem is fixed."

After we finished eating, we went up to Representative McSally's office and met with her staff. We all walked to an area outside in front of the Capitol building. Some reporters were setting up their equipment. I spied two bearded men in blue suits.

"Ben, Max!" Our Change.org advisers turned and smiled. I gave them each a hug. I waved for Mom to come over to us. "This is my mom."

"It is an honor to meet you," Ben said as he and Max shook Mom's hand in turn.

"Thank you for all your help," Mom replied.

I saw Senator Ernst and Representative Davis arrive. They got hugs from me too.

"Senator Ernst, this is my mother, Terry," I said as she and Mom shook hands.

"It is wonderful to meet you Terry," Senator Ernst said with a smile.

"It is an honor to meet you. Thank you for everything you're doing to support this," Mom replied.

I spotted Representative McSally in a blue blazer walking across the lawn and waved to her.

"Hey there, good to see you," she said as I gave her a hug.

She gave Mom a hug too and then started explaining to Senator

Ernst what had transpired earlier in the day. Coincidentally Representative McSally had been in a hearing with Patrick Murphy, a former congressman who was now the Acting Secretary of the Army. She had questioned him about who exactly was going to change the regulations at Arlington for the WASP. "Can you believe this? He said legislation would be the fastest way to fix this issue!"

We all laughed at the irony of claiming that action by the notoriously inefficient Congress was the most expedient way to resolve the problem with Arlington.

The staff rounded us up behind the microphone podium. Senator Klobuchar showed up just before we got started, she also got a hug from me. She was a little late because she had been at the White House Rose Garden when President Obama had announced his new Supreme Court nominee.

Representative McSally stepped forward and started the press conference by thanking everyone for coming and giving a brief overview of the situation before introducing Senator Ernst.

Senator Ernst spoke about some of the WASP from her home state of Iowa, one of whom was Gleanna Roberts, a classmate of Gammy's who had died in service. "There is no doubt in my mind that these women are heroes."

Senator Klobuchar recalled how she had spent time with Betty Strohfus the prior month. "An incredible woman who just died this last week in Minnesota. Her funeral is actually today." She went on to explain how women like Betty were denied not only recognition as veterans because of discrimination, but denied a career in aviation after the war. "We aren't going to be able to change history, but we can change how these brave women are honored."

As Representative Susan Davis was finishing her remarks, Representative McSally turned to me and whispered that I was next. "I guess I should think of something to say," I quietly replied. She laughed, but with everything I had been doing, I had forgotten to write any remarks for the press conference.

Representative Davis finished her remarks and turned the podium over to me. After thanking the members of Congress who were leading the charge to amend the 1977 law to recognize the WASP service as eligible for Arlington National Cemetery, I explained what I thought Gammy would have thought of all this effort. "If my grandmother were here she would probably say, 'I can't believe you're making such a fuss about this, you can just put my ashes over there in the park, I really don't care.' However, I know that for the WASP as a whole she would want everyone to make sure that the WASP are recognized as veterans in Arlington Cemetery and honored for the role that they played."

At the end of the press conference, Representative McSally took questions from the reporters. One reporter asked about the irony of the situation with Arlington National Cemetery given the military's recent decision to integrate women into all roles. Representative McSally agreed that it was indeed ironic. "I think it's ridiculous that at a time that the Pentagon is deciding to open up every single military position to women, which I support, they are closing the gates to Arlington to the pioneers who paved the way."

After the formal speaking finished, Mom and I spoke to a few reporters and then said goodbye to the staff. We had some time to kill before our meeting at the Change.org offices so we sat on a bench nearby. I was updating our social media accounts on my phone with information and news links from the press conference when I received a text message from Caroline.

Caroline: Did you see Yahoo news? The WASP are the top story! There is an interview with Katie Couric and McSally and Ernst

Me: What? Watching now! Thanks!

"Mom, Caroline sent me a link to an interview with Katie Couric about the WASP."

"Can we watch on your phone?" Mom asked.

I clicked the link on my phone and we watched the interview together on that bench in the shadow of the Capitol building. Representative McSally and Senator Ernst argued passionately that the WASP deserved recognition at Arlington National Cemetery.

"What did Martha just say?" Mom asked, straining to hear the sound from the phone speaker.

"She said Elaine's family has been amazing and even though her ashes have been sitting on a shelf in the closet, they don't want an exception to the policy, they want a change for all the WASP. She said they're our wingwomen in Congress, pushing to get this change so we can bury Gammy."

"Cool," Mom said.

Senator Ernst explained that the Secretary of Defense would be appearing before the Armed Services Committee in the Senate the next day and she would be asking him about this situation.

Katie asked the Senator, "Well why wouldn't he just change the policy?"

Senator Ernst and Representative McSally both smiled and shook their heads. "That's a wonderful question Katie," Senator Ernst replied.

As we continued watching the interview, and as Senator Ernst and Representative McSally continued to talk about their efforts in Congress and dealing with the Department of Defense, it occurred to me how insane it was that so many high level government officials were spending time working on this issue in order for our family to be able to bury Gammy. I was grateful for all the help, but it was unbelievable that it had reached this level.

"Why did Katie ask about the election at the end?" Mom wondered out loud.

"This election is crazy. It is unavoidable," I told her. "Come on, time to go."

We grabbed a ride across town to the local office for Change.org.

Ben greeted us at the door and introduced us to the staff. Mom and I sat with Ben in the back of the open space loft style office, at a large butcher block table near the kitchen. One of the staff members set up a camera to record our conversation while others gathered around.

"Usually, the staff here don't get to meet the people behind the petitions, so we are all excited to have you here so we can learn more about your experience with your campaign," Ben explained.

Mom talked about growing up with Gammy. The way she spoke of Gammy as a mother, was similar to what I told people about Gammy as a grandmother. "She raised us to be independent." Mom talked about camping trips without a tent and sleeping outside under the stars. Mom and I explained the WASP history and their fight to be recognized as veterans in the 1970s.

Ben asked Mom about Gammy's involvement in the lobbying for veteran status during that time period.

"I remember her sitting up for hours typing at the dining room table, letters, and you know, using the correction stuff," Mom explained, using her hands to mimic blotting correction fluid on the typewriter paper, "working to lobby Congress."

Ben asked about what happened when Arlington told Mom that Gammy was denied a place in the cemetery.

"I was so thrown off," Mom replied. "First I thought, well I'm glad I don't have to decide whether to tell my mother about this or not. My second thought was I don't want to have to tell these other WASP that they have to go through this fight to be recognized as veterans again. They're all in their nineties, or I think a few are a hundred. But it's important, given that they're in their nineties that their families are made aware of this."

Then Ben and I discussed the development of the campaign for Arlington recognition and the flurry of media coverage. Ben turned to me and asked, "What's it been like? You haven't had a public face before."

"It's been weird," I replied. "But at the same time, I am very focused on what I am trying to accomplish. So I'm not really thinking about it that much. I'm just looking at each day as, what can I do today to accomplish our mission? Literally every day I think about things that I can do and what I have done today to advance what we're trying to get."

When Ben asked to discuss something interesting I had noticed about talking to members of Congress and their staff, I mentioned the petition. "When I pull my phone out and say, we have a hundred and seventy thousand people supporting us, people respond. It's been such a good tool."

We continued our conversation with Ben and the other staff members for so long that the batteries ran out on the video camera.

That evening, the beautiful weather continued while I walked the dogs around the neighborhood. My mind drifted over the events of the day and how much had developed since the previous summer when Arlington had rejected Gammy from the cemetery. Gammy had gone from being my grandmother who had flown planes in the Second World War to having her image broadcasted across international media outlets as the face for legislation in Congress to grant the group of little known women military pilots known as WASP the ultimate recognition of acceptance as veterans at Arlington National Cemetery. Last year at this time I saw that Gammy's final flight was imminent. A little over one month remained until April 21st, the one year anniversary of her passing. Mom wanted the legislation to pass before this anniversary did, but even with Congress moving relatively quickly, it seemed unlikely that in the next few weeks the House and Senate would both vote on the bill and it would be signed by the President. As had become almost a daily routine, I spent the rest of the evening updating our social media with news clips and developments from the day, corresponding with legislative staff, and sharing everything with the family – my version of spending the evening hunched over a typewriter.

* * *

March 22, 2016

I was elated when I woke up on Tuesday morning, anticipating the day ahead and taking stock of the progress that had been made so far. As usual, while still in bed, I checked the news and social media on my phone and my excitement was immediately extinguished when I saw the news reports of multiple terrorist attacks in Belgium. These incidents were increasingly common, especially since the Paris attacks the previous November. And now with my hypersensitivity to the news cycle, I absorbed every story going on in the world. In a consciously selfish moment I wondered if this news would change the schedule for the day, but nobody had emailed about it yet. Granted, it was not even six a.m. yet. I went ahead as if everything would be fine.

The vote wasn't until the afternoon, so I could have gone to work for a while in the morning. But I was too excited. And nervous. *What if my car broke down? What if there was an accident? What if some random event happened and I had to shelter in place in my office?* The day had already begun with terrorist attacks; I didn't need to increase the odds on additional problems. Instead, I walked the dogs and went running.

My heart was beating hard as I was going through the security line at the House office building. Today was probably the most significant hurdle we would have to face, even though getting this bill passed in the Senate was not a given. A lot of bills get through the House of Representatives and then go to the Senate to "die."

I grabbed the door handle and entered Representative McSally's office as I had done many times and greeted everyone. "Good Afternoon! My favorite office on the Hill!" The staffers stopped and smiled gave a little cheer.

I approached Keeley, one of the staff members. "I know I am here earlier than you suggested but I didn't want to be late."

"No, it's good, now we think the vote might be earlier than we thought. You know things here are always changing. We're figuring it out right now," she explained. "I will take you over to the Capitol soon."

"Thank you so much. All of you have been so helpful," I replied.

"We are really happy to see this getting across the finish line," Keeley said. "The whole office has been excited to work on this issue."

"I named it!" Chase exclaimed from behind his desk, partially obscured by two giant computer monitors.

"You did? That's great!" The official name was the Women Airforce Service Pilots Arlington Inurnment Restoration Act. Short version: WASP AIR Act. "What were the other options?" I asked.

Chase made a face indicating they were not worthy of discussing. I leaned on the couch for a while until Keeley indicated we were ready to go.

We had gained two visitors from Arizona as Keeley led us through the halls of the office buildings to the underground tram.

"Have you been to DC before?" I asked.

"This is my first time here. He's been living here for a couple years," one of them replied.

Once we arrived at the Capitol we hurried up a narrow stone staircase winding up to the main level and then up a wider stone staircase to the gallery level where we could watch the floor proceedings. We approached the security desk where we handed over our cell phones to a Capitol police officer. The security line was long but Keeley pointed out to the officer that she was a staffer and she was going to escort us to the line.

"You still have to wait in line unless the member is here with you," the officer retorted.

"Really? We've done this before. I think it's okay," Keeley replied.

"I don't know that rule," the officer responded.

We all stepped back from the desk.

"Okay, I think we can go around on the elevator. This way," Keeley motioned for us to follow as she walked down the hall to more stairs and eventually to a set of two elevators. After arriving at another level, Keeley asked another officer about a different security entrance.

"You have to take this elevator down to the basement, and then get off and get on that elevator back up to the other level," the officer replied. "The elevator doesn't go to that level from this level."

At this point, one of the guys from Arizona chimed in, "Wow, this is crazy."

"This is your first trip to DC right? Welcome to your federal government," I said.

Instead, Keeley led us back to another set of stairs. After running around for fifteen minutes we returned to the first security desk. However, a new officer was on duty. Keeley showed him her staff badge, the officer nodded, and we all walked by straight to the express security line.

"Have fun! Call me when it is over if you need help coming back to the office," Keeley offered before hurrying away.

"Thank you so much," I replied. "Shall we?" I said to the two guys from Arizona. The three of us headed for the gallery doors where an escort took us to a few available seats and then remained in the aisle to ensure the audience adhered to the rules of the gallery, which mostly consisted of being quiet and not putting your feet up on anything.

We settled into three seats at the top row of the middle of the gallery seating area situated like a balcony above the floor of the House of Representatives. Visitors quietly watched from up high as representatives spoke about the bills coming up for vote. As one representative droned on about an unfamiliar bill, I turned to the guys from Arizona and whispered, "Don't fall asleep before it's our turn!" They laughed. The escort eyed me. I was so excited, I was sure I would end up doing something to get myself kicked out of the gallery. I had to keep reminding myself to stay quiet so I didn't get ejected.

Finally they announced debate for H.R. 4336. I poked the guys from Arizona and said, "This is it!"

I leaned forward, resting my head on my folded hands, and watched Representative Jeff Miller, the Chairman of the House Committee on Veterans' Affairs, introduce Representative McSally as the sponsor of H.R. 4336 down on the House floor. As Representative McSally approached the dais, I turned to the guys next to me and whispered loudly, "I want to get up and cheer. Would that be bad? I think Congress needs cheerleaders. It's too quiet in here." They laughed and shook their heads. Some people in the gallery turned to look at me, likely wondering why anyone would be excited to watch government officials give speeches.

Representative McSally began to speak, thanking the Chairman and highlighting the role of the WASP as forerunners to today's women in the armed forces. Her exuberance for this issue radiated in her voice throughout the gallery.

One of the guys from Arizona turned to me and said, "Hey, she's pretty good at this, huh?"

"Yes, she's good at this! Hello, where have you been?" I retorted, as if I had some authority to make such a proclamation when I didn't even know who she was three months earlier. The gallery escort looked at both of us. I folded my hands back in my lap and turned back toward the front of the balcony.

Representative McSally mentioned Gammy's name and remarked how our family had brought this problem to the media instead of relenting to the Army's new policy.

"These women were feisty. They were strong. They were not going to take no for an answer. In that spirit, her children and granddaughter – and Erin Miller is with us in the gallery today – said, 'We are not going to take no for an answer. We are going to get awareness on this, and we are going to get my grandmother and the WASPs the right that they deserve,'" Representative McSally continued.

At the mention of my name I put my hands up in the air and smiled, but remained quiet. Half of the audience in the gallery looked at me in confusion. The escort stared at me again. I prepared for the possibility of getting kicked out of there and hoped the video was available on my new favorite channel, C-SPAN.

Representative McSally concluded her speech by mentioning how the WASP had helped her personally while she was a pilot in the Air Force and she encouraged all the members of the House to pass the bill. When she ended her speech, I put my hands up again and said to the guys from Arizona, "Can I clap now?" One of them smiled and pointed down to the floor. We all looked down as Representative McSally motioned up in our direction.

"What is she doing?" one of the guys asked.

"It looks like she says she is coming up here. Does that make sense?" I replied.

We found out a few minutes later when Representative McSally appeared in the gallery and sat at the end of the row next to the guys from Arizona. She started explaining to them what was going on as a few more representatives talked about the WASP bill down below. A woman seated in front of Representative McSally turned around and started asking questions. Representative McSally explained some procedural rules to the woman and her family.

"Do you think that woman knows she's talking to a member of Congress?" one of the guys asked me.

"No. There is no way she knows," I replied.

"I think she knows," he argued.

"No way," I responded. "She has no idea."

After a few minutes of discussion on the intricacies of House floor proceedings, the woman finally asked, "How do you know all this stuff?"

Representative McSally motioned her hand toward me and replied, "I'm a congresswoman. I was just down there talking about this bill for the WASP. Erin's grandmother was a WASP."

The woman and her family looked over at me. I smiled and waved.

The woman's eyes lit up with recognition and she said, "Oh, right! Thank you for explaining this."

I poked the guy next to me and said, "See, I told you."

He smirked.

Representative McSally leaned over the guys to get my attention and said, "Erin, I want to take you downstairs for the vote."

"What? Okay!" I replied. This was a surprise. I had no idea I would be able to go down by the floor and watch the voting take place. Now I really wanted to do a cheer.

"Let's go, come with me," Representative McSally stood up and I followed her. I gave the dour escort a smile and a wave as I left the gallery.

Representative McSally led me downstairs via the marble staircase, down a long corridor, and finally through a door to the cloakroom. The cloakroom is a small private area where the representatives gathered in between votes to chat or eat. There were old phone booths lining one wall, but the representatives inside them were talking on their cell phones. We walked over to the doorway leading to the voting floor where the carpet changed to royal blue featuring large gold medallions of laurel leaves.

"This is as far as you can go, but you can see the votes up there." Representative McSally pointed to the front wall of the gallery as we stood in the narrow doorway while a couple of representatives squeezed by us.

"I appreciate you doing this," I said to her as we waited for the voting on the first bill to start. "Not only bringing me down here, but everything. I don't know what else to say. Thank you."

She smiled and placed her hand on my arm. "Of course," she responded. "Isn't this exciting? Let's take a selfie!"

We positioned ourselves near the doorway so the gallery showed up behind us as she held up her cell phone.

"Excuse me, ma'am," a young security officer said as he approached us. "You can't take photos here."

"Oh?" Representative McSally said and then clicked the camera button on her phone a couple of times. The officer was not amused.

He stared at us until she put her phone away. Then he sauntered off.

"You're in trouble," I said laughing.

"That's twice," Representative McSally replied.

"Twice? What else did you do?" I asked.

"Didn't you hear the speaker after I was finished? I got in trouble for mentioning that you were in the gallery during my speech. We are not supposed to talk about the people watching in person," she explained.

"You've gotten in trouble twice in ten minutes with me," I said, laughing. "Sorry."

Representative McSally waved her hands and laughed it off.

"Are you going to send me a copy of that selfie?" I asked.

"I have to think about it," she replied with a grin.

"Fine," I said.

Losing Gammy had not been the difficult part of this journey. She was elderly and sick and although it was sad to watch her pass on, her loss was also expected. However, the denial of a funeral and its accompanying emotional closure as a result of the Army's decision meant that almost a year after Gammy's death the grief lingered. The associated emotions that should have been processed months earlier continued to percolate to the surface regularly and were exacerbated by the anger and frustration of fighting with the Army for Gammy's peaceful rest. The support our family was receiving propelled me forward, ahead of the conflicting and exhausting emotions. Representative McSally seemed to operate with heightened awareness of and sensitivity to the unique stress that the situation created for our family. This welcome personal attention from her in having me present at the vote in Congress epitomized her actions thus far in allaying not only that stress but also my ever-present anxiety about whether Gammy's ashes would be in a closet forever.

The voting for the first bill started and Representative McSally left me in the cloakroom. While she was gone, Representative Mark Takano from California appeared in the doorway, shook my hand, and then recited a long poem from memory. Although I was impressed, I was also stunned and confused, but I thanked him and shook his hand again before he smiled and walked away. As other members stopped to say hello, Representative McSally introduced me to them in between her trips to vote on the floor.

"It's our turn!" Representative McSally smiled and pointed to the digital vote tally board projected high on the front wall of the chamber with the names of the 435 members of the House of Representatives that now also displayed, "HR4336."

"Make sure you vote yes!" I joked.

"Everyone better vote yes on this!" she responded as she walked out to the floor with her voting card in hand.

I stood at my boundary line in the doorway and watched as representatives approached the electronic voting recorders in the gallery to insert their voting cards. The board lit up with a green letter "Y" next to the names of the representatives who voted yes. Logically, I figured the House leadership would not schedule a vote on the bill if there was any doubt it would pass. There were 191 cosponsors and many more offices who had told me they would support the bill but hadn't ended up on the list. It seemed unlikely that reaching 218 votes, the minimum for it to pass, would be a challenge. Even so, I was nervous and excited to see the votes going up on the board while the digital timer in the gallery counted backwards from five minutes.

Representative Susan Davis, the lead cosponsor of the WASP bill, walked by. Representative McSally introduced her to me. "It's nice to meet you, I didn't get to say hello at the press conference," I said.

"This is so exciting, isn't it?" Representative Davis asked.

"Yes! I can't stop saying thank you! Thank you!" I said.

She laughed. The three of us stood together for a minute by the doorway watching the board overhead light up with green Y's. Watching Representative McSally's enthusiasm as the vote proceeded demonstrated to me that this was not a rote political exercise but was an equally meaningful moment for her as it was for me.

"Wait, who is that red 'N,' who is that? I can't read it," Representative McSally asked while squinting at the array of names projected across the front of the chamber.

"I can't read it either, the names are too fuzzy!" I replied.

"I see who it is!" Representative Davis announced. "I am going to see about this," she said before walking away.

Representative Davis returned quickly with a smile on her face. "It was a mistake," she said and pointed to the board where everything was once again a sea of green letter Y's. Most of the board was full and the countdown timer approached zero. When it expired, the WASP bill known as H.R. 4336 had passed with a yes vote from all 385 members present.

"Eh, look at that! Unanimous!" Representative McSally exclaimed.

I embraced Representative McSally and said, "Thank you so much for this! And congratulations!"

"I'm so glad we could make this happen," she replied.

We made our way out to the hallway to take photos. I hugged her again before she left for a meeting. After she walked off I realized I still had not given her the book which had been living in my bag for weeks. After running to chat with a few other offices, I arrived back at her office and sat on the couch in the waiting area for her to return. The staffers were discussing an event that night and I realized what it was for.

"Wait, is it Martha's birthday?" I asked.

"Yes!" they replied in unison.

"Good day for a birthday," I said.

Representative McSally returned and I followed her to her office with the book in hand.

"I'll be quick. I want to give you this book. I've been carrying it around for weeks and I kept forgetting about it. This is *Yankee Doodle Gals*. It was my grandmother's favorite book about the WASP. But I am giving you this particular copy because my grandmother signed it." I opened the front cover of the book to show her Gammy's signature on the title page.

"Thank you, this is amazing," she said while tracing her finger over Gammy's signature.

"I don't have anything else of hers to give you but I wanted you to have this. I think she would have been happy for you to have it," I said. "Thank you for everything." After one more hug, I turned for the door and remembered what I had heard earlier in the office. "Oh, and happy birthday!"

As I meandered out of the marble hallways of the congressional office building, I realized how anticlimactic this was about to become. And I was alone. I texted Caroline to see if she was still at work over at the Senate so we could eat dinner together. Fortunately, she was around to celebrate with me.

Walking past the Capitol building on the way to the restaurant, everything that had happened in the past few months leading up to this day ran through my head. Then I thought back to the days immediately after Gammy had died when we cleaned her house out and I helped Mom with paperwork. I had assumed Gammy's funeral at Arlington National Cemetery would require a routine request. Instead it had turned into a major undertaking culminating in today's step toward ultimate victory for which surreal was the only appropriate description. I had walked by the famous Capitol dome so many times in my life, yet I never imagined that the activity inside would ever affect me on such a personal level.

14

Final Flight

When I returned from my semester abroad in South Africa, I resumed taking Gammy to her medical appointments and chemotherapy sessions. By this time, she needed a wheelchair, so I loaded it into the trunk of her old car each day when I picked her up. The VA hospital had free valet parking, which was a wonderful amenity that I did not truly appreciate until it was suspended during a construction project.

"Gammy where did this wheelchair come from? It weighs a ton!" I asked Gammy as I helped her from the passenger seat of her old Honda into the wheelchair I had dragged from the trunk. I pulled her WASP tote bag from the car and tucked it onto her lap. I began pushing her up the hill in the parking garage and around to the pathway leading to the hospital's main entrance.

"What did you say?" she asked.

"I think this wheelchair weighs more than you do." I leaned into it, holding tight onto the hard plastic handles as I pushed her along. "I should just carry you over my shoulder."

"I don't know, Rob found it somewhere," she replied, indicating

Mom's brother had come home with it one day.

Later, on the way home from the hospital, we stopped once again at the traffic light on North Capitol street by Rock Creek Cemetery. As usual, Gammy pointed toward the cemetery and said that my grandfather was buried "over there." I looked over at her as we waited for the green light, examining how she had changed in the few months since I had been gone. She had a thinner frame and the left side of her face continued to droop. My eyes stopped on Gammy's ring-bare left hand resting on her thigh.

"Gammy, you never got married again. You weren't that old when he died. Why didn't you get married again?" I asked.

She cocked her head and wrinkled the side of her face that still worked, and retorted, "Marriage? Once was enough!"

I burst out laughing. "But did you ever date again?"

Gammy shook her head. "I kept my wedding ring on for years. People thought I was being sentimental, but really I wore it so men wouldn't talk to me. I only took it off when I got fat some years ago and then I had to ask someone to cut it off."

"I never knew that! It's hilarious."

She shrugged. We spent the rest of the ride home laughing.

Gammy's health declined over the next few months leading into spring and law school graduation in May of that year. I asked if she wanted to come to graduation but she said no. It was the first big event of my life she would miss. It was going to be a busy weekend because Whitney was getting married the day after my graduation, so I thought she wanted to take it easy and save her energy for the wedding.

Whitney got married at the beach the day after graduation. We wheeled Gammy out in a big wheelchair with special tires that rode across the sand so she could be up front for the nuptials. Because the chair sat a few feet off the ground, Gammy looked like a queen presiding over an important ceremony in her throne. "When is your graduation?" she asked me as we prepared for the ceremony.

"Gammy, it was yesterday. You said you didn't want to come." I could see disappointment even in her half drooping face.

"Well, I don't know why I would have said such a thing!" she told me.

Shortly thereafter, I took Gammy for a PET scan at the VA hospital. I waited in the prep room with her while the radioactive tracer made its way through her body. I could see she was shivering, so I grabbed another blanket for her. I tucked it all the way up around her neck as she lay back on her hospital gurney. She was so thin; I got cold looking at her trying to stay warm under all the blankets.

"Oh wait," she tugged the blanket down. "Can you take this off?" She pointed to her gold WASP wings necklace. I obliged and slid it into the pocket of my jeans – aware that the necklace was one of the few material possessions Gammy would be distraught about losing.

I tucked the white blanket back up over her shoulders and around her neck. "Are you tired? You can sleep. I think it will be a while." She nodded and closed her good eye, while her droopy eyelid meant the other eye remained partially exposed. I sat and watched her sleep for a bit, wondering what it must be like to have had death scratching at her door for almost a decade. She was a fighter. She rarely complained. Even suggestions from her doctors for complex and potentially painful procedures got a response no more dramatic than, "Okay, if you think that's best."

Upon reading the PET scan results the doctors said the tumor was growing, so they increased her chemo treatments to once a week. Over the next year, the doctors continued to work on her eyelid, check up on her hearing aids (which she said didn't help), and monitor her cancer. I went to the VA with her on many of these visits. They were altering the chemo treatments or stopping them altogether based on how they thought the tumor would respond. It was shrinking and they hoped it would disappear. Gammy got recurring episodes of shingles as well. At the beginning of 2014, I took her for another PET scan to see how the tumor was developing. The doctors said it shrank significantly and was not growing back.

Mom had been doing the bulk of the caregiving for Gammy and she had a break when Gammy was in the hospital. After this, the VA provided a visiting caregiver for ten hours a week at Gammy's house, which took some of the stress off of Mom. The caregivers helped Gammy walk around the house during the day and reminded her to eat.

By December, Gammy was complaining about her vision and hearing loss getting worse. She started forgetting things, although she had always been mentally sharp, even if her body was getting weaker.

"Can you write the names on the people?" Gammy handed me a marker and a book of photos from her seat on the floral sofa. I sat next to her and flipped through the photo album, writing names in the margins of the pages next to each photo. "I know I should know these people, but I don't remember their names," she explained.

Because of her declining mental acuity, the doctors ordered another MRI. In contrast to what the doctors had predicted a few months earlier, the new MRI showed that the tumor had not only grown back, but had grown in such a way that it was spreading like a spider web throughout Gammy's brain. The doctors said radiation was not an option because the tumor was no longer one mass, but a network. The chemotherapy treatments were not preventing the tumor from growing either. And now the tumor was affecting her brain function. The day she had wished for almost two years earlier was fast approaching now.

15

Final Fight

March - May 2016

I was ecstatic when the bill passed the House, but we had to make
sure it passed the Senate also. I had no idea what to expect
regarding that phase of things. I had been to about 50 Senate
offices and I knew we had a lot of support, but I didn't know whether
that would translate into action to pass the bill. The House passed
a lot of bills that for various reasons ended up going nowhere in the
Senate.

Since Senator Mikulski and Senator Ernst were the lead sponsors of
a companion Senate bill, I felt confident that there would be attention
to the House bill. Senator Ernst had already given media interviews
about the issue and had spoken at the press conference in March as
had Senator Klobuchar. The only other obstacle had been that some
senators did not want to support a bill which only granted rights
to the WASP and not the other groups, but now all the groups were
included since the House bill had been amended. There was one Senate
office which had told me it had no interest in supporting the bill at
all. However, everyone else was supportive and I hoped they would
all drown out the one naysayer I knew about and any others that I did

not know about.

The Senate was in recess until April 5th, so things were quiet until then. I didn't like it. I wanted to get it done immediately. It was frustrating to be forced to take a break.

The morning after the House vote, I had an interview with BBC television at Gammy's house. Mom had been trying to sell the house since Gammy had passed away, but had not closed on a deal for it yet. She had some interest from potential buyers that week, so it was fortunate they hadn't moved on it. I had not arranged any other news interviews at Gammy's home because it was empty and seemed uninteresting as a background. I explained this to the reporter, but she didn't seem to mind.

When I arrived at the house, I expected to see the reporter waiting, but she wasn't there. I went inside and found her chatting to my uncle, who had not changed out of his sleepwear – an old T-shirt and blue flannel pajama pants. After showing her around the house, the reporter and I set up chairs in the empty dining room that she had decided made for the best interview spot, lit by sunshine from all the windows. Due to the preparations to sell the house, Gammy's beloved metallic bird wallpaper was gone, replaced by freshly-painted cream colored walls.

The interview initially proceeded as the previous ones had. I explained Gammy's patriotic spirit and her history with flying and entering the WASP program. The reporter requested a rundown of the procedure in Congress and the status of the legislation. I was elated to share the success of the prior day. "So now that the bill has passed the House, we have to wait for the Senate to actually pass the bill as well."

"I think that's all the questions I have," the reporter said. "Is there anything you would like to say that I did not ask about?"

I paused for a moment, about to reflexively decline. Instead, I responded that I was grateful for all the support our family had received. I wanted to thank everyone from the media to the people at

Change.org to the lawmakers. I thought about how long Gammy and the other WASP had been seeking this basic recognition and now she wasn't even here to enjoy it. 70 years ago, Congress did not support recognizing my grandmother and the WASP as part of the military. So I had to say that I appreciated how supportive the members of Congress were being this time around. I could feel tears forming in the corners of my eyes. The outpouring of emotion that I had imagined the reporters over the last three months had been searching for was coming to the surface. *Hold it together. Don't cry. A few more sentences.* In particular I had to thank Representative McSally. She and her staff worked hard and were so supportive. I could not have imagined a better person to take the lead on this legislation in Congress.

After the interview, I headed to work. I managed to avoid bursting into tears in the car on the way there. However, by the afternoon, I felt overcome with the same physical exhaustion I had experienced the day after Gammy died – grief, illness, or some combination. I left earlier than I had planned and went home.

The next morning I felt no better than the day before, but I went to work anyway. I didn't know what was wrong and I thought work would distract me from worrying about it. On the drive to the office, all my thoughts on the past few months were on overdrive. *I can't believe that we needed a law passed to bury Gammy and it is actually happening. People are learning about the history of the WASP because of Gammy being denied at Arlington National Cemetery.* I looked around the car for tissues to wipe away the tears that were flowing. I was overjoyed. Things were going well. Yet I spent twenty minutes crying as I drove down the freeway. I fared no better in the kitchen that evening – trying to eat while crying over a plate of food. I stopped trying to figure out why I was upset and let myself cry. I had been unaware that I needed to.

* * *

"Hey. Are you doing better?" Mom asked as she passed through the living room toward the kitchen to toss her purse down and take off her coat.

I was stretched out on the sofa, my laptop perched on my chest. A pile of used tissues littered the coffee table. "A little," I responded, my congested sinuses adding a nasal pitch to my voice.

Mom came back into the living room. "What's happening with the Senate?"

"The Senate is on recess," I replied.

"Can't you get them to hurry up? Why are they taking so long?"

"Mom. I am not in charge of the United States Senate. I am doing my best."

Mom exhaled. "So, what are you doing then?"

"I have more media interviews," I replied. I reached for a tissue and blew my nose. "*Huffington Post*. The BBC story will be on, tonight I think."

Mom grabbed a key from a hook by the front door and went outside. When she returned, I heard an envelope tearing as she replaced the key on its holder.

I looked over as Mom started laughing. "What's so funny?"

Mom held up a few sheets of paper. Even from across the room I could see strips of black covering almost the full area of each page.

"I got a response to one of my FOIA requests." Mom walked over to hand it to me.

It was a copy of the memorandum from the US Army regarding changing the policy on WASP inurnment at Arlington National Cemetery. The entire three page document was redacted – every line covered with a stripe of black ink – except for the title, subject, and signature.

"What is the point of having a FOIA law if replying with the equivalent of a blank document is an acceptable response?" Mom asked.

"That's a good point. I doubt that any of the information in this memorandum about active duty designees at Arlington would be classified," I replied. "At most it would make the Army look bad, which is why I assume it is all redacted. Hopefully in a matter of weeks this whole thing will be over and the information in the memorandum will be irrelevant."

"I hope so," Mom replied. "Well, let me know when the Senate is done so I can call Arlington." Mom stuffed the redacted memorandum into her enormous black purse and walked upstairs.

The Senate resumed its session the next week in the beginning of April. I felt like things would move ahead, even if more slowly than in the House. Gammy's friend Lorraine Rodgers was kind enough to have me over again, this time accompanied by a reporter from NBC news.

I received a call mid-week from Senator Ernst's office to inquire if the senator could call me later on that day.

"Are there people who say no to this question?" I asked.

The staffer who had phoned laughed and gave me a time to expect a call. I had become friendly with Senator Ernst's office staff during this process. I didn't know them as well as the staff at Representative McSally's office, but I had been keeping in touch as the bills moved through Congress.

Later that afternoon, my phone rang and showed an extension used at the Senate switchboard.

"Hello, Erin? How are you?" Senator Ernst greeted me.

"I'm well, thank you senator," I replied.

"I wanted to call and assure you that we will be working to move the bill ahead. I was so glad to see it pass the House and come over to the Senate."

"I am glad to know you all are there to carry on the work from the House side. My grandmother passed away on April twenty-first, so we are a couple weeks away from the one year anniversary. This timing is weighing on my mother. I was hoping this bill could be hotlined as soon as possible," I told her, referring to the procedure of announcing a bill for passage without a vote – if no senator objected, the bill would pass by unanimous consent.

Then the senator explained to me that there was a request to incorporate our bill into a package of other bills related to veterans. "I promise you if that package seems like it is not moving forward, then I will try to separate the bill out and pass it on its own. I know this is a sensitive situation."

"I appreciate the personal attention to this. I will trust your judgment on how this proceeds," I told her. "Thank you for the phone call. It means a lot to me that you took the time to call me yourself. I'm sure you're busy."

"You are welcome," she replied.

"One more thing, I want to let you know that your staff has been great – friendly and helpful. I appreciate all their assistance."

"Thank you, I love to hear that!" Senator Ernst replied.

* * *

From: Mom

Subject: Fwd: "Assist Sec of Army"

Message: He wants me to call him.

"Mom, what's going on?" I asked over the phone after reading her email.

"I got a message from the Acting Secretary of the Army's office that he wants me to call," Mom replied.

The suggestion of an exception for Gammy's burial at Arlington had been floating around since the previous summer when the cemetery called Mom the first time to deny the request. The Army had for

241

months been without an official secretary since the Senate had yet to hold a confirmation hearing for the nominee, so Patrick Murphy, the Under Secretary of the Army, was filling in. I assumed that he was calling about the exception but I had no idea. Now that the Army had formally declared a few weeks prior that they were supportive of the legislation, I didn't understand why he would be calling.

"I don't like this. I don't think you should call. Or I should call instead," I told Mom.

"I think it would be rude not to call back," Mom replied. "I think you're overreacting."

"Fine, then let me ask around and see if anyone knows why he's calling before you call. I don't trust the Army."

Mom agreed to wait. I asked the staff at Representative McSally's office if she had talked to him or if something had happened that we didn't know about. They said they didn't know of any reason for the Acting Secretary of the Army to call us. I dialed Mom's number.

"Mom, nobody knows why he would be calling. Just remember to say no if he asks about the exception. I have no idea what else he would say. And call me back as soon as you hang up. And tell them to expect a call from me too."

"Okay, okay. Again, I think you're overreacting," Mom replied.

I waited to hear how the conversation turned out. I didn't care if Mom thought I was paranoid. Almost one year to the day since Gammy had died and now the Army decided to reach out to us while this legislation was sitting in the Senate? I found it suspicious. Then my phone rang.

"Mom, how did it go?" I asked.

"Fine. He has a very nice voice," Mom replied.

"What?"

"The Under Secretary of the Army, he has a nice voice," she replied.

"Mom! He may be a nice person, I don't have a problem with him personally, but he represents our enemy! I hope you didn't say yes to something because he has a nice voice."

"Erin, relax. He said he wanted to reach out to our family since he hadn't spoken to us yet. He did bring up the exception and I told him that wasn't what our family wanted at this point."

"Okay, good job Mom."

"And I told him to expect a call from you," she informed me.

* * *

Tiffany was in town that same week. She told me she wanted to go meet some people at Congress because she lived in California and felt removed from a lot of the things that had happened over the past few months. I imagined that finding available members of Congress with 24 hours' notice for meetings was not generally successful, but I hoped that some of the people I had been speaking to during this process would help out. Since it would be a Wednesday, I hoped Senator Ernst would consider chatting with us for a few minutes during her regular Iowa constituent morning meeting. Then I emailed a few other offices to see if any of them could chat for a couple minutes the following day as well.

We took the Metro down to Union Station and walked over to the Senate building first to see Senator Ernst. I handed Tiffany one of the blue WASP scarves and I put one on as well for our day ahead. Senator Ernst was gracious enough to take a few minutes to chat with us so I could introduce her to Tiffany. We also chatted with the office staff for a while, who had been helpful during this process. We headed over to the House offices, with a stop for a sister selfie in front of the Capitol building. We met with the staff member at Representative Rice's office who had seen Tiffany on MSNBC back in January and who had also been very supportive during this process. While meeting with her, I got an email that Representative Tulsi Gabbard would be able to meet with us after lunch. I had tried to meet with her a couple other times before, but it hadn't worked out, so I was glad she was available that day.

Then we walked down to Representative McSally's office so I could introduce Tiffany to some of the staff. While we were there, they said the representative was at a hearing in another building but if we walked over there she could probably say hi in between sessions. I led Tiffany back to the other building we had cut through after lunch to wait for Representative McSally's break during the hearing. Once she appeared, we all chatted and my sister's comments had both of us laughing hysterically, although I don't even remember what she was saying. It was like a comedy show at the House office buildings.

"How is the bill doing at the Senate?" asked Representative McSally.

"We are waiting for them to work on this veterans' package," I replied.

"They need to move faster. Your family has already been waiting so long," she said.

"I know, but I am giving them time to work on it this way. I have already spoken with Senator Ernst about moving the bill forward alone and hopefully hotlining it if things seems like they aren't going well."

"Keep on top of them," she suggested.

"Thank you for taking a few minutes to talk with us," I said and gave her a hug.

"Of course and I am glad to meet your sister," she replied.

Then Tiffany and I grabbed some food and went outside to eat in front of the Capitol building since it was a nice day. Tiffany had fun posing at the podium installed where we had done the press conference back in March. After we finished eating and playing at the podium, we walked over to meet up with the granddaughter of WASP Lorraine Rodgers. We had been chatting online but I had yet to meet her in person. It was great to meet her and we all had fun talking about our grandmothers and the Arlington situation. Then Tiffany and I had to run off to meet Representative Gabbard. When we got to her office, they offered us Hawaiian macadamia nut treats while we waited. Eventually we had to walk over to the Capitol with one of her staff members because the representative was in the midst of voting and didn't have time to come back the office. Tiffany was excited to take the subterranean tram to the Capitol as we made our way to the meeting.

When I arrived back home that evening, Mom was hanging over the answering machine on the breakfast counter. I took off my coat and walked over to her.

"What are you doing?" I asked.

"Listen!" Mom pushed the play button.

A familiar voice emanated from the speaker.

"Oh my gosh, Mom."

"What?" she asked. "I responded to his email the other day, I didn't realize there was a voice mail from him."

I laughed. "How many times have you listened to this message already?"

Mom smiled. "Did you speak to him yet?"

"Yes. He said he wanted to touch base with our family when the situation came to his attention, but had been waiting for the Army to formally approve of the legislation," I told her. "I informed him we were putting our efforts toward supporting the legislation. An exception would not only miss the whole point of pursuing a law but would also diminish the power of the story behind it. He said he understood and wanted us to know that he supported our efforts."

"Okay, but don't you think he has a nice voice?" Mom asked.

I rolled my eyes. "I guess he has a nice voice."

* * *

After waiting on the Senate for a month to move forward on the package of veterans' legislation, I started contacting Senate offices again during the week of April 25th. I told them I didn't want to wait around for this package deal and that our bill needed to pass on its own. My strategy was to call and email offices until they became annoyed enough to pass the legislation to avoid hearing anything further from me. If that did not work, then I would go in person again. It had now been more than one year since Gammy died.

Senator Ernst was supportive of hotlining the bill. Some of the other offices were not as keen on the idea for reasons that remained a mystery to me. After I inquired at the Senate Veterans' Affairs Committee chair's office about singling our bill out a few times, a staff member replied that they were working with Senator Ernst to move the bill ahead separately. I assumed there were things going on behind the scenes that I didn't know about, but at least Senator Ernst's office kept me informed about the general status of the legislation.

Finally, on Wednesday, the news came that the bill was being hotlined. I was thrilled to hear this since I had been unaware of any movement on the bill for the past month. Then it became a matter of waiting to see if anyone had any objections to the bill.

The next day I learned some news which I thought would irritate me more than it did. For unexplained reasons, the hotline process was not completed. We had to wait ten more days, if not more, until at least the week of May 9th when the Senate returned from another week of recess to try again. I was upset, but knowing all this was not under my control – I was not in charge of the United States Senate, as I kept telling Mom – I focused on what would happen after the Senate finished with the bill. I also learned that the Senate had changed two words in the House bill. Those changes, although minimal, meant that after the Senate passed the bill and finished the process of modifications, it had to go back to the House of Representatives for yet another vote.

I called Patrick. "Hey, have you heard about the Senate changing two words?"

"Yes, we were talking to Senator Ernst's office earlier," Patrick informed me. "Don't worry, Martha has already talked to the leadership here about voting on it right away."

"Just what I wanted to hear!" I replied. "Thank you!"

During the recess week, time was dragging. I knew the representatives and senators were in their home states, but it meant ten more days that Gammy's ashes were sitting in the closet. Things were quiet. No emails or phone calls to respond to all day. The media outlets were waiting for the Senate to pass the bill before doing new stories. All I could do was wait with them.

I worked at my paying job. I ran. I walked the dogs. At the suggestion of Max from Change.org, I wrote another op-ed to submit once the bill passed. I tried not to cry while running in the Race for the Cure, an event to raise money for breast cancer research that Gammy had participated in before the disease took her life.

Finally those ten days came and went. I hoped the bill would pass without any drama via the hotline. But I prepared myself for the possibility of having to go bang on more doors at the Senate. When I told Mom that I had faith that the bill would pass, but no concrete answers as to when or how, I could tell her patience was wearing thin. On May 10th, the dogs got up at 4:51 a.m., so I had an early start to what I hoped would be the last day of waiting for Congress. I got my running clothes on and went out. The early morning spring air had a chill, perfect for outdoor exercise.

Throughout the day I received responses to the email inquiries I had sent the day before or early that morning. *It is moving. Not sure exactly when it will happen.* Congress had been trying my faith in our system of government over the past ten months, but I had to trust that this was about to end.

"All right dogs, let's go." I clicked the collars and leashes onto the dogs and opened the front door just as Mom was arriving home that evening.

"Any news?" Mom inquired.

"Don't ask." I replied. "I think we have a few more days to go."

Mom frowned.

The dogs paused to sniff a tree along our neighborhood walking route. The pocket of my hooded sweatshirt vibrated. I pulled out the cell phone and clicked to activate the screen.

There was an email from Senator Ernst's office.

Subject: VICTORY!!!!!

"Yes! Yes! Oh my gosh!" I startled the dogs as I shouted and jumped in the air. I bent over to pet them. "We did it you guys! Almost done!"

Even my two dogs that were approaching geriatric status managed to jog home so we could give Mom the good news.

"Mom!" I yelled as I removed the leashes.

No response.

I walked upstairs and popped my head in Mom's bedroom. "Mom!" Mom looked up from her computer perched on her lap.

"It just passed the Senate."

"All right!" Mom yelled. "Now to the president?"

"No. The Senate changed a couple words so it has to go back to the House for another vote," I informed her.

"What?" Mom asked. "How long will that take?"

"I don't know. I already spoke with Martha's office. She knew about this before the recess and I think they will get a vote quickly," I assured her.

"They better," Mom said.

The following morning, I went to the office still elated from the night before. I concentrated on work and not the emails filling my inbox inquiring about the status of the bill. I didn't have a good answer for them anyway.

I checked my phone before the drive home that evening. Seeing no news about the bill, I thought I would have to wait another day or two for it to pass in the House again. As I cut through a residential neighborhood to avoid some heavy traffic, my phone rang, so I pulled over to answer. Rain drops streamed down the windshield.

"Erin?" the voice on the other end asked. "It's Martha McSally!"

I hoped from the tone of her voice that she was about to convey good news.

"Yes! It's me!" I replied.

"I'm calling to let you know that the bill just passed the House for the second time!" She sounded as excited as I was.

"Awesome! Thank you!"

"We are going through the process to send it over to the president's desk," she informed me.

"Thank you for letting me know," I said. "And thank you for calling me yourself, I appreciate it."

"I wanted to let you know as soon as possible, I know your family has been waiting for this," she said.

"Thank you for everything. Thank you so much."

I hung up the phone and sat in the car listening to the rain while I processed the news: only one more step – a signature from the President of the United States.

* * *

The Constitution gives the president ten days to sign a bill into law. I hoped President Obama would not wait that long to sign this bill for Gammy. But again, when Mom inquired about it, I didn't have a definitive answer.

The day after the House had passed the bill for the second time, a reporter at the afternoon White House press briefing inquired about whether the president intended to sign it. The little light on my phone started blinking. I clicked the screen on and saw a tweet by a CBS News reporter sitting in the White House press room.

"Mom," I said into the phone.

"Yes," she replied from the other end, followed by a cough. She was at home in bed.

"The White House press secretary said that the president will sign Gammy's bill."

"Today?" she asked.

"I don't know, it said he confirmed the president will sign it."

She replied, "Well just tell me when I can call Arlington."

"Hey, I know you are sick, but can you take the dogs out? I am going to be home late."

"All right," Mom replied. "See you tonight."

I relaxed on the table as the needle worked the ink into my skin. I thought about everything that had happened in the past year to get to this point. Now calm had come over me. The constant state of anxiety was gone, replaced with excitement and gratitude.

I greeted the dogs when I got home and went straight to Mom's bedroom. I poked my head through the door to see if she was awake. I waved and she looked up.

"Hey," I said. I walked over and sat down on the bed in front of her.

"What's up?" Mom asked.

I held up my right arm. She took my forearm in her hand, held it three inches from her face, and squinted to try to discern the image.

"What is that? A tattoo?" she asked.

"Mom, where are your glasses?" I grabbed her glasses off the bedside table and handed them to her.

"H.R. Four. Three. Three. Six. One hundred and fourteenth Congress, second session." Her face showed confusion and disappointment as she read off the letters and numbers on my arm. "Isn't that... excessive?"

"Excessive?" I replied and laughed. "No way!"

She thought for a moment. "At least you can get it removed one day for a lot of money."

"Mom, I am not getting it removed," I said as I turned to walk out of her bedroom.

"Well," I heard her say. I paused to hear the rest of her thought. "It is excessive, but cool."

"Thank you." I smiled.

There was another burst of media stories after the White House confirmed the bill would be signed. Max confirmed that my op-ed would be published with Fox News. I wrote statements for a few press releases and did a couple interviews. I couldn't stop smiling and saying thank you to everyone.

Mom came home from picking up some things at Gammy's house, which had finally been put under a sales contract over a year after she passed away. Mom pulled out a familiar black velvet bag.

"Look what we found in the kitchen cabinet!" She pulled out the pen that President Obama had used to sign the Congressional Gold Medal bill for the WASP.

"Mom. Don't you remember that I found that in Gammy's desk last year and handed it to you to put with her WASP memorabilia? How did it end up in the cabinet?" I asked. "I am glad it didn't get lost!"

"Oh. You're right. I have no idea how it ended up in the cabinet," she replied.

"I think we need to give that to the College Park Aviation Museum immediately before it gets lost again," I suggested.

"Good idea." Mom continued to fish things from her big black purse while she stood in the living room. "We found this too." She held up Gammy's small replica Congressional Gold Medal attached on a chain by a holder fashioned by her WASP friend Shutsy Reynolds. "Rob and I talked. He suggested, and I agreed, that you should have this for all the work you did for Gammy in the past year."

"Thank you." I stood up from the sofa and went to take the necklace in my hands. I was moved. More than I thought I would be. I rubbed my thumb across the two faces of the coin depicting the women of the WASP on one side and the planes they flew on the other. The image of a few of the WASP pilots stepping across a line encircling their image portrayed their role in history of breaking barriers for women in military flight.

By Friday, May 20, 2016, I was wondering if the president would ever sign the bill as his press secretary had claimed he would eight days earlier. I watched my phone all morning, waiting for news. Around midday, I saw a tweet from the same White House reporter stating that the president had just signed our bill. The media stories had started back in December with a tweet to Andrea McCarren at the local news station, and here everything was coming full circle with a tweet about the bill signing. It was exciting but anticlimactic to learn from a tweet that the President of the United States had signed a bill into law to allow our family to finally lay Gammy to rest after more than one year of fighting.

I messaged my sisters and called Mom.

"Mom," I said as soon as she picked up the line. "You can call Arlington now."

"What?"

"The president just signed the bill," I informed her.

"All right!" she shouted. "Should I call now?"

"Actually, maybe you should wait until Monday," I told her.

She agreed.

I could not concentrate so I left work early and told my cousin I was coming over for her homemade mojitos.

Mom called Arlington National Cemetery the following Monday to ask about getting a date. As she started to explain the request, it became clear that the person on the other end of the phone was not familiar with anything that had been going on regarding the WASP. A lieutenant colonel within earshot of the conversation took over the phone call. He explained to Mom that the cemetery had reopened our case file from the previous year and placed Gammy back in line. He estimated it would be a week before he knew what dates were available, but he would call as soon as he had the information.

My first thought was that Congress was going into recess soon for the Memorial Day holiday. I had to make the first official invitation to the funeral. And it seemed like the kind of thing I should do in person.

* * *

"I came here to invite you to my grandmother's funeral at Arlington National Cemetery. Would you like to come?" I asked with far too much enthusiasm considering the topic of the request.

"Yes, of course!" Representative McSally was even more enthusiastic than the day I had first met her five months earlier sitting in this same office on this same space on her couch. I was relieved she was finding this a happy occasion too because I was so elated, even though I was discussing funeral arrangements, I couldn't stop smiling. The sun beamed in from the window behind her and over the photo of her dog which I remembered noticing back in January because Gammy would have appreciated it. "When is it?"

"We don't have a date yet. I hope that we get one when you are in town," I replied.

"It doesn't matter what day it is, I will fly back here for one day if I need to," she stated. She glanced at Justin, her chief of staff sitting across from me, who nodded in agreement.

"Really?" I asked. "Thank you. I hope that you don't have to though. They said they might be giving us a date this week, so I wanted to be sure to talk to you in person before the recess. They opened our old file and put us back in line..." I saw her eyes darting around as I spoke. "What?"

"Sorry, I can't help it, I am very distracted by your arm," she said.

"Right, you haven't seen this." I held my arm up for closer inspection.

"Wow. That's... big," she said with a smile. "Were you drunk when you did this?"

Justin and I both started laughing at her question.

"No! I've been thinking about this for months!" As she continued to marvel at my arm, probably convinced that I had indeed been intoxicated, I made more requests. "After the funeral, we are having a service at the Women In Military Service For America Memorial. I think my mom, and my sister Tiffany, and I, and somehow the WASP are going to speak. I haven't figured that part out yet. Would you like to speak at the memorial service?"

"Yes, I would be honored to speak," she replied.

I smiled. "And, because you haven't done enough for us, I have one more request." She laughed as I explained. I had learned a few things about her over the previous five months, one being that she often sings at community events. "My mom wants someone to sing, but I am a horrendous singer, as is most of my family. She thinks the Air Force song is something my grandmother would have liked. So, will you sing the Air Force song for us?"

She laughed again. "Yes, I can do that."

I thanked her profusely and gave her a big hug. "Oh, wait, we should take a photo," I exclaimed.

We stood together on one side of her office and I handed my phone over to one of her staff. Representative McSally turned to me and said, "You have to hold your arm up so we can see the tattoo in the picture!"

I gave her another hug, thanked her yet again, and headed for the door, but she stopped me. "Wait, I have to tell you something funny. When this started, another representative wanted to take the lead on this." My face changed at this revelation. "No, he's my friend, he's a good guy," she assured me.

"I'm sure he's great, but this would not have worked out the same way without you. You know that, right?" I explained.

"When I found out, I went to him and told him we can't have multiple people leading this. And he was like, well, how are we going to decide? So I asked him, 'Do you have pilot wings and ovaries?' And he said, 'No.' So, that's how it was decided." She laughed.

"What? That's hilarious," I replied. I was already on a high because of the funeral finally coming together and now there was such relief in this laughter after so many months of anxiety. The previous year, Congress seemed uninterested, and now I learned that back in January, representatives were actually arguing over who would help us. And now there was finally a funeral to plan.

16

Final Fight

May 2016

A Memorial Day tradition in the WASP community for many years was a gathering of the WASP and their families and friends in Sweetwater, Texas where they trained during World War II. The women of the WASP shared stories and signed autographs for fans surrounded by vintage planes. The National WASP World War II museum hosted the event, which it called "homecoming," in the hangar at Avenger Field, the dusty strip where Gammy and her cohorts earned their wings in the first half of the 1940s.

Around the time the bill passed the House, the author Sarah Rickman had suggested I come to the WASP homecoming. I couldn't commit at the time because I felt glued to Washington while the legislation was still pending. But after the president signed it into law on May 20, I bought a ticket to Texas. Whitney had moved to Texas so we arranged to go to the homecoming together. When I told the organizers at the WASP museum that we would be attending, they asked if I would speak at the luncheon and dinner and talk about the new law.

"Look what I got," Whitney held up a new onesie with "Gammy flew planes" printed on the front. Then she folded it and placed it into the suitcase in the middle of her living room floor. Isabella had outgrown her original onesie she had worn in January when we first met Representative McSally. After Whitney picked me up at the airport, we stopped by her house so she could finish packing. Then we headed out with Isabella in her car seat for the three and a half hour drive to Sweetwater.

I watched the hill country fade into a desert landscape and the expansive Texas sky opened up for all the stars to shine in the absence of city lights. "What a strange year," I said to Whitney as I stared out the window. After Gammy passed away, the furthest thing from my mind was that we would end up having to get a law passed to bury her.

"I can't believe how all this worked out. It is amazing," Whitney replied.

"This could have been a nightmare. We lucked out," I said. "We had exactly the right people to help us each step of the way."

"I know. We are so lucky," Whitney agreed.

* * *

The next morning, we made our way to Avenger Field and the WASP World War II museum for "Homecoming 2016." Unfortunately, neither Whitney nor I had ever attended with Gammy during her many trips to Sweetwater. Our first experience was bittersweet without her.

The day started at the wishing well, a legendary spot for the women of the WASP to toss coins for luck in passing through the program and to toss each other after completing their first solo flights. There were twelve WASP attending the reunion, a good showing for the hundred or so who were still alive. They sat side by side on the edge of the wishing well for a photo, some with their blue WASP scarves tied around their necks, others sporting their Congressional Gold Medal necklaces. Despite their current infirmities and gray hair, the exuberance of the young pilots who had flown at Avenger 70 years earlier was evident in the wide smiles of the twelve WASP gathered together that day.

Whitney and I finally met history professor Kate Landdeck in person. She greeted us with hugs and a big smile. I also finally got to meet WASP Nell Bright, who I had conversed with for media interviews by phone. I waved to Caroline, who had her long blond hair tied up in a bun, as she roamed the crowd in her green flight suit and tended to the WASP as if she was also one of their granddaughters.

Shutsy Reynolds recognized me immediately. She was a tall, no-nonsense lady with a gruff voice and a big heart. Shutsy pulled no punches and said exactly what was on her mind. "I'm so glad you're here," she exclaimed while holding tightly to my shoulders in a bear hug. "Thank you for what you did, and your family. I have no desire to be buried at Arlington, but you know, it's the principle of the thing!"

I started wondering if I had actually met any of these WASP before. I remember Gammy's friends being around the house when I was young, but whether it was these WASP women or some other friends, I couldn't say. Watching all the people in attendance who were so excited to be in the presence of these women made me think I had been taking Gammy's history for granted my whole life. At least two hundred people had traveled great distances just to be able to shake hands with one of the WASP, have her sign a poster, or speak for a few minutes with her. I had the honor of having one in my life for 38 years and we rarely talked about her WASP experiences. What I did gather from my years with Gammy was that more than anything she wanted her children and grandchildren to forge their own paths in life, unrestrained by the societal pressures that had permeated the lives of women from her era.

Everyone started making their way over to the building where the luncheon was being held. The organizers had asked us if we wanted to speak for a few minutes. Whitney said she didn't feel compelled to speak, so I spoke on behalf of our family.

As I was about to get up from our table and go to the podium, Whitney reminded me, "Make sure you include the 'Army said no to the wrong family' line, people love that!"

I hadn't written a speech, and I was only going to talk for a few minutes. I wanted to convey the good news and thank everyone for their support. I briefly explained that after Gammy passed away and her last request to be at Arlington National Cemetery was denied, we knew we wanted to fight for her and the other WASP to have the right to be at Arlington National Cemetery. I declared as Whitney had suggested, "The Army said 'no' to the wrong family!" The audience cheered. "I bring good news from Washington, D.C. I am proud to report it here in front of twelve WASP who are directly affected. Last week the president of the United States signed into law the bill to recognize the WASP as eligible to be at Arlington National Cemetery." The crowd stood up, clapping and cheering. The twelve WASP who were there smiled. I saw tears in the eyes of two or three of them.

Lieutenant Colonel Christine Mau, who flew the newest fighter plane in the Air Force, the F-35 stealth fighter, started her keynote speech. Gammy had told me on many occasions how happy she was when she saw the next generations of female military pilots succeeding in a career where women like herself had been excluded. Shortly after Christine started speaking, WASP Jean McCreery beckoned me from the next table over. I got up and moved over to her side, crouching to the floor so as not to block the view of the audience.

"I'm so happy about what your family has done. Did your grand-mother get the blanket I sent?" Jean said to me as she squeezed my hand.

"What do you mean?" I asked, trying to speak as quietly as possible, aware of being at the table directly in front of the podium.

"I sent a blanket with the WASP logo on it to her."

I thought for a moment and suddenly realized what blanket she was referring to. "Yes! She did receive it and she had it on her bed her entire time in the hospice. I have a photo. I can show you after lunch."

"I would love that," she told me. Then I snuck back to my own table to watch the rest of Christine's speech.

After lunch, everyone went to the WASP museum down the road from the wishing well. As Whitney and I walked to the entrance, we found WASP Marty Wyall, one of Gammy's close friends. For many years, especially during the 1970s during the lobbying for veterans benefits, Marty was the historian of the WASP. She helped keep track of the WASP and their documents. She stayed over many times at Gammy's house when she came to Washington, but I didn't remember if I ever spoke with her. Marty was a petite and sharp woman with striking gray hair and blue eyes. Caroline called Marty "the most full of love" person she had ever met and someone who was always generous with her time and flying stories. She exuded positive energy. Whitney and I both hugged Marty, who knew exactly who we were and conveyed condolences for our loss.

Inside the museum, there were tables set up for the WASP to sign autographs and chat with visitors later in the afternoon. Just beyond the museum's hangar doors was an exhibit with dozens of cement hand impressions and short biographies of the respective WASP. Whitney and I found Gammy's hand prints in cement. My hand fit right inside Gammy's hand impression. We looked up near the ceiling and searched for Gammy among the large headshot photos lining the periphery of the hangar. A display on one side of the museum held WASP memorabilia and explained the history of the WASP.

We passed to the hangar doors on the opposite side of the museum and went outside to see at least a dozen World War II era planes that enthusiastic pilots had flown there for the special occasion. We were excited to meet Alex Esguerra and his wife Tia, who spent twelve hours flying a restored BT-13 trainer from San Francisco all the way down to Sweetwater. Alex had taken Tiffany up for a ride earlier in the year in San Francisco. The BT-13 was the type of plane that Gammy spent many hours in as a WASP while training other pilots.

Whitney and I met more kids working on National History Day

projects about the WASP. One group was doing a performance piece about the history of the WASP. The teacher leading their group came and asked if we would be willing to talk to the kids about Arlington because they had been updating their performance with the information about the bill. I also met a pair of young ladies from Texas as well named Priscilla and Danielle who were doing their own project on the WASP for the national competition.

We mingled some more; there were so many people to talk to. I met several authors who were writing books or screenplays about the WASP or World War II. We took photos out by the WWII planes. I chatted with a few of the WASP. Then the history day kids performed for the WASP. They had even incorporated a song that the WASP used to sing during their training. As the young students recreated the vintage musical notes, I noticed a few of the WASP had tears in their eyes.

I spotted Jean McCreery chatting to a couple of people. I sat next to her and said, "I found the photo." I held up my phone for her to look at. I could see tears form in her eyes as she took in the scene: Gammy lying in the hospice bed, thin as ever, and sleeping under the blue blanket featuring the WASP logo that Jean had sent.

"Your grandmother was a great friend and a great person. I am so glad I knew her," Jean told me after looking at the photo for a while. At that point tears started welling up in my eyes too. I held them back as the couple she had been talking to recognized me from the luncheon and started asking questions about Gammy and Arlington National Cemetery.

There was a break for a few hours before dinner, so Whitney and I headed back to the hotel. While she and Isabella rested, I went to hang out with Caroline. I was happy to spend some time with her since we didn't get to see each other too often, despite the fact that she was living in Washington for the year.

"Come on, we have to go to Lana's room," Caroline instructed me. Lana had been a WASP supporter for years, even hosting the WASP at her home in Texas and organizing flights in private planes for them to the reunion.

Upon arriving at the room down the hall, Lana embraced me. Her positive energy poured out as she both consoled me on my loss and congratulated me about Arlington.

"I met your grandmother and I know she is proud of you and what your whole family did, standing up for the WASP," she beamed. "We were all following your story. I cried when I heard that the law was passed. I did, really!"

"Thank you," I replied, "I know there were a lot of people following along and supporting us. I can't stop saying thank you to everyone! I'm grateful that I can meet and thank some of them in person too."

When we arrived back at the WASP museum for dinner, there was a band playing military standards outside near some chairs organized to face the grass landing strip.

"Hello." The museum director greeted Whitney and me. "You all should have seats right in the front, come with me."

"Excuse me," I asked him. "What is going on?"

"Two WASP are having a memorial ceremony. Their ashes will be scattered over the air field. You two should have a front row seat," he explained.

I recalled that the WASP museum had asked us if we wanted to scatter Gammy's ashes there, but we declined and said we would fight to make sure she got into Arlington. Whitney and I sat down among the WASP in attendance and the families of the WASP who had passed on. As the sun set, a band member played taps while the honor guard lowered the United States flag. They folded and presented two more flags to the families of the WASP there who had taken their final flights that year: Gayle Mildred Snell, from Gammy's class 44-W-9, and Patricia Nethercutt Weaver, class 44-W-3. Christine, who had given the keynote speech earlier, and another military officer, carried the urns out to the grass landing strip and scattered the ashes in the wind as a World War II era plane did a low flyover across the setting sun.

I gave my condolences to each of the families of the WASP who had passed away. Then Whitney and I met WASP Shirley Kruse. I started calling Shirley "The Queen of Bling." Even in her WASP uniform, she brought style with oversized sunglasses and giant turquoise and silver rings adorning each finger on each hand.

I realized that in the not too distant future – likely two or three years – the annual WASP Memorial Day gathering at Sweetwater would transform from a reunion for these women pilots of World War II – all over 90 years old – into a remembrance of their lives, history, and legacy. I wondered if there would be enough enthusiasm and motivation for succeeding generations to carry on the tradition in their absence.

It started to get dark and we all headed inside for dinner. I gave another rendition of my speech from the luncheon. Whitney and I mingled with a lot of people while trying to eat our barbeque dinners. I talked some more with the National History Day kids and I promised to coordinate a visit with them when they arrived in Maryland for the national competition. Popular swing tunes from the 40s band playing in the background echoed throughout the hangar. Whitney headed back earlier than I did to take Isabella to bed. I stayed and sat with Caroline on a bench outside watching thunderstorms rage in the distant dark sky across the air field while I sipped a cocktail.

"This is so surreal," I said to Caroline. "Like maybe my grandmother sat here seventy years ago watching a thunderstorm too."

"I feel a certain energy when I'm here, like connecting with the past," Caroline replied. "I know what you mean."

"Hey, you have your Fifinella patch on," I pointed to the patch on the arm of her flight suit depicting the WASP mascot.

"I wear it every time I fly. I think I got it when I was an instructor pilot. I've probably flown two thousand hours with this patch on. I always think of how much I owe the WASP for doing what they did so I can do what I do."

"How did you learn about the WASP? At the Air Force Academy?" I asked.

"No. I decided I wanted to be a fighter pilot when I was pretty young. My dad was a pilot in Vietnam. But instead of discouraging me when I learned that women were not allowed to be fighter pilots, he took me to this air show where one of the WASP was. He said he wanted me to know about these women that flew during World War II, so ever since then I've been a fan," Caroline explained.

"Oh right, you said that at your talk at the Senate that one day," I replied.

"But I feel a deep connection with them. I think because we are all pilots, like they're my sisters. It sounds weird because they're so much older than me, but we can all relate because of our experiences flying."

"Making sure my grandmother got into Arlington helped me learn about another side of her that I never experienced growing up, the side you know as a pilot," I told her. "Today, meeting these women, it was like talking to my grandmother, they all have similar characteristics. Now I understand why people who aren't related to them find them so fascinating. I understand why being in Arlington was so important to my grandmother, to preserve this shared history. Today when Shutsy, Marty, and Shirley told me my grandmother would be proud of us for fighting for her, I felt a new connection to my grandmother even though she's gone."

Caroline smiled and held up her drink. "To the WASP!"

"To the WASP!" I said in response, clinking my glass to hers.

17

Final Fight

S weetwater was only the beginning of a busy summer.
Two weeks later, it was time for the National History Day
finals and the start of the formal funeral planning process. It
had taken that long to get an assigned funeral date from Arlington
because the cemetery administrators had Gammy's name recorded as
"Florence Harmon." Knowing Gammy would have come back from the
afterlife if possible to chastise us for letting that name be marked on
her plaque, Mom had to get the original birth certificate and prove to
Arlington National Cemetery that Gammy's official name was Elaine.
I never understood where Florence had come from. It was not on
her birth certificate, but had ended up on her marriage certificate. I
recalled a similar situation when I had taken paperwork to the Social
Security Administration office a few years earlier on Gammy's behalf
to correct her name with that agency. The employee at the desk said a
lot of people "from that time" started informally using other names
which had created inconsistent documentation. He wasn't surprised
by it. I didn't understand why Gammy had ever voluntarily taken on
the name Florence if she hated it. Another question I had failed to ask

her.

After sorting out the name problem, the cemetery offered us three dates. We had to nix the one at 9:30 a.m. because Caroline had informed me that flyovers were only allowed from 10 a.m. to 2 p.m. Finally we settled on September 7 at 10 a.m. and hoped it would work out for everyone.

The ceremony at Arlington National Cemetery required much less organization than a funeral elsewhere would have. The inurnment ceremony is performed multiple times a day there and they know their routine. We only needed to show up on time with Gammy's ashes and a burial flag, and then fill out paperwork.

The memorial service and flyover required more thought and preparation. The Women In Military Service For America Memorial was the obvious choice for the service location, especially since Gammy had approved of a gathering there in her funeral arrangements letter. Since this would no longer be the small informal collection of family Gammy had predicted, I had an idea to address each main facet of her life: the mother, the grandmother, and the WASP pilot. Mom contacted the family. I asked Caroline to be in charge of arranging the flyover since she had offered months earlier. She understood the logistics and permits required and knew the guys with the planes. Besides Scott, Caroline's friend who owned a P-51 named "Quicksilver" and had offered to do a flyover, a pilot named Brian with a T-6 had been calling Tiffany earlier in the summer to offer his plane for the funeral.

"Mom, I have been talking to this man from Idaho about the urn. I think it's cool," I said to her when she got home from work one day that June.

"Explain to me again," Mom replied as she put her purse down and started looking in the refrigerator for dinner.

"A man named John Sword in Idaho called. He told me he saw me in a news story on television that showed Gammy's box of ashes in the closet," I told her. "John makes urns and he said he couldn't imagine, after everything that has happened, us placing that generic plastic box of ashes from the crematorium in Arlington National Cemetery's Columbarium, so he wanted to donate an urn to us. He makes urns at his business called Everlasting Tree in Boise, Idaho and donates some of them to the families of veterans."

"Okay, but what is it going to look like?" Mom asked.

"I already got an email with photos, here look." I held my phone up for her to see.

Mom peered at the screen from a couple inches away since she did not have her glasses on. "Wow, that is beautiful! Is that wood?"

"It's called Padauk wood. He carved it himself. Cool right?"

"Do you think we can get Gammy's wings attached to the urn?" Mom inquired.

"Yes, he is going to put a plaque on it. We have to tell him what to inscribe and then he can also weld on the wings too," I explained.

"You know," Mom said. "Of all the things that have been going on for the last year, I did not even think about having to get a proper urn for her ashes. How lucky is it that this man called us?"

"I know," I responded. "Hey, you are going to meet the history contest girls tomorrow to see their project, right?"

"Yes, I think I understand where to go," Mom replied.

"Tell them good luck and I will see them on Tuesday," I said.

3,000 students from across the United States and other countries descended on the University of Maryland for the National History Day competition in the middle of June. Since the situation with Arlington National Cemetery began, I had met not only Avery and Jessee from Michigan, but several students in Texas, along with others who had contacted me online. Gammy would have been thrilled to know how many students were doing projects about the WASP – and how many more had learned something because of the press surrounding her posthumous fight with Arlington National Cemetery.

I met up with Avery, Jessee, and their families at the Metro station and we got to know each other as we rode down to Capitol Hill together.

Since their families were Michiganders, our first two stops were to visit with Senators Stabenow and Peters, who each congratulated Avery and Jessee for their achievement in making it to the final rounds of the National History Day competition. An aide gave us passes and had an intern escort us to the Capitol to watch the floor proceedings at the Senate, where we spotted Senator Stabenow chatting with her colleagues.

As we exited the Capitol, Avery asked me, "Is it time to meet Ms. McSally now?"

I laughed and checked my phone for the time. "We still have an hour and a half until our appointment. We can eat lunch while we wait."

We walked across Capitol Hill and parked our group of about a dozen people at a pizza place. The restaurant was crowded but we managed to find a spot outside on the patio where we talked and ate in the warm late spring weather.

"The office is small, not like the Senate offices we were in earlier," I said to Avery and Jessee. "If only you two and maybe just your moms could come, it will be less crowded."

The girls exchanged glances with their moms and then replied in unison, "Okay."

"Are you all ready to go?" I asked.

The girls hopped up and sprinted to the sidewalk.

"I think they're excited," I said to their moms who were both laughing.

As I began to walk down the sidewalk, I heard Avery's mom say, "Wait, we have a shoe change in progress."

Avery had stopped to put on her fancy sandals.

I laughed. "You are smart. I did the same thing when I was lobbying."

The five of us walked down Independence Avenue toward the House office buildings and the Capitol. "Have you two thought of any questions to ask Representative McSally?"

"Yes, I have a list," Avery said.

"What about you?" I turned to Jessee.

"I think I am going to be spontaneous," she replied.

"Oh, let's take a picture here, with the Capitol in the background," I suggested. We handed our phones to their mothers and posed for a photo.

As I had noticed was often the case, Representative McSally's office was a flurry of activity. A large group of people chatted to her in the hallway and several more waited in her office. After a couple groups had moved in and out of her interior office, Representative McSally emerged.

"Hey there!" she greeted me with a hug.

"Hi! I know you are busy, I appreciate this so much," I replied.

"Of course. No problem. Come in," she motioned for the girls to follow her.

Avery and Jessee settled on the couch near Representative McSally, who sat in an adjacent chair. The moms and I sat at the opposite end of the room to observe.

"Thank you for coming to see me. What would you all like to talk about?" Representative McSally asked.

Avery and Jessee glanced at our end of the room.

"Don't look at me! We've been talking all day," I said to them and laughed.

Avery spoke up. "We've been studying the WASP for our National History Day project and I learned that you were very inspired by the WASP. Could you tell me more about that?"

Representative McSally smiled and began to talk about how her career as a pilot in the Air Force resulted in her developing a friendship with some of the WASP and learning more about their historic achievements as pilots. Jessee chimed in with her spontaneous comments between Avery's meticulous questioning. More than once the girls broke out in hearty laughter at the responses from Representative McSally.

As the conversation came to a close, Avery's mom pulled out two envelopes. "The girls brought these for you and Erin." She handed one to me and passed one down via the girls to Representative McSally. Inside were thank you cards containing necklaces featuring the WASP Fifinella logo.

Representative McSally put her necklace on immediately and stood up to thank the girls. "This is so cool, thank you!"

As we left the building, Avery had to stop and change back into her sneakers out on the front steps.

"Did you all enjoy your meeting?" I inquired of the girls.

They both gushed and Avery replied, "That was amazing."

We had to hurry back to the Metro station and make our way to the College Park Aviation Museum. Our meeting with Representative McSally had started later and gone on longer than originally planned, which was good, but we needed to move along quickly. Fortunately the family members who had been waiting at the pizza place had already walked over to Union Station. These were my kind of people: efficient!

The College Park Aviation Museum was close to the Metro station, so we arrived on time. The assistant director gave us a personal tour of the museum and explained that the airport outside the windows was the oldest continuously operating one in the country. The Wright brothers had even done some training there. Andrea, the museum director, took all of us back into the archival area. They had already laid out a few of Gammy's documents on a table. The girls smiled as they put on the gloves Andrea had given them to handle the documents and photos. Andrea showed them around the collections room too.

"I have a few things to formally donate to the museum," I announced. I pulled out a small bag and a folder from my purse. "This is my grandmother's diploma from the WASP program. A letter from Jackie Cochran to my grandmother. And the pen that President Obama used to sign the Congressional Gold Medal bill in 2009."

"Wait, so you've been carrying those things around in your purse all day?" Jessee's aunt asked.

"Yes. I didn't want to leave them in my car," I explained. "And my family has already lost that pen twice."

Out in the parking lot after our visit, I had to rush off to see the other students at the competition down the street. I pulled two autographed copies of Amy Nathan's book, *Yankee Doodle Gals*, out of my car.

I leaned into the minivan. "I wanted to give each of you a copy of this book. This was my grandmother's favorite book about the WASP. My mom suggested I give you copies." I handed the books out to Avery and Jessee.

The girls smiled and replied in unison, "Thank you!"

"Erin, thank you for taking the time to do this," said Jessee's aunt. "You never know how small interactions with inspirational people will impact someone's life later on down the road."

"I'm happy to help some young people learn more about the history of the WASP, that's what my grandmother really wanted," I replied and waved as their van drove off.

* * *

In keeping with our family's realization that it was impossible to thank people too much or too often for their support on the campaign, Tiffany had planned a party in California. As we closed in on the end of June, we celebrated the passage of the law one beautiful evening at the Oakland Aviation museum, the perfect venue for such a gathering of aviation history enthusiasts. The tunes of the 1940s era singing group, The Jeweltones, echoed throughout the museum and family, friends, and supporters of the campaign chatted in the shadows of the vintage planes on display.

* * *

Each summer since 1970 (and earlier, before the event was moved to Oshkosh), hundreds of thousands of aviation enthusiasts gather in Oshkosh, Wisconsin for a week-long convention hosted by the Experimental Aircraft Association (EAA). There are air shows, lectures, workshops, souvenirs, history lessons, films, the latest industry news, exhibitions by businesses and schools, and planes. So many planes. Military planes. World War II warbirds. Vintage planes. Homebuilt planes. Aerobatic planes. Commercial planes. Helicopters too. The local air traffic control tower is the busiest one in the world during the week of the Oshkosh Airventure.

I had never heard of this Oshkosh airplane extravaganza prior to Caroline convincing me a few months earlier that it would be a good idea for me to accompany her when she flew up there to attend.

"It will be great," she told me. "I know a lot of people. I can introduce you to my favorites. I'm hoping to borrow a plane so we can fly ourselves." I thought it sounded fun, so I agreed to go along, not thinking much about what I was getting myself into.

Coincidentally, someone in the WASP network had also suggested giving a lecture about the Arlington situation would be a good feature for Oshkosh. The convention organizers agreed and invited me to give a talk.

"That's amazing!" Caroline replied when I told her about the Oshkosh lecture. "I was going to call you today. I can't go to Oshkosh."

"You're going to send me up there all alone?" I pleaded.

"You'll have fun, I promise! The WASP will be there, you'll be fine," she consoled me.

Once I started looking into it, I realized what a production this Oshkosh show was. Since I had to give a talk, I figured it would be best to be close to the event grounds. Apparently that meant camping, as I interpreted from Caroline's advice and from the online discussions.

As I approached the showgrounds in my rental car with my tent and sleeping bag in tow, I saw miles of open campground, rapidly filling up. Tents, motorhomes, and cars dotted the landscape, with ATVs and bicycles scurrying about.

"Welcome to Oshkosh!" came a hearty greeting from behind the check-in counter from a tanned clerk who looked like he had weathered many years of air shows.

"Thank you! It's my first time here." I presented my printed tickets.

"Great, you'll have fun. What brings you to Oshkosh?" he asked as he flipped through my tickets and searched for the appropriate wristbands and paraphernalia to give me.

"I guess the main reason is to give a lecture," I replied.

"Oh, what about?"

"My grandmother was a WASP, you know, from World War II? And she wanted to be buried at Arlington National Cemetery..."

"Wait! I know this story. I know you!" he interrupted. "And I know that!" He pointed to the tattoo on my arm, resting on the counter. "Hey, you guys, come here, it's the woman from the Arlington cemetery thing!" he announced to his co-workers who came over to say hello and marvel at my arm.

"Do you know when your lecture is?" he asked and flipped open the program schedule.

"Friday. But I don't know where to go," I said.

He opened the map and pointed out the Forum area where the lectures were held, then showed me a general area in the campground where I could set up my tent. The campground holds over 50,000 people during the show, and it requires its own street map to get around.

"Thank you. You've been so helpful." I didn't realize in that moment that I was about to repeat that conversation with almost every person I encountered for the next six days. It seemed like everyone there knew about "the Arlington cemetery thing."

I got back in my car and headed out to the campground to search for a spot to pitch the tent. I was in a hurry because I had made arrangements to meet some social media connections in person that evening and realized I would now be late because of the vastness of the event grounds. I didn't set anything up. I parked the car and walked off knowing that I would be setting up everything in the dark later on. I waved to a few people relaxing and preparing dinner at their campsites as I made my way through the maze of motor homes and mini tent cities.

When I arrived at the meeting location, there were only a few groups of two or three people left there chatting and I wasn't sure I was even in the right place. Most had huge professional cameras and media badges dangling around their necks.

"Hi. I am looking for Dave," I said to a friendly looking guy in a T-shirt and baseball hat.

"That's me! And who are you?" he extended his hand and I shook it.

"Erin Miller."

He looked a little confused, then exclaimed, "Oh! From Twitter! Right! Welcome! Did you get any bacon? We're all about bacon here." He pointed at a table with a dwindling supply of bacon of various flavors. He called over a couple other guys who wore aviation related T-shirts.

"Nice to meet you," I said as I shook their hands.

"You too," replied Ryan, a young guy about twenty years old with a camera around his neck. "How do you know Dave?"

"I don't... I just met him. I found him on Twitter. He said I could stop by, so here I am," I replied.

Dave chimed in, "You guys, this is the granddaughter of that WASP that wanted to be at Arlington cemetery."

Their eyes widened in recognition and we then proceeded to repeat the conversation from the campground check-in.

"But where are you staying?" Dave inquired.

"In the campground," I informed him.

"Where in the campground?" he asked. "It's big."

"I might have to get the map out. I went through the gate, then right for a while, then right again, then into a field..." I described my car trip through the campground.

"What? Way out there? No, no. You have to come to our camp area. Right guys?"

The guys nodded in agreement.

"Our camp would love to have you. Come on, you can have dinner. Elyse is making gumbo. Okay, it's decided."

After retrieving my car and setting up the tent among a group of RVs and tents, I walked into the main area of the self-proclaimed "Camp Bacon." This group of aviation enthusiasts, specifically, Oshkosh enthusiasts, had been coming here for years and had grown into a little community within the air show campground. About thirty people milled about sitting in lawn chairs and at picnic tables, and standing by a central campfire. I spotted Ryan and Dave from earlier and they introduced me around to the denizens of Camp Bacon as well as the "mayor."

I sat down with a bowl of homemade gumbo at a picnic table full of campers. They were all chatting excitedly about aviation issues, half of which I didn't understand. A blonde-haired woman across the table extended her hand across to me. "I'm Tracey, nice to meet you."

"Erin. Nice to meet you too."

"You're new here, how did you end up here?" she inquired while she ate.

"I just met Dave earlier and I guess I looked like a lost puppy so they brought me here. I've never been here before. It's so nice of you all to let me stay," I explained.

"Well, we are happy to have you! Are you a pilot?" Tracey asked.

"Nope," I replied.

"We'll have to change that." She squinted at my arm. The sun was down but the twilight sufficed to discern something unusual there. "What is that?"

I held my arm up. "It's a tattoo for my grandmother. She was a WASP and..."

"The Arlington cemetery thing! Right? That's you? I followed that!

275

I signed your petition! It's so nice to meet you!" She squealed with excitement. "You definitely belong here! You're like a celebrity!"

I laughed. "I don't know about that."

"Trust me," she offered. "Around here, you'll see how it is. Did you come to Oshkosh for fun? Or some other reason?"

"I am giving a talk on Friday."

"Oh, where? I'll come," Tracey offered.

"Thank you! That's nice of you. At least I know there will be one person there." I gave her the information. After mingling with the rest of the campers for a while, I headed back to my tent in my new little temporary home in Wisconsin.

The next few days were a blur of WASP-related activities. The first stop was the Women in Aviation International breakfast. After learning I would be speaking at Oshkosh, I realized how many activities the Women in Aviation International (WAI) group would be sponsoring to encourage and promote women's participation in the aviation industry. Having organizations with hundreds of thousands of members, like WAI, publicly supporting the campaign, had added to its legitimacy and helped publicize our mission. Their leadership and members had been supportive of the Arlington campaign since the beginning, so I wanted to thank them in person.

I arrived a couple minutes late since I misjudged the expanse of the event grounds. I found an open pavilion teeming with hundreds of women in green shirts chatting at rows and rows of picnic tables. I grabbed some food and found my way to the front of the room. I greeted Dr. Chabrian, the President of WAI, as she was making her way to the microphone to start off the speeches. I was flattered that they were letting me speak for a few minutes given the impressive résumés of the main speakers: Sherry Carbary, a Vice President from Boeing, Jackie Nesselroad, Boeing director of the teams building the rocket to go to Mars, and Jessica Cox, who, despite being born without arms, had qualified as a pilot.

Everyone was cheering as I came up to the microphone after Dr.

Chabrian's kind introduction. I looked out at the sea of over 400 faces and realized it was a group of people who all knew exactly how much the WASP had contributed to their own chosen profession or hobby of flying. I had been explaining the WASP history for months, often to people who had no idea who they were. I didn't need to explain the historic role of the WASP here; these women were aware that females still made up a tiny percentage of pilots – military or civilian. I did my best to convey how much their support meant to our family and to the women of the WASP who were still alive, four of whom were sitting there in the front of the room.

"I want to thank Dr. Chabrian for letting me speak for a few minutes. I wanted to thank you all for your support. I am happy to say we had so many people supporting us, it was impossible to respond to everyone personally. But I want you all to know that each signature on the petition, comment on a news article, Facebook post, Tweet, call to a congressperson, we saw it and our family felt all of it."

After the speeches, I went to chat with the WASP who were there: Shirley Kruse, Marty Wyall, and Shutsy Reynolds, all of whom I had just seen in Texas, and Dawn Seymour, another of Gammy's friends who I was meeting for the first time. People kept coming to take photos of them and to thank me for standing up for the WASP.

"Come on Erin, we have to go." Shutsy ushered me out of the pavilion.

"Where are we going now?" I asked.

"Hold on to my arm. I need someone to lean on. This way," Shutsy instructed me. We meandered away from the pavilion across a grassy area with our arms linked while Shirley walked alongside.

We arrived at a tent nearby. Inside, about 50 teenage girls eagerly awaited the arrival of the famous World War II pilots. The four WASP set themselves up front on stools and passed a microphone between them while telling flying stories. I had never seen Gammy at any of her numerous talks but I imagined her being as animated as these four. Watching them speak was stoking a growing fire of regret inside me. I had missed out on so much with Gammy, but not intentionally. I didn't recall ever being invited to her talks. It was so much a part of her identity, but not something she seemed to want to overwhelm us with, but now I wished that she had.

The girls in the audience were mesmerized by these women of history talking about barrel rolls, dusty air fields, and being told to "look pretty" when they had been flying around in the Texas heat and dust all day sweating into their oversized men's jumpsuits. I knew from the letters Gammy received that she had the same effect on schoolkids during her life. I also recalled her telling me that Jackie Cochran expected them to brush their hair and put on lipstick after they landed and that Gammy had begrudgingly complied by carrying around a hairbrush and lipstick along with her parachute.

"They didn't want women to fly. They tried to stop us. But we did it anyway. And you can too. Don't let anyone stop you," Marty advised the enchanted girls. Gammy had said similar things to me and to all her grandkids throughout our lives. The four WASP must have talked for an hour but for me it passed in an instant. I saw how revered and respected these women were by both the girls in the audience and the adults dotted around the edge of the tent. One woman was crying. I had teared up seeing what the WASP represented to people who were not their blood relatives. People took all their stories to heart – stories that harkened back to a time when many women didn't even have driving licenses. Here was a group of women who had flown military planes in a time when women "just didn't do that." Yet I knew Gammy and all these women didn't think about blazing trails or breaking glass ceilings, all they cared about was serving their country and flying planes. They became inadvertent symbols of equality, but it took decades.

Each year at Oshkosh, Women in Aviation International also gathered as many female attendees as possible sporting their organization's T-shirt in the color of the year (this year was Kelly Green) to take a photograph from high above the crowd. I was distracted and had forgotten to ask for a shirt. I ended up in the middle of the crowd in a black dress, with my blue WASP scarf, huddled among Shirley, Dawn, Shutsy, and Marty. There were over 400 women at breakfast, and even more had appeared for this photo – a huge crowd of female pilots and aviation enthusiasts encircling four women whom they each might name as an aviation inspiration. After the photo, like rock stars rushed by fans, women surrounded the WASP to request autographs and photos. I spotted Dawn signing the back of one woman's green shirt with a black marker.

When I described learning more about the WASP from a different perspective, people often said that I took Gammy's presence in my life for granted. I didn't think that was accurate. I thought of taking something for granted as having an understanding of it and then not appreciating it. What happened while I was growing up was that I appreciated what Gammy had done, but I didn't fully understand it.

Some grandmothers did needlepoint. Gammy went off to schools and gave lectures about being a pilot during World War II. I wasn't involved with her endeavor to educate the world about the WASP. I knew there weren't that many of them, but I didn't know exactly how rare they were. Like most people of the "Greatest Generation," Gammy didn't boast about her wartime flying experience. She saw it as a necessary service for which she held a rare qualification. It generally didn't come up in conversation unless she was preparing for a talk or event, or had received a letter from a student or one of her WASP friends. As a child, I interpreted her humility to mean her service was not important.

The day after the breakfast panel, I watched Gammy's friends chat about their time in the WASP program in a panel discussion moderated by Professor Kate Landdeck. A theater full of admirers listened as Marty, Shutsy, Shirley, and Dawn talked about their time flying during World War II. Dawn was another no-nonsense lady like the rest of the WASP. She was in one of the earlier classes in 1943 and had accumulated a wider range of flying experiences than Gammy had during her service. Dawn trained to be a B-17 pilot, eventually spending 200 hours in the aircraft. She also co-piloted the B-26.

"I always think of our motto: we live in the wind and the sand but our eyes are on the stars," Dawn said before passing the microphone on.

What I learned from Marty that day was that she was supposed to be in Gammy's class. "I arrived in Sweetwater, ready to go for class 44-9," she explained. "But they told me that my medical certificate had never arrived so I had to go home and get it. I went all the way back to Indiana to the military doctor who had done my exam. I asked where my medical certificate was. He told me that he didn't think women should be flying so he had not mailed it to Texas. Well, I about got up and stomped on his desk. I said well I should at least have the chance to try and if I fail, then I fail, but I should at least have a chance. I may have said some other things too," she winked as she said this and the crowd laughed. "So finally he gave me the certificate, but I was too late then to rejoin my class back in Texas, so that's how I ended up in the last class."

I learned about one of Shutsy's experiences with discrimination. "I saw an advertisement in the paper for the Civilian Pilot Training Program. I knew I had wanted to fly since I was a kid. My family thought I was crazy. I grew up on a chicken farm! But I signed up anyway. I learned after signing up that there were flight scholarships for the top five of the class. And I was in the top five, so they gave me a scholarship. But a little while later they called and said they were rescinding it because it was supposed to go to the men. I told them they had given it to me and they couldn't take it back. That was stealing! We had some arguments, but I won in the end and they let me keep the scholarship."

Shirley strolled into the theater near the end of the discussion. She had been off flying around in a warbird, a P-51 Mustang. She radiated from the excitement of her flight, and gave the audience a wave with her bejeweled hand.

At the end of the panel discussion, the audience crowded around these four women. They took photos, asked questions, and got autographs. Being in the presence of the WASP brought joy to these admirers of all ages, ranging from little kids to adults who looked almost the same age as the WASP. I imagined Gammy getting the same treatment from her lecture attendees and was glad that she had brought happiness into the world along with her history lessons.

On the morning of my lecture, I did my best to look professional – more of a challenge while camping. I blow dried my hair outside in the sun and did makeup in a small spotty mirror attached to the exterior wall of the shower building. I put on my backpack and walked across the fairgrounds to the lecture pavilions.

The pavilion was empty when I arrived. As I set up the presentation on the computer, I wondered if anyone besides Aunt Chris and her family, and Tracey from the campground would show up. People trickled into the pavilion as the assigned time approached. It ended up being a packed house with over 200 people.

"Welcome everyone. Thank you for coming." I spotted Tracey in the front row and gave a small wave. "My name is Erin Miller. I am here to talk about my grandmother, Elaine Harmon, one of the Women Airforce Service Pilots, and my family's campaign to grant her last wish of being laid to rest at Arlington National Cemetery."

In the middle of the lecture I noticed that Shutsy and Dawn had snuck into the back row, along with Professor Kate Landdeck. After my last slide, I announced, "If anyone wants to thank a WASP, there are two right there in the back row!" Everyone in the audience stood up and cheered while facing the back of the pavilion. Dawn and Shutsy made their way to the front of the hall. Audience members surrounded them, wanting to shake hands or take a photo.

18

Final Flight

April 2015

T he last photograph I took of Gammy was solely of one of her hands. Gammy had been in hospice care for ten days since she had experienced a series of seizures causing her body to spasm uncontrollably on April 10, 2015. At the hospital emergency room, the doctors determined that there was nothing to cure her, so her health directive came into play, meaning they would take no more life-saving measures. Since Gammy's body wouldn't stop seizing, the doctors administered drugs to relax the seizures and reduce pain, but nothing to cure her or extend her life like food or water. An ambulance transferred Gammy to Casey House Hospice near Rockville, Maryland.

Casey House was a beautiful hospice center — a relaxing, tranquil place to temporarily accommodate people leaving this world. The staff members were all angels doing amazing work. It was open to visitors 24 hours a day. Families could bring their dogs and there were also organized therapy dog visits. Mom slept in Gammy's room at night on a chair that folded out flat. And fortunately because of the veterans benefits that Gammy and the other WASP had fought for decades earlier, the hospice was part of her VA healthcare plan.

I came to visit every day. Mom did not go to work for the duration of Gammy's stay, spending almost 24 hours a day at the hospice. Other relatives came and went. We had a stream of visitors for the first few days including Navy nurses and doctors from the Veterans Affairs hospital in Washington, D.C.

It was surreal knowing what was happening but being powerless to help. I hoped that by being present we all assisted in some way because there was nothing else for us to do. I lay in the bed with Gammy sometimes or just held her hand. On a regular basis, about every four hours, she started writhing and scratching at her skin. The nurses came in and changed her morphine patch which calmed her down again. We kept a blue blanket with the WASP logo emblazoned in gold draped over her. I believed she felt our presence even if she couldn't acknowledge it.

I incorporated the hospice into my daily routine. I went to work, walked the dogs, and then went to the hospice for the night. There was a particular smell there, a combination of the extreme sanitary odor of a hospital with a more welcoming smell of fresh linens – a smell I will never forget.

Since I was there in the evenings, Mom and I usually got takeout for dinner from a nearby restaurant and ate together at the large table in the dining area of the hospice's common room. One night as I was eating chicken and rice, a woman frantically exited a patient room and yelled "My daughter just died!!" Then she started sobbing and hyperventilating. The staff went to comfort her and carry on their responsibility to the deceased patient. Even though visitors consciously knew why they were there, it still came as a surprise when the patient died. Life went on for those left behind. I continued eating my meal and wondered to myself when Gammy's last moment would arrive.

The hospice gave us a booklet which outlined the last stages of life. I thought of it in my head as the "countdown to death" book. Based on this book, Gammy had fewer than 14 days to live.

The first two days, she had been somewhat alert. She could not speak clearly, but could acknowledge yes or no to simple questions. It was obvious she was confused about her situation, being in a foreign room after spending her entire life at home. Mom had brought photographs and mementos from home per the advice of the nurses. She tried repeatedly to get out of bed and leave. Gammy was strong enough to stand up, but couldn't maintain balance. We held her for a while in her half-erect stance and then eased her back into bed after she reluctantly acquiesced to her own inability to walk away.

Perhaps the only good thing about the slow demise was the time it gave the family to say goodbye. My sister Tiffany came from California as soon as she could after I told her the book predicted Gammy had 12 to 14 days remaining. Whitney was in and out since she did not live too far away. My cousin brought their family's dog that had been living with Gammy for several years to the hospice each day as well. Even after Gammy could no longer communicate or react to us, I liked to think she felt the dog's presence. Mom went and picked up Gammy's lone surviving sister one day so they could have a final visit. She brought flowers.

Gammy adored dogs and she especially loved my Shiba Inus with their curly tails and fluffy coats. I showed her photos of them on my cell phone. She reached to touch the screen and smiled. The screen changed photos when she touched it, which confused her. Then I brought the dog photo up again. I realized she was trying to pet my dogs. Videochatting one day with Tiffany's husband and daughter in California also brought joy to Gammy's face. She didn't seem to have any idea that photos or video chats were only electronic. It looked to me like Gammy thought the dogs and my niece were right there with us. I was glad her brain was playing that trick on her. That was the last day she actively responded to anyone.

Although she slept most of the time in the hospice because she was on so many medications, it was obvious when they started to wear off as she began to fidget and to try to remove her clothing. Those were the opportunities to hold Gammy's hand and talk to her, even if she didn't acknowledge us. The nurses came in to administer more medication. It was hard to watch her agitation, remembering what she had said to me before her surgery a couple years earlier. She wanted to escape from this world, but was trapped here. She was essentially starving to death and being medicated through the pain of the process.

Her decline continued as predicted by the death book: increasing agitation, inability to communicate, weight loss, reduced output of fluids, and removal of clothing. The nurses at the hospice had comforting words about this process. One told me that Gammy was at the train station, but hadn't gotten her ticket yet. Mom and I had some discussion about the sudden attractiveness of euthanasia. "This makes me wish we had taken her to Oregon," Mom commented from a bedside chair. As I watched Gammy in a rare moment of peaceful rest, all I could do was tilt my head with an understanding nod.

After about ten days, I peeled back the WASP blanket and saw her extremely blue hands. According to the book, this was one of the final signs in the "hours remaining" category. I took a photo to send to my sisters. This was the last photo I took of Gammy, of her mottled blue hand. Shortly thereafter, the "death rattle" began. According to the book, that meant death was imminent.

More than one hospice staff member told me that they had observed patients who waited to pass away until they had seen everyone they needed to see. Even if the presence of visitors seemed unacknowledged by the patients, they held on for that missing link. I guessed for Gammy that missing link was Aunt Chris. Many members of the family and others who knew Gammy had stopped by or had been there regularly like Mom. After ten days, Aunt Chris still had not visited. She showed up on April 20 and Mom decided to let her younger sister sleep in their mother's room that night. Her hands were blue and she had lost a lot of weight. Gammy's breaths were rattling like the crunch of pebbles underfoot in a shallow puddle.

I looked at Mom while I squeezed Gammy's hand. As I walked out the door, I turned toward the bed and said, "Goodbye, Gammy." I guessed that I would not see her alive again after I walked out. I was right. Gammy passed away after midnight that evening, April 21st, 2015.

19

Final Flight Final Fight

September 7, 2016

I was awake before the alarm went off and got in the shower before everyone else woke up. I hadn't slept much, but it didn't matter, I was energized for the day ahead. Everything had been leading up to this day. With so much time to plan ahead, it was only a matter of execution now. We had waited almost 17 months for Gammy's funeral.

The weather predictions for this momentous day had varied over the previous week since a hurricane had brought wind and rain and floods to the southeastern part of the country. Fortunately the hurricane had dissipated by midweek and the sun was out in Arlington, Virginia for the day we had been anticipating. Weather was more of a concern than usual because six World War II planes were planning to make a pass over the ceremony and hurricane force winds would have grounded them. Considering people had volunteered such effort to provide this special honor for Gammy and the WASP, it would have been a shame to cancel it. The weather was one of the few things we could not control and we had lucked out.

The house was full with Whitney and Tiffany and their families in town. An important day for laying the matriarch of our family to rest had become exponentially more so given that people around the world were following our family's story. Tiffany had been working on her speech until at least midnight the prior evening. Mom fretted about whether we had all our necessities: the printed speeches, the flowers, bowls of Hershey kisses, and of course Gammy's urn. There were my two nieces to dress, both under two years old and not quite ready for such an early wake-up call. Although the limousine arrived fifteen minutes early, we left at least fifteen minutes late. With car seats, infant accessories, and getting eight people prepared for a funeral, it took time.

"We have the flowers?" Mom asked.

"Yes, they're in the limo. Let's go," I encouraged everyone.

"Where is Gammy?"

"I put her on the floor in the limo," I responded.

"Should she be on the floor?" Mom inquired.

"Well, what if one of us is holding her and then the limo driver brakes hard and we drop her? That seems bad. The floor is safer," I said. The last thing we needed was to spill ashes that we had been safeguarding for a year and a half.

The blue neon interior lighting shone on Mom's face as she studied her eulogy while the limousine crawled through the heavy Washington rush hour traffic. Tiffany tried to keep her toddler daughter from wailing too much. Isabella wanted food. I spent the entire ride fielding emails and phone calls from reporters and guests needing information.

"Hello. Hi!" I said to the caller on the other end of the line. "Yes, number two Arlington Drive. Right. Okay! I am so glad you're coming! Okay, bye."

I hung up but had to check the information that I had given over the phone, leading me to realize I hadn't put the address of the memorial on the invitation.

"Oh crap," I blurted out. I started dialing my phone.

"What?" Whitney asked.

"Ugh, I just gave the wrong address to Greta Van Susteren, I am such a jerk." I turned to speak into the phone. "Hi, Greta? Sorry, the address is number two Memorial Avenue, I am so sorry! Yes, we are still in traffic, so we are going to be there later than I wanted to be there. See you there." I started laughing after I hung up. "I am so awful, people are coming to the funeral and I am not even giving them the right address!"

As we exited onto George Washington Memorial Parkway, cars were stopped for the usual rush hour traffic to the Pentagon. The limousine crept along for the final mile until we made it to the entrance of the cemetery about an hour after we had left the house.

"Oh man. You have to be kidding me!" I exclaimed.

"What?" Whitney asked. I pointed and she turned around to look behind her. A group of cemetery workers with signs were picketing at the gates of the cemetery.

"The cemetery workers are on strike? Today? Of all days? Well, this fits right in with everything else I guess, the blizzard, the terrorists, the crazy election." We reached the police officer directing traffic and he waved us through to the back gate. The officer said nothing about the impact of the striking workers, so I assumed everything would go ahead as planned.

As we pulled up to the administration building, I saw Greta leaning against the railing outside. I was glad that she had arrived despite my mishap with the address. There was already a huge crowd there gathered in the building and spilling out onto the entryway. I spotted three of the WASP in their blue jackets and scarves with people swarming to chat with them. I grabbed the flag and Mom took the urn inside. Tiffany and Whitney unloaded their respective children.

"I'm so sorry!" I apologized to Greta as I made my way up the ramp to the administration building where guests gather prior to the funeral ceremonies at Arlington National Cemetery. "Come inside." I gave awkward hugs with the flag tucked under my arm to several people on the way in and greeted everyone. We made our way to the small waiting room assigned to us, which in no way would fit over 200 expected guests.

I had wanted to be there first so I could greet people as they arrived, but traffic had thwarted that plan. We made our way into the reception room and I first tried to find the folks that were participating in the memorial service. John Sword, who had made and donated the urn, had traveled all the way from Idaho with his wife. He had some sand from Avenger Field which he wanted to insert in a special compartment below the ashes in the urn. Since we hadn't arrived as early as planned, we had to figure out how to do this with all the guests around.

Mom placed the urn on the table in the waiting room, flanked by flowers in the two wooden vases also made by John. People kept commenting on John's beautiful custom woodwork. It was sad to think we would be placing the urn in a wall soon, never to be seen again.

Mom found Petula Dvorak from *The Washington Post* in the lobby and proceeded to explain that her article back in March had single-handedly restored Mom's faith in that newspaper to report on worthwhile stories.

Guests continued to stream in. Gammy's three WASP friends, Shirley, Shutsy, and Marty, barely even made it inside with all the photo requests and conversations. Two of Gammy's favorite authors were there, Amy Nathan and Amy Goodpaster Strebe. Amy Nathan brought a copy of *Yankee Doodle Gals*, one of Gammy's favorite books featuring the WASP, and she had some of the guests sign it for us. Kate Landdeck came from Texas; she said she would not have missed Gammy's funeral for anything. WASP Helen Cannon's grandson came with his family. Julie Englund, who had fought with Arlington National Cemetery in 2002 over military ceremony rites for her mother who had been a WASP, was there as well.

I went back outside to check on the WASP and instead encountered

FINAL FLIGHT FINAL FIGHT

Senator Ernst, dressed in a bright purple blazer, Gammy's favorite color. I gave Senator Ernst a big hug and thanked her for coming. I had seen recent news stories stating that the approval rating of Congress was at an all-time low – nine percent in one story I saw – meaning almost everyone in the country thought Congress was doing a terrible job. And here all I wanted to do was give everyone in Congress a hug for making sure this day happened.

I accompanied Senator Ernst into the building where we came upon Mom, who handed me the urn so she could hug the senator and then introduce the chaplain, who was on her way out to the grave site.

Then the funeral coordinator came to get Mom and me to fill out the official paperwork to transfer the urn to the cemetery. We sat in a small cubicle behind the front desk in the lobby and listened as he explained the procedures and Mom signed documents. There was so much excitement surrounding us, it left no time to dwell on this formal act of giving Gammy away.

Then he asked for the burial flag, so I handed over the one Caroline had given us. He opened the box and told us it was the wrong kind of flag because the stars were too small. Mom was annoyed because the directions she had received from the cemetery had not explained the flag requirements in such detail. I had read on the website for the cemetery that the flag had to be burial length, 9.5 feet, which it was. However, there was no explanation of flags coming with different sizes of stars. In any case, the cemetery representative said this happened "often," which I interpreted as a sign that they don't clearly explain the requirements for the flags. Fortunately, they had one to give us. I was disheartened, but couldn't show it because Mom was unaware of the surprise related to the flag from Caroline. I ceded my seat to John so he could place the special sand in the urn.

I found Greta and Representative McSally chatting together in our assigned room.

"You're here!" I reached out to embrace Representative McSally. "Thank you for coming."

"Of course," she replied. "I wouldn't miss it."

"And you're wearing your necklace!" I pointed to the WASP Fifinella necklace around her neck that Avery and Jessee had given her when we visited a few months earlier. She held it up proudly. I took a photo and sent it to the girls.

The funeral coordinator came back to the room to funnel everyone outside to start the vehicle procession to the grave site. The limousine pulled up and we all climbed in. It followed the funeral coordinator's car carrying Gammy's urn. At the grave site, we poured out of the limousine in front of a roped-off line of at least 30 reporters and photographers who immediately began snapping away. There were some unfamiliar faces in the media gaggle but I recognized most of them as they had been covering the story since the beginning of the year. I waved to Andrea McCarren and Bunce, the service dog in training, and knew Gammy would be happy that a dog was attending the funeral. Bunce was even dressed in a bow-tie for the occasion. I spotted Shannon Perrine from WTAE in Pittsburgh, who had paid her own way to come down and cover the funeral because the story was that important to her.

As the rest of the family arrived and emerged from their vehicles, most were taken aback by the level of media coverage facing them. I knew Gammy would not have been interested in reporters for herself, but I imagined that the exposure to the history of the WASP because of the news stories from the funeral and the fight to ensure it happened would have made her proud. We even had a reporter from the Czech Republic news service. When he had contacted me to ask about attending, he said people there were fascinated by this positive story about a World War II veteran.

David Martin, the reporter who had done the *CBS Evening News* interviews, broke away from behind the press gaggle's rope to shake my hand before the Air Force guards began the ceremony.

"Erin, I wanted to say hello before everything started," David said quietly as he shook my hand.

"Thank you for being here, I appreciate it," I replied.

As the designated family photographers and videographers, Shane and his team from DC Visionaries, and photographer Scott Nolen, recorded the event for us unencumbered by the official press rope line.

We all gathered in the street near the small ceremony pavilion and waited. Representative McSally asked if she should hold on to Shutsy and the other WASP. I told her yes please, if she wouldn't mind. She took it to heart, because every time I saw her after that she was holding onto the arm of at least one, if not two, of the WASP ladies, and smiling. It was obvious that she enjoyed being around her World War II aviation predecessors.

A tradition at many military funerals, especially for pilots, is to have planes fly over the ceremony. Arlington National Cemetery will arrange when possible for high ranking generals to have flyovers of armed services planes. Gammy was not of high enough rank (her status as an officer was a fight for another day) to qualify for the cemetery's official flyover. But, as with many things during the campaign, we had volunteers offer to perform a special flyover.

Caroline had mentioned a flyover back in January and had been itching to make sure it happened. A friend of hers named Scott Yoak owned a P-51 Mustang called "Quicksilver" that he flew regularly at air shows. Scott volunteered before we even knew the funeral would happen. Then a man named Brian, who had contacted Tiffany initially through the petition, offered to participate in the flyover with a T-6 Texan named "Miss Olympia," that he owned with two friends. It was only after they had acquired it that they started looking into the history of the plane and discovered the military serial number inside. After further research, they found that the plane had been flown at Avenger Field during World War II. Scott, along with Brian's group of friends, and several other pilots volunteered with a total of six vintage planes – three T-6 Texans and three P-51 Mustangs – to do a flyover.

Scott and Caroline arranged the paperwork with the FAA for the flyover. Since Arlington National Cemetery is within the restricted air space over Washington, a flyover there requires special permission and detailed flight plans. It was supposed to take place at the closing of the funeral, but I got a text from Scott while we were in the administration building signing the funeral paperwork that the time had changed to 10:04 a.m. – the start time of the funeral ceremony.

A loud buzz signaled the arrival of the T-6 Texans and everyone looked up to the sky searching for them. Three appeared from the east over the Pentagon, including "Miss Olympia," which had possibly been flown by one of the WASP watching from the cemetery below. Shirley, Shutsy, and Marty smiled and poked each other on the arms when the planes flew overhead.

I heard Representative McSally ask one of the WASP, "Does this bring back memories?"

"Oh yes," was the reply in a wavering voice of one of the WASP, holding back tears. Two P-51 Mustangs followed (instead of three, one of the pilots had thrown his back out that morning), including "Quicksilver."

The official ceremony commenced when we all followed the chaplain and two airmen carrying the urn and the burial flag to the pavilion for the ceremony. There were ten chairs arranged in two rows of five set in front of the table where the urn rested. Mom and her siblings sat in the first four seats as we had discussed earlier in the week. The three WASP sat in the back row and Gammy's set of triplet great grandchildren smooshed themselves in the remaining two chairs. I took Representative McSally's arm and started leading her to the remaining empty chair in the first row.

"You sit up here," I said to her.

"Are you sure? Shouldn't someone in the family sit there?" Representative McSally asked.

"You're basically family now. Come on," I replied with a smile. I squeezed her arm and then ushered her over to the seat. I walked back to stand behind Mom. I never even considered sitting in the other chair. If Representative McSally hadn't helped us, I don't know that we even would have been there. Regardless of how many petition signatures we got, how many articles supporters wrote, or how many news stories we did, the bottom line was we needed a law passed in Congress and someone there to stand up for Gammy and this little known group of female veterans from World War II. That is what Representative McSally did for our family and for all the women of the WASP. The perfect person to help us had found us. I wanted Representative McSally to have a front row seat to what she helped accomplish.

The remaining two hundred or so guests, including Senator Ernst who I had unfortunately lost track of after the flyover, gathered behind and around the ceremony pavilion as the chaplain began the ceremony. She opened with a bit about the history of the WASP and recited some of the anecdotes Mom and I had told her about Gammy. Occasionally, an airplane taking off from Reagan National Airport drowned out the chaplain's words and she paused to allow the noise to taper off. It reminded me of the *NBC Nightly News* interview we had done on the cemetery grounds nine months before.

The chaplain closed out the ceremony with a poem called *Celestial Flight*, written by one of the WASP named Elizabeth Magid for her friend and classmate Marie Robinson, who died in a plane crash while serving as a WASP. Elizabeth was buried at Arlington National Cemetery in May 2004, alongside her husband.

After the chaplain finished her recitation, everyone stood for the honor guard to fire off the 21 gun salute. As the bugler played taps, the honor guard began its meticulous process of folding the American flag into a triangle over the urn. I caught Mom wiping away tears as she watched the white-gloved airmen performing this tradition to honor her mother. The Air Force Honor Guard captain with her blond hair gathered meticulously above her collar, bent down on one knee to present Mom with the flag and recite the words heard at all armed services funerals, "On behalf of the President of the United States, the

United States Air Force, and a grateful nation, please accept this flag as a symbol of our appreciation for your loved one's honorable and faithful service."

We all followed the chaplain and the cemetery assistant carrying the urn as they made their way to the Columbarium across the road. Our immediate family, the three WASP and Representative McSally (holding onto two of the WASP), and the rest of the guests gathered together tightly in front of the wall of niches. I waved to my coworkers Brandy and Gina among the crowd. Marty wiped a tear from her cheek with a tissue. The Chaplain led a short ceremony and recited a prayer as a cemetery attendant atop a ladder slid the urn into a niche at the top row of the wall, leaving Gammy in her final resting place after 17 long months.

Gammy's was one funeral out of the 30 performed daily at Arlington National Cemetery, so the cemetery assistant reminded us all to move along to the memorial service to ensure other families had timely ceremonies. Guests meandered to their vehicles, engaged in conversation. Our limousine crawled along behind a caisson before we arrived at the Women In Military Service For America Memorial, housed in what used to be the ceremonial entrance to Arlington National Cemetery.

Once again, many of the guests had arrived before us and were milling about in the atrium. Sunlight filled the memorial space through the floor-to-ceiling glass windows. Reporters captured interviews with some family members, the three WASP, and Representative McSally, before the memorial service was scheduled to start. The caterers prepared for the post-service meal. A framed photo of Gammy, flowers, and the service programs decorated a small table by the doors to the auditorium.

"Erin!" I heard a familiar voice call out to me. I turned to see the reporter Andrea McCarren, accompanied by Bunce, the service dog in training. "Can we get a quick interview before you start?"

I gave Andrea a hug and patted Bunce on the head before answering.

296

"Of course! Look at Bunce, wearing a bow-tie, so cute."

"I wanted to make sure he dressed appropriately! It's a big day!" Andrea replied.

In the aisle of the auditorium, I answered Andrea's questions, almost nine months after our first interview. Unlike that first interview, where I was concerned about whether anyone would come to our aid, about whether Gammy's ashes would sit in the closet indefinitely, I was now giddy – anyone who didn't know the backstory would wonder why I was so happy at a memorial service for my deceased grandmother.

Shannon Perrine from WTAE television station in Pittsburgh interviewed Shutsy at the other side of the atrium. "Why is it in my particular life, and the lives of the other one thousand, one hundred and two WASP, can't even rest in peace? Here they are on their final flight and they have to fight to be recognized to get in," Shutsy said to the camera. "I felt today when I saw those ashes up there and I saw the wings on 'em, I thought finally the battle's over. That's like pinning a medal on your chest. We won! We won!"

We could have ended the day after the funeral service at Arlington National Cemetery. After all, that is what we successfully fought for – to have Gammy's ashes inurned there. But I thought a memorial service would serve multiple purposes. It would be a proper way to honor Gammy's life and to celebrate the legacy of the WASP. We could thank everyone who helped us achieve the goal. And given the international media attention, we could teach millions of people about the WASP service during the war. Gammy didn't want the WASP to be forgotten and even though she was physically gone, her dream of keeping the history of the Women Airforce Service Pilots alive was coming true.

As I stood at the podium on stage to begin the memorial service, dozens of reporters stacked along the aisles and the back of the auditorium began recording the event and taking notes. I started the ceremony by explaining that Gammy was a patriotic woman and the best way to honor her patriotism was to stand and recite the pledge of allegiance to the American flag. The audience in the packed auditorium complied with a smile.

Next up was Trisa, Gammy's niece, to read an old poem written by her mother, Gammy's sister Jean, who was unable to attend the funeral. Just before the memorial service programs were printed, Mom had added Jean's poem entitled, "Wingprints," dedicated to her sister Elaine.

<u>Wingprints</u>
By Jean (Danforth) Thompson

When I first decided to fly I didn't think of the sky as a man's world. I thought of it as my sister's world. She was the only pilot I had ever known.

Her wingprints in the sky gave me the courage to try. Because she had done it, I knew I could.

When my parents and boyfriend discouraged me, I thought of her. When I had no money for lessons, I thought of what she would do, and I found a job after school.

When I became frightened by small aircraft on a windy day, I knew she had gotten beyond that fear.

When I soloed, I crossed my fingers and thought of her first time to fly. When I thought I would never be able to make a good landing, I knew she had.

My sister's wingprints in the sky gave me the courage to fly.

So I propose a toast to all my sisters who went first.

To all the WASP who pioneered the sky leaving trails through the night, wind, and weather.

To all who proved the sky belonged to them.

Thank you for your wingprints.

Mom followed with the eulogy she had been working on for several days. She opened by explaining that Gammy's wish was to be laid to rest at Arlington National Cemetery and "not to make a fuss" about her. The audience laughed along with Mom at the obvious unheeded instruction. Mom's stories about growing up with a Great Depression era mother who loved the dime store and made cheap lunches from processed cheese product, mayonnaise, and white bread, gave the audience a glimpse of Gammy's personality. Mom included Gammy's pride and honor at being a part of the Women Airforce Service Pilots, but she finished her speech with an excerpt from a letter in which Gammy called her children her "big accomplishment."

Tiffany came to the podium next as the representative of the grandchildren. I knew Tiffany's sentimentality and nostalgia for our childhood times with Gammy were perfect traits to write a great speech to honor Gammy, and she did not disappoint. Tiffany compiled shared family memories of Gammy – her Halloween fun, patriotism, and silly but stern nature – along with how Gammy's personality is exhibited in each grandchild – artistry, tenacity, or continuing "the lost art of letter writing." Tiffany recalled how Gammy declared that our cousin Oakley's music was "complete rubbish," and Tiffany guessed that Oakley likely considered that to be a compliment.

As Tiffany's speech wound down, I turned around and waved at Caroline and Heather seated behind me. I thought it would be nice to have some words from other WASP who were friends with Gammy. However, knowing they were all over 90 years old and however much they wanted to attend, it would not be possible for most of them, I had emailed and asked if they wanted to send along sentiments to read at the funeral. Several had sent back notes of varying lengths. I had enlisted Caroline and Heather to read the notes, thinking it would be appropriate to have today's female fighter pilots reading notes from their predecessors. However, Caroline had a surprise presentation first, so Heather followed by reading the WASP notes solo.

Another tradition to honor pilots is to fly a United States flag, often in a plane on a special mission. When people learned that H.R. 4336 had been signed by the president and that Gammy would finally be laid to rest, pilots started messaging Caroline to ask how they could best honor Gammy's legacy as a WASP. In addition to arranging for the flag to be flown over the United States Capitol, Caroline organized a special cross country trip for that flag. I hadn't put this on the memorial service agenda because we wanted to surprise Mom.

Caroline began by explaining that she owed her career to the WASP. She was able to fulfill her childhood dreams of becoming a fighter pilot, eventually flying over 3000 hours in fighters, 1700 of them in the F-16, with 200 hours in combat, and spending three years as the Thunderbirds right wing. Then Caroline read entries in the small black diary that had accompanied the flag in which pilots added their squadron stickers and left notes reflecting on the role of the WASP in history.

The entries varied from flights "in undisclosed locations" over the desert of California, to a commercial 737 flight, to an F-16 training mission over Arizona where the pilot "got it up to 8.7 G's and supersonic just for fun," to a training mission in a T-38 in Texas, an F-15 training flight in North Carolina, and it had all started out with Caroline and Heather's check rides for their airline transport ratings in a Piper Twin Comanche in Virginia. All the comments referred to the WASP as the women who paved the way for today's female pilots.

"...thank you for your example in paving the way..."

"...I've always looked up to the WASP and I use them as an inspiration and motivation for what I do today..."

"...I've been blessed to fly many different aircraft in my 18 plus years in the Air Force, I started out as a T-38 instructor, moved to fly the mighty A-10 Warthog, followed by the Predator, Reaper, and Talon."

At the mention of the "mighty A-10 Warthog," I heard Representative McSally – seated next to me – say out loud, "Awesome."

Before reading the notes from the WASP, Heather began with a short commentary on her respect for the WASP, how she thought often of them while she was the only woman in her fighter pilot training class and then the sole female again in her fighter squadron at the District of Columbia Air National Guard. According to Heather, the WASP made it possible that "one day on the eleventh of September, that I was standing at the ops desk when we got the call to go after flight ninety-three," the plane hijacked by terrorists that eventually crash-landed in a Pennsylvania field after the heroic efforts of the passengers. Heather conveyed that although she had never met Gammy, we should all know that her spirit and the spirit of all WASP lived on in the successive generations of female aviators, and to "please know that she is still alive."

Jean Harman, classmate of Elaine, 44-W-9

Elaine was a very special friend of mine both during WASP training and until she passed away.

We were lucky enough to be able to visit each other through those many years, in spite of living on opposite coasts.

She fought hard for causes she thought were righteous; particularly matters that pertained to the WASP and even when her health started to deteriorate, she traveled to events far and wide to continue to be active. She faced adversity with such courage and acceptance. Being surrounded by such a loving family must have helped.

I still miss her, but even in her passing she has given me the gift of getting to know her family: daughter, granddaughters, great granddaughter! Tigers...each and every one. And loveable. Just like Elaine.

Fondly, Jeepie.

Bee Haydu, class 44-W-7

I have only fond memories of Elaine. She was always willing to help. 1975 -1977 when we were asking Congress to give the WASP recognition as veterans of WWII, she was extremely helpful. She worked in our DC Headquarters, compiled information as proof of us having been treated as "military," organized the scrap books of news articles from all over the country by states so WASP visiting their representatives could show how much publicity we were getting, hosted visiting WASP, attended all functions. She was not only helpful but I considered her a good friend. I do miss her.

Nadine Nagle, classmate of Elaine, 44-W-9

Elaine and I were very good WASP friends. We shared the same concern over our flight tests and same excitement about flying! We were in the same class. We had ground school and flight training together and we marched everywhere together. Elaine and I always had a happy time together at WASP reunions.

I am so thankful that the WASP have been acknowledged to be buried at Arlington!

Nell Bright, class 43-W-7

Wish I could be there for the funeral, but we will all be with you in spirit. I didn't know your grandmother until we started having all our reunions and gatherings, but we hardly had time to know anyone in training except the ones in our own class. But when we started getting together later, we all loved it and were all bonded like sisters, regardless of our class number. She was great, and we always enjoyed "hangar flying" sessions. She did so much for all of us when we were fighting for our veteran status. It was always a fun "catch up" time when we got together. Such a great "gal." I miss her!

Dawn Seymour, Class 43-W-5

Elaine Dear,

You can smile now and rest in peace, in this sacred place. Please know that your strong delightful granddaughters accomplished your last request; to the benefit of all WASP and the progress of all women.

Farewell dear friend, farewell.

As the audience applauded and Heather exited the stage, I turned to Representative McSally and asked her, "Should I introduce you?"

She smiled and nodded and we headed for the stairs to the stage.

Again, as with the television interviews earlier, in a manner slightly too giddy for a memorial service, I introduced Representative McSally by explaining how I first learned of her interest in our problem with Arlington National Cemetery when Greta Van Susteren's show contacted me. Seven months later, it was still difficult to hide my excitement when discussing how a person who could change the law came forward to help our family.

"Our self-proclaimed wingwoman in Congress, from the second district of Arizona, Representative Martha McSally," I announced. I turned to hug her as she approached the podium.

After telling a brief history of the WASP and their fight to be recognized as veterans, Representative McSally's eyes lit up when she began to describe her personal experience with the WASP she had encountered in her lifetime, three of whom had been particularly influential: Dawn Seymour, Eleanor Gunderson, and Ruth Helm. She cocked her head and smiled from behind her tortoise shell glasses as she described how her often lonely journey as a female fighter pilot moving through the flight training process was made easier with the occasional encouragement of those three women who had done something similar 40 years earlier.

"They shined the light for us, who came after them, but literally they held up our wings at times when they were tired to allow us to continue to serve to follow in their footsteps and their contrails," she described how meaningful knowing some of the WASP during her career had been. The three WASP Representative McSally mentioned were at her change of command ceremony when she became the first woman to take command of a fighter squadron.

When Representative McSally moved on to discuss the legislation, her face reflected the personal slight she had felt upon learning that the WASP were being denied entry at Arlington National Cemetery.

"We tried to get the Pentagon to change the policy," and she laughed as she described the answer she received. "No kidding, they said we think the fastest way to fix this is an act of Congress, which is a pretty... interesting statement."

The audience laughed as she paused to let them absorb the absurdity of what she was describing. The fortunate thing for our family and for all WASP was that a former Air Force fighter pilot had decided to run for Congress a few years earlier.

"Okay, well, if it takes an act of Congress, I happen to be there!" Representative McSally recalled her response to the suggestion of

FINAL FLIGHT FINAL FIGHT

the Army that legislation was the most expedient resolution to the problem. She continued summarizing the main points of the legislative process and ultimate victory when the bill was signed by the President of the United States.

She finished with a reading of *High Flight*, the famous poem by pilot John Magee, Jr. When I was about ten years old, I had come across that poem for the first time in a magazine. I liked it so much that I copied it by hand using a metallic silver ink pen into a small hardcover address book. As Representative McSally read those words in honor of Gammy, I was reminded of how many times I opened that little book to search for a name only to be delayed by reading again the poem that expressed how I imagined Gammy felt when she had flown so many years before I came into the world. I was sure that in her 26 year career in the Air Force, Representative McSally had many unfortunate occasions to refer to that poem when a fellow pilot died. It was an honor to have her read it at Gammy's funeral. Representative McSally then closed her remarks with, "God bless you Elaine. May you fly and rest in peace."

As Mom and I had planned earlier, I ushered Representative McSally over to the middle of the stage after she finished speaking while Mom took her position at the podium. Representative McSally looked perplexed about why I was preventing her from leaving, but she obliged nonetheless. She and I stood in the middle of stage while Mom spoke.

"Representative McSally, to show our gratitude on behalf of the Harmon family, we wanted to come up with something. We can't thank you enough for all you have done to get us here to this day. My first thought was perhaps to get you a gift certificate to a tattoo parlor so you could get a forearm tattoo." The audience laughed and Representative McSally's concerned facial expression turned to joy as she joined in. I laughed too; Mom had not told me what she was planning to say. Representative McSally touched my arm and motioned to hold it up. I complied and the audience clapped. "But I rethought it. And what you have here is silver WASP wings." I opened the blue jewelry box that I had carried with me. "And they're not just any silver WASP wings; they were made by WASP Shutsy Reynolds."

At this, Representative McSally turned toward Shutsy in the first row and whispered, "Oh Shutsy," as she saw what was in the box.

I pulled the bracelet out of the box to show to Representative McSally while Mom continued, "And on the reverse side, we have engraved 'thank you' on the back of the left wing, and 'one hundred and fourteenth Congress, H.R. four, three, three, six' on the back of the right wing. Thank you so much on behalf of our family." I reached over and fastened the bracelet on Representative McSally's wrist. She promptly displayed it to the clapping audience.

After another hug from Representative McSally for both Mom and me, I began the last speech of the day. The sole purpose of the speech was to thank everyone who had contributed to making the day possible: those who had traveled long distances to be at the funeral, who had flown a flag in honor of Gammy, family and friends who put up with our endless requests to take action, others who had signed the online petition at Change.org or called their members of Congress, the media who had reported on our progress, the representatives and senators who wrote and passed the legislation. I tried to convey how I had never seen Gammy's service as less valuable than that of any other veteran. But when Arlington National Cemetery told us she was not the right kind of veteran, I learned that not everyone viewed her service, and the service of the WASP, in the same way. Fortunately, thousands of people worldwide disagreed, and those were the people who came forward to support our family in this 17 month quest to ensure Gammy made it to her final resting place. In the end, I thanked the most important person of all, Gammy. "I want to thank my grandmother and all the WASP for volunteering to serve in such a unique way during World War II, that seventy-two years later, when the value of that service was deemed as less than that of others, hundreds of thousands of people came forward to say, 'no it is not.' We will miss you and I think I speak for everyone here today when I say how proud we are of you."

As if Representative McSally had not done enough on our behalf, she now came on stage to fulfill one last request: to lead us in singing the Air Force theme song.

She motioned to me to stay up and sing with her at the podium. "First verse only? And you're singing here with us?" she asked and I confirmed. Then she spoke into the microphone to the audience, "We're just doing the first verse. And by the way, the real words are 'at 'em boys, give 'em the guns,' but we changed it to 'at 'em girls.' Well, the WASP changed it too, right?"

From the podium on stage, I looked out at over 200 faces – family, friends, media, academics, government officials, uniformed armed services members, veterans, three WASP, a Tuskegee airman, and an A-10 pilot turned member of Congress – and knew that the history of the WASP was in good hands. Then we all sang a hearty rendition of the appropriately altered Air Force theme song as we celebrated victory after 17 months, ushering Gammy's spirit into the wild blue yonder.

– THE END –

Epilogue

One of the staff members from the Women In Military Service For America Memorial called me a few weeks after the funeral.

"Erin, can you tell me the Columbarium location of your grandmother's grave in Arlington?" she asked me.

"Yes, hold on." I walked to the high counter between the kitchen and dining room and grabbed the scrap of paper I had written the numbers on when the funeral representative had called to tell us this information back in September. "Court 9. Section N42. Column 12. Niche 6," I recited into the phone.

"Thanks so much. I searched on the Arlington National Cemetery website for Elaine Harmon and I couldn't find her name," the staff member explained from the other end of the line.

"They have it under Florence in the computer system. Mom requested to change it but they haven't done it yet," I replied. "Why are you asking?"

"People have been calling to ask where her grave is so they can pay their respects," she informed me.

In that moment, hearing that strangers were searching for Gammy's grave site, I realized Gammy was still here. Each time that spark of inspiration ignited in someone learning about the history of the Women Airforce Service Pilots, Gammy was here.

But now I imagined she was happy to be here.

Elaine Danforth Harmon, WASP WWII, 1944

HEADQUARTERS ARMY AIR FORCES

OUTGOING UNCLASSIFIED MESSAGE

PRECEDENCE	DATE	FROM (OFFICE OF ORIGIN)
PRIORITY	3 APRIL 1944	DIRECTOR OF WOMEN PILOTS

NAME OF OFFICER PREPARING: JACQUELINE COCHRAN   PHONE: 71207

I certify that the following message constitutes official business and is necessary in the military service.

TYPED NAME: JACQUELINE COCHRAN   SIGNATURE: s/m 70
GRADE AND TITLE: DIR OF WOMEN PILOTS

TO: MRS FLORENCE RIAINE DANFORTH HARMON
SAN CARLOS HOTEL
PENSACOLA FLORIDA

AF RWP .... PD

THESE ARE YOUR OFFICIAL INSTRUCTIONS TO REPORT TO COMMANDING OFFICER THREE HUNDRED EIGHTEENTH AAFFTD AVENGER FIELD SWEETWATER TEXAS ON EIGHTEEN APRIL ONE NINE FOUR FOUR AT YOUR OWN EXPENSE FOR ADMISSION TO WOMEN'S FLYING TRAINING BRING THIS WIRE PILOT CERTIFICATE AND LOGBOOK PD BUS LEAVES BLUEBONNET HOTEL SWEETWATER AT NINE THIRTY AM ON REPORTING DATE PD YOU WILL BE EMPLOYED ONE HUNDRED FIFTY DOLLARS PER MONTH DURING SATISFACTORY PURSUANCE OF FLYING INSTRUCTION UNDER ARMY CONTROL NO ALLOWANCE IS MADE FOR SUBSISTENCE AND MAINTENANCE DURING TRAINING PD ACKNOWLEDGE RECEIPT OF THESE INSTRUCTIONS SIGNED COCHRAN

ARNOLD
COMMANDING GENERAL ARMY AIR FORCES

OFFICE SYMBOL	1	2	3	4	5	6
SIGNATURE OF RESPONSIBLE OFFICER						
INTERNAL OFFICE COORDINATION						

1944 Telegram orders to Sweetwater

1944 Elaine D. Harmon

1944 Elaine D. Harmon

1944 Log book, Elaine D. Harmon

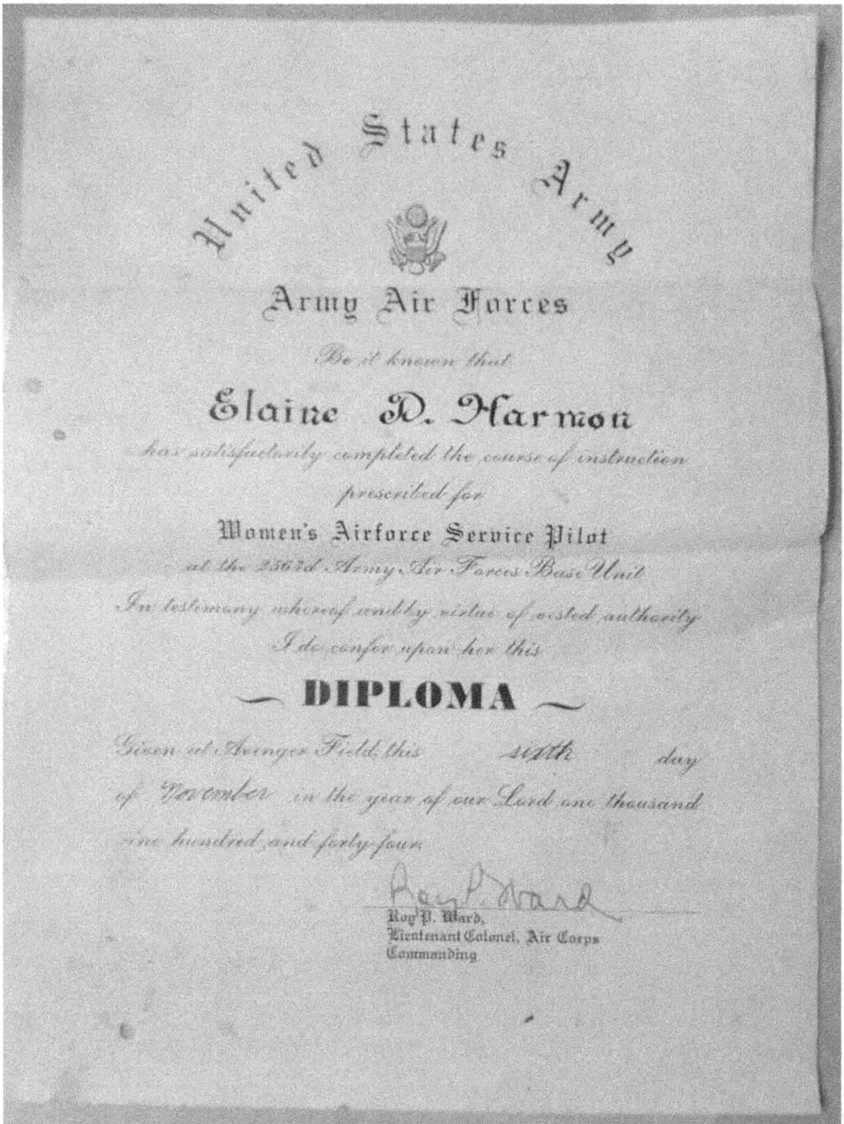

United States Army

Army Air Forces

Be it known that

Elaine D. Harmon

has satisfactorily completed the course of instruction

prescribed for

Women's Airforce Service Pilot

at the 2563d Army Air Forces Base Unit

In testimony whereof and by virtue of vested authority

I do confer upon her this

— DIPLOMA —

Given at Avenger Field this sixth day

of November in the year of our Lord one thousand

nine hundred and forty-four

Roy P. Ward

Roy P. Ward,
Lieutenant Colonel, Air Corps
Commanding

Elaine D. Harmon, WASP WWII diploma

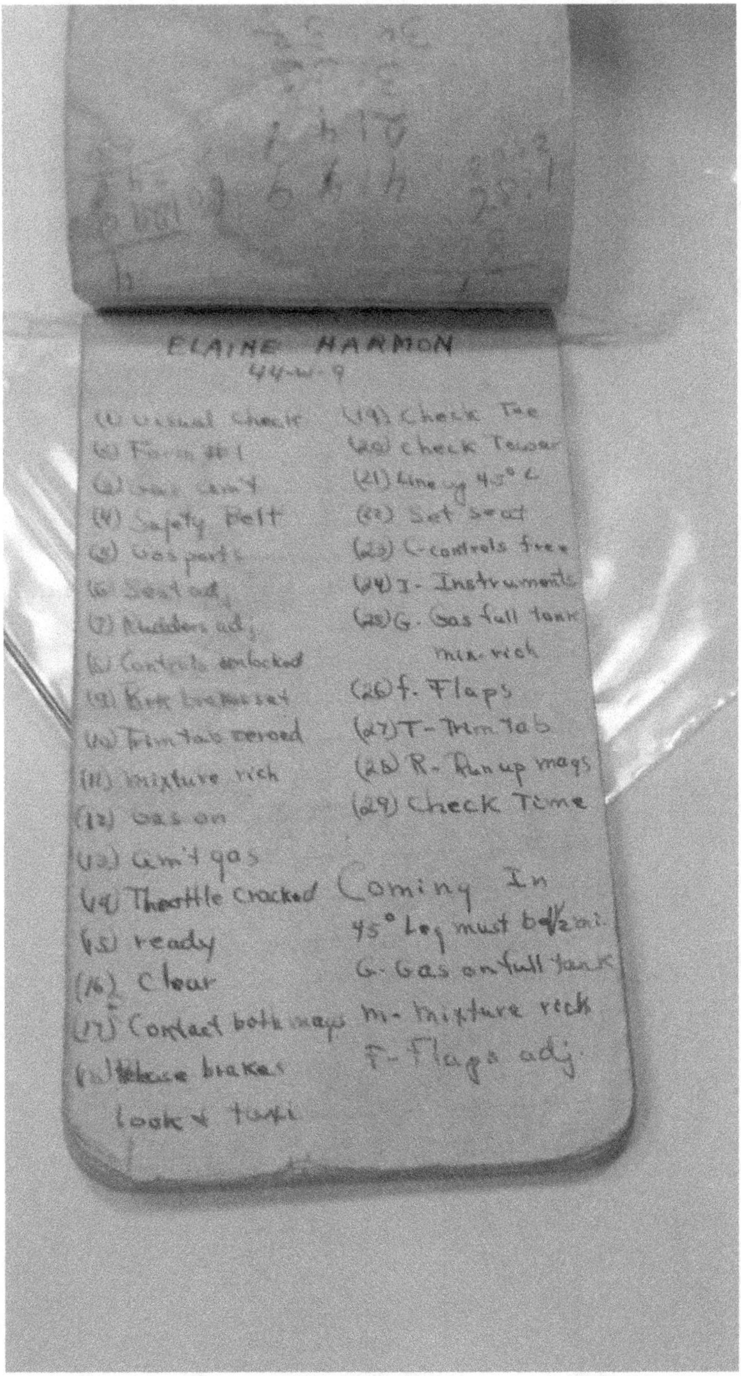

Elaine D. Harmon, cockpit checklist 1944

WASP reunion, 1969. Maggie Gee (front left) Elaine Harmon (front right)

EPILOGUE

Elaine Harmon with baby Erin, 1976

WASP meeting at Elaine's home, Sep 17, 1977. (Notice Elaine holding her dog.)

TO PROVIDE RECOGNITION TO THE WOM-
EN'S AIR FORCE SERVICE PILOTS FOR
THEIR SERVICE DURING WORLD WAR II
BY DEEMING SUCH SERVICE TO HAVE
BEEN ACTIVE DUTY IN THE ARMED
FORCES OF THE UNITED STATES FOR
PURPOSES OF LAWS ADMINISTERED BY
THE VETERANS ADMINISTRATION

HEARING
BEFORE A
SELECT SUBCOMMITTEE
OF THE
COMMITTEE ON VETERANS' AFFAIRS
HOUSE OF REPRESENTATIVES
NINETY-FIFTH CONGRESS
FIRST SESSION
ON
GRANTING VETERANS' STATUS TO WASPS

SEPTEMBER 20, 1977

Printed for the use of the Committee on Veterans' Affairs

*Transcript from Sep. 20, 1977 House of Rep. hearing with note from Rep.
Heckler*

Erin in her "Gammy flew planes in WWII" T-shirt

Me, giving a report to the Subcommittee on Implementation of Title IV of Public Law 95-202 related to WASP and other similarly situated groups. 1975

Elaine testifying before Congress. (I think this is 1981, not 1975 as marked)

Elaine with Senator Bob Dole & Rep. Kaptur at a WWII Memorial meeting

Elaine with the Duke of Kent, 2005

Mom and I with Gammy for Veterans Day at Applebee's, 2011

A special pen that I found in Gammy's desk after her death

Erin, Rep. McSally, Whitney (with baby Isabella), Mom. Jan. 2016

Caroline Jensen and I visit WASP Lorraine Rodgers, Feb. 2016

A visit with Senator Klobuchar

Tiffany (right) and I visit with Senator Ernst

WASP at the wishing well in Sweetwater, 2016

Mom receiving the burial flag at Arlington National Cemetery, Sep. 7, 2016

Whitney, Tiffany, WASP Shirley Kruse, Rep. Martha McSally, WASP Shutsy Reynolds, Erin (behind), WASP Marty Wyall, and Mom (left to right) at memorial service

I would like to be buried in Arlington Cemetery. Proof of my veteran status is necessary. It requires a copy of my DD 214. I have put copies of that form in various places. One is inside the frame for my Honorable Discharge which is on the book shelves in the den. Another copy is in the file marked "Death" in the steel fireproof box in the den.

If for some reason (and there should be no reason) I can't be in the Columbarium at Arlington, there is still one burial site available in Back Creek Cemetery where Daddy is buried.

Carpe diem,
Elaine
(Sometimes called Mom)

Elaine's funeral request letter

Elaine Danforth Harmon, Columbarium stone at Arlington National Cemetery

Beyond the Book

For more photos and documents, please visit the website:
finalflightfinalfight.com

The website also lists organizations, projects, and other ways you can be involved in keeping the history of the Women Airforce Service Pilots alive.

About the Author

Erin Miller is the granddaughter of Elaine Danforth Harmon, who was one of the Women Airforce Service Pilots (WASP) of World War II. She has a J.D. from the University of Maryland School of Law, a Master's in international studies from the University of Leeds (UK), and a B.A. in History from the University of California, San Diego. Erin has now become an ambassador for the Women Airforce Service Pilots of World War II - giving talks and supporting projects to keep their history alive. Erin is a licensed attorney in Maryland, where she lives with her two Shiba Inus.

Twitter: @millerlawmd

Instagram: @millerlawmd

Facebook: @officialerinmiller

Website: finalflightfinalfight.com